THE
AMERICAN PRISON
Issues in
Research and Policy

Edited by
Lynne Goodstein

Pennsylvania State University
University Park, Pennsylvania

and
Doris Layton MacKenzie

Louisiana State University
Baton Rouge, Louisiana
and National Institute of Justice
Washington, D.C.

PLENUM PRESS • NEW YORK AND LONDON

Library of Congress Cataloging in Publication Data

The American prison: issues in research and policy / edited by Lynne Goodstein
and Doris Layton MacKenzie.
p.   cm.—(Law, society, and policy; v. 4)
    Includes bibliographies and index.
    ISBN 0-306-43197-1
    1. Corrections—United States. 2. Prisons—United States. I. Goodstein, Lynne. II.
MacKenzie, Doris. III. Series.
HV9469.A777   1989   89-35536
365'.973—dc20   CIP

This limited facsimile edition has been issued
for the purpose of keeping this title available
to the scientific community.

10 9 8 7 6 5 4 3

© 1989 Plenum Press, New York
A Division of Plenum Publishing Corporation
233 Spring Street, New York, N.Y. 10013

Printed in the United States of America

THE
AMERICAN PRISON
Issues in
Research and Policy

LAW, SOCIETY, AND POLICY

Series Editors: Joel Feinberg, Travis Hirschi,
Bruce Sales, and David Wexler
University of Arizona

CONTRIBUTORS

GEOFFREY P. ALPERT, College of Criminal Justice, University of South Carolina, Columbia, South Carolina 29208

ALFRED BLUMSTEIN, School of Urban and Public Affairs, Carnegie Mellon University, Pittsburgh, Pennsylvania 15213

JOHN P. CONRAD, 544 Reed Drive, Davis, California 95616

FRANCIS T. CULLEN, Department of Criminal Justice, University of Cincinnati, Cincinnati, Ohio 45221-0108

TIMOTHY J. FLANAGAN, School of Criminal Justice, State University of New York at Albany, Albany, New York 12222

PAUL GENDREAU, Centracare Saint John Inc., Saint John, New Brunswick E2M 4H7, Canada

LYNNE GOODSTEIN, Administration of Justice Department, The Pennsylvania State University, University Park, Pennsylvania 16802

J. DOUGLAS GRANT, Nicasio, California 94946 (Formerly of the Social Action Research Center)

KENNETH C. HAAS, Department of Criminal Justice, University of Delaware, Newark, Delaware 19716

JOHN R. HEPBURN, School of Justice Studies, Arizona State University, Tempe, Arizona 85287

KAY A. KNAPP, Institute for Rational Public Policy, Inc., 40 Philadelphia Avenue, Takoma Park, Maryland 20912

CHARLES H. LOGAN, University of Connecticut, Storrs, Connecticut 06268

DORIS LAYTON MACKENZIE, Louisiana State University, Baton Rouge, Louisiana 70803, and National Institute of Justice, U.S. Department of Justice, 633 Indiana Avenue NW, Washington, DC 20531

HANS TOCH, School of Criminal Justice, State University of New York at Albany, Albany, New York 12222

NICOLE HAHN RAFTER, College of Criminal Justice, Northeastern University, Boston, Massachusetts 02115

KEVIN N. WRIGHT, Center for Education and Social Research, State University of New York at Binghamton, Binghamton, New York 13901

PREFACE

Despite the dire forecasts of others who had themselves edited books, we proceeded with the project of an edited volume on the American prison, although with more than a little trepidation. We had heard the horror stories of authors turning in their chapters months or years late or never at all, of publishers delaying publication dates, of volumes that read more like patchwork quilts than finely loomed cloth. As if to prove the others wrong, our experience in editing this volume has been marvelous, and we think the volume reflects this.

Most likely, the success of our experience and of the volume stems from two elements: first, the professionalism and commitment of the authors themselves; and second, the fact that early in the life of this volume, most of the authors convened for a conference to critique and coordinate the chapters.

This book brings together an illustrious group of criminologists and correctional scholars who wrote chapters explicitly for this volume. Cohesiveness was furthered by the charge we gave to each author to (1) present the major issues, (2) review the empirical research, and (3) discuss the implications of this work for present and future correctional policy. The goal of this project was to examine the major correctional issues facing prison systems. The chapters scrutinize the issues from the perspective of the system and the individual, from theory to practical and daily management problems, from legal to psychological concerns. The advantage of this approach is revealed by the depth and richness of the chapters. No one or two individuals could have adequately covered so many of the issues relating to research and policy in today's prisons with such sophistication and comprehensiveness.

To insure editorial integrity and cohesiveness, the authors met in Nags Head, North Carolina, in late 1987 to review each other's drafts and to provide suggestions and feedback to each author. Arriving at the conference with completed chapters, authors distributed copies to all participants, and time was scheduled to discuss, evaluate, and offer suggestions for improving chapters that were already superb. Participants approached these tasks with the perfect combination of seriousness and good humor to enable the conference to proceed not only efficiently and productively but enjoyably as well.

Thoughts of the conference bring back wonderful memories of sitting on the beach reading chapters, meetings to critique others' work, being on the "chopping block" when one's own chapter was critiqued, sharing sunsets and swims, picnics and wind. It was a time to build new friendships, share time with old friends, and discuss issues in research and policy.

The results of all this fun and sharing of talents is a volume that we believe has a cohesiveness not usually found in an edited book. Our job, of course, was also simplified because the burden of editorship was shared by all conference participants. Moreover, after the conference when the new editions of the chapters were received, they were ready to go to press. We are indebted to numerous colleagues for their encouragement and advice on this project, but most importantly, we would like to thank the authors whose work appears in this volume.

CONTENTS

PART III. MANAGING THE PRISON

Chapter 8. Prison Labor and Industry 135
TIMOTHY J. FLANAGAN

Chapter 9. Prison Classification: The Management and
Psychological Perspectives 163
DORIS LAYTON MACKENZIE

PART IV. LIVING IN PRISON

Chapter 1

INTRODUCTION
Issues in Correctional Research and Policy

LYNNE GOODSTEIN and DORIS LAYTON MacKENZIE

Many books have been published on prisons over the past several decades. Why another one? One might take the cynical approach and say that the book provides another line to add to each author's and editor's curriculum vitae, another potentially successful project for the publisher. But, as we prepare to cross the threshold to another century, there are more substantial reasons for bringing out a new volume that investigates the prison, one of the most intriguing and intractable of our social institutions.

The title of this book was selected carefully to capture the essence of the authors' contributions. All chapters focus on the contemporary prison and explore the part research has played in uncovering insights about prisoners, staff, the prison as a complex organization, and the correctional system within a broader social and political context. It is a book in which the authors consciously attempt to take the relevant research in their area and explore its implications for correctional policy for the remainder of this century and the next.

This was not an easy charge to be given, and the problem of ad-

LYNNE GOODSTEIN • Administration of Justice Department, The Pennsylvania State University, University Park, Pennsylvania 16802. DORIS LAYTON MacKENZIE • Louisiana State University, Baton Rouge, Louisiana 70803, and National Institute of Justice, U.S. Department of Justice, 633 Indiana Avenue NW, Washington, DC 20531.

1

dressing implications of research for correctional policy and practice was perhaps more challenging for authors writing in some areas than in others. Yet what has resulted is a volume that illuminates the critical issues in contemporary corrections in ways that interweave the authors' understandings of social science research with the complexities of managing correctional institutions. The editors have sought to make the volume useful not only to students and reseachers in corrections but also to practitioners and policymakers. With its emphasis on the interrelationships between research and policy, this book is clearly a product of the 1980s.

The book includes contributors who, throughout their distinguished careers, have been committed to developing critical perspectives on and strategies for improving correctional policy and practice. Some authors examine historical and political events that have shaped the current correctional scene. Some chapters focus upon the current state of crisis in corrections, its causes, potential solutions, and projections for correctional systems into the twenty-first century. The strength of all the chapters lies in the care with which the authors have conceptualized these issues and with the abundance of high-quality research performed over the past several decades that has been integrated and presented.

Although each chapter is intended to review the most current research in a specific area in corrections and the implications of this work for correctional policy, several themes unify the volume. One theme concerns the emergence of the rational bureaucratic model of correctional administration, with its increased attention to due process and accountability. A second important thread running through several chapters concerns the impact of the nation's political climate on prison management and on the interaction between the private sector and correctional systems. The issue of the individual prisoner and his or her relationship to the correctional environment is the focus of several chapters as well. Finally, the book deals with the problem of utilization of significant research findings for improved correctional management within a climate of limited resources. We will discuss each of these themes in turn and briefly introduce the chapters that reflect these themes.

1. THE PRISON AS A RATIONAL ORGANIZATION

Scholars familiar with the history of American correctional institutions are aware that for most of their hundred-plus years of existence, the actual operation of the facilities was left virtually exclusively to the discretion of local prison administrations. Although public interest in correctional institutions, fueled by the belief in correction's ability to reform offenders, was strong during the latter part of the late nineteenth century, it rapidly waned as the hoped for evidence of inmate reformation was not forthcoming. This diminution of interest—coupled with the geographical isolation of most correctional institutions, which further removed them from the public eye—enabled local authorities to maintain extraordinary degrees of authority and control over the daily operations of these institutions well into the twentieth century.

Over the past several decades, local correctional authorities have lost much of their autonomy. Central offices have become significantly more instrumental in setting correctional policy than are individual wardens or superintendents. Accompanying this centralization of policy-making authority, and to some extent a cause of it, is the increased intervention by the courts in the daily operations of correctional institutions. As a result of these two forces, centralization of authority and increased intervention by the courts, concerns for accountability and due process have increased. Correctional institutions are no longer individual fiefdoms controlled by wardens, some benevolent, some not. Instead, the model for contemporary prisons is that of a rational, accountable bureaucracy.

The discussion of these issues in the correctional arena are not new, as readers of Jacobs's *Stateville*, written over a decade ago, will recognize. Yet the reasons that some of these changes have come about, especially the significant impact of certain court decisions, are less well known. Moreover, recent developments in corrections have again challenged inmates' rights to the courts and, for some classes of inmates (particularly women), have restricted the satisfaction of their demands for equity. These issues are the foci of two of the volume's chapters.

In "American Prisoners and the Right of Access to the Courts," (Chapter 5), Kenneth C. Haas and Geoffrey P. Alpert trace the courts' rejection of the "hands-off doctrine" in the late 1960s and the broad-scale litigation concerning prison conditions and prisoner representation in court which ensued. Nicole Hahn Rafter's chapter (6), "Gender and Justice: The Equal Protection Issue," complements Haas and Alpert's through a review of some significant court cases that focus on the conditions of confinement for women prisoners. Starting from a review of the historical inequities in the treatment of women prisoners, she illustrates how women prisoners have been the victims of sex discrimination in a wide range of areas. She focuses on court cases litigated within the past 20 years, which have served to address equal protection issues for women. Although pointing to significant contributions by the courts to the amelioration of conditions of confinement for men and women, both chapters include a word of caution concerning the potential of the courts to continue to impact significantly on prison conditions.

John R. Hepburn's chapter (10), "Prison Guards as Agents of Social Control," looks indirectly at the impact of court intervention and centralization of correctional policymaking by focusing on the changing roles of correctional officers in contemporary prisons. Pointing to increased prison bureaucratization and court intervention, he argues that over the past two decades, correctional officers have experienced a reduced level of control that threatens—or at least is perceived to threaten—their abilities to perform their jobs adequately.

Independent of the impact of the courts on correctional policy, the past 20 years have also witnessed a profound change in the nature of correctional decision making. There has been a movement for decisions that were once at the discretion of individual court and corrections personnel to be regulated and systematized, with the goals of ensuring greater fairness, reducing capriciousness, and increasing system efficiency. Two chapters in the volume focus on methods aimed at regulating discretion in the treatment of criminal offenders. Kay A. Knapp (Chapter 7), in "Criminal Sentencing Reform: Legacy for the Correctional System," discusses determinate sentencing, the restructuring of the sentencing process that began in a number of states in the 1970s. The implementation of sentencing guidelines, which regulate judicial discretion in meting out penalties for criminal offenses, has resulted in correctional systems in which inmates are handled with greater uniformity than was previously the case. Although Knapp's chapter looks at the decisions of whether, and for how long, to confine offenders, Doris Layton MacKenzie (Chapter 9) looks at where confined offenders should be placed and what should happen to them during their confinement. In her chapter "Prison Classification: The Management and Psychological Perspectives," MacKenzie discusses new technologies for classifying inmates and illustrates how these methods are supplanting discretionary decision-making methods traditionally used for prisoner classification.

2. PRISONS, POLITICS, AND DEMOGRAPHICS

The increased intervention of the courts had its roots in broader changes in the political consciousness of the nation. The turbulence of the 1960s brought prisons back again into the public eye, and the conditions of confinement became objects of journalists' articles and activists' energies. The U.S. Supreme Court, still comprised of a majority of liberal justices, reflected the dominance of a perspective that was sensitive to issues of individual rights and social justice.

This period can also be characterized by a revived general belief in the power of prisons to rehabilitate offenders. The dominant ethic of the 1960s was the rehabilitative model, and it manifested itself in a plethora of programs for prisoners and evaluation projects designed to assess their effectiveness.

Ironically, as Alfred Blumstein (Chapter 2) remarks in his chapter, "American Prisons in a Time of Crisis," that just as the public began to revive—after almost a century—its interest in prison reform, other factors had begun to take precedence in shaping correctional institutions. These forces, a dramatic rise in crime rates due primarily to a unprecedented increase in the proportion of the nation's population to reach the crime-prone years, coupled with increased political conservatism, ultimately resulted in an extraordinary 500% increase in the number of individuals incarcerated in prisons and jails from 1970 to 1988. Moreover, the widely publicized results of social science research aimed at identifying the effectiveness of correctional treatment, the "nothing works" doctrine, provided the justification political conservatives needed to recast the goals of corrections away from rehabilitation and solidly into the domain of incapacitation, retribution, and deterrence.

In "The Effectiveness of Correctional Rehabilitation: Reconsidering the 'Nothing Works' Doctrine," Francis T. Cullen and Paul Gendreau (Chapter 3) review the political controversies surrounding the redefinition of correctional goals that occurred in the 1970s and into the 1980s. They confirm that the public and politicians alike have declined in their support for the goals of rehabilitation. Notwithstanding this decline, they demonstrate that the public retains a commitment to rehabilitation; although in a state akin to pluralistic ignorance, politicians appear to underestimate this sentiment and believe only in the public's punitiveness.

This embracing of punitiveness by judges, legislators, parole boards, and other criminal justice professionals provides part of the explanation for the dramatic increases in prison and jail populations, according to Blumstein (Chapter 2). He discusses the relative effects on the prison overcrowding problem of various decisions made by legislators and criminal justice professionals. Over the past two decades, decisions regarding the institution of mandatory sentences and the "tightening up" on parole decisions have had an impact on overcrowding. He argues that in the spirit of regulating sentencing discretion, determinate sentencing has resulted in sentencing proportionately more offenders to prison. But, in his opinion, the most significant factor in the prison overcrowding crisis, and the one most difficult to change, is the demographic one.

In discussing the origins of sentencing guidelines, Knapp (Chapter 7) also acknowledges the political impacts of both liberals, intent upon regulating sentencing discretion, and conservatives, who pushed for punitiveness. Yet her chapter goes beyond a discussion of political forces to provide an insight into the potential of such reform to aid in the control of the prison population crisis. Critical of some guidelines models that she contends no longer embody the objectives of uniformity and proportionality, she advocates for sentencing guidelines as a means to regulate both sentencing discretion and prison overcrowding. Indeed, she argues that one cannot be successfully effected without the other.

3. THE PRIVATE SECTOR AND THE PRISON

The conservative political climate of the 1980s, coupled with states' concerns for constructing and managing rapidly expanding correctional systems, has led to another recent development discussed by two authors—initiatives to reduce prison costs. Several directions have been pursued, with the two most significant being privatization and a new interest in prison industry and labor. Charles H. Logan (Chapter 4) writes about proprietary prisons, an area that has only recently become a subject for study by corrections researchers. His chapter reviews the status of private prisons in the United States and articulates some of the issues that are generally raised about the "propriety" of proprietary prisons. Hard data on private prisons, however, are scarce; and Logan cautions that conclusions about the relative costs of private versus public prisons must wait until the necessary research is performed.

A good deal more is known about the area of prison labor and industry, as Chapter 8 by Timothy J. Flanagan illustrates. Although many advocate increased reliance on prison labor and industry as a means of cutting costs, Flanagan reminds us that from the inception of the correctional system, prison industry has been viewed as a method of resocialization for prisoners who were deficient in work habits and skills. He traces the decline and resurgence of prison industry and ties this process to the inversely correlated rise and fall of the rehabilitation model. Like Logan, he is cautious about arguing too strongly for the accrual of significant economic gains (or even social benefits to prisoners) through prison industry, suggesting instead that correctional policymakers must realistically articulate the mission of prison industry and, then, not expect too much from these efforts.

4. THE PRISON AND THE PRISONER

In his brief review of the effects of prison industry on recidivism, Flanagan is less than optimistic about the potential of prison work to reduce one's likelihood of returning to prison. However, Cullen and Gendreau (Chapter 3) are considerably more affirmative about the prospects of successfully reducing recidivism through correctional programs, at least for some inmates. Integrating the research findings of hundreds of studies, they provide an important conceptual framework for analyzing types of programs attempted and characteristics of these programs that increase or decrease their success in reducing recidivism.

Several chapters focus upon the theme of the adjustment to and behavior of the individual prisoner in the prison setting, reviewing research and new strategies that seek to reduce management problems whereas, to the extent possible, aiding prisoners in their growth and development. MacKenzie's chapter (9) on prison classification underscores the potential effectiveness prisons can have in facilitating inmate self-improvement, in this case through appropriate classification of prisoners to programs and settings which meet their individual needs. The two chapters (12 and 13) by Kevin N. Wright and Lynne Goodstein, "Inmate Adjustment to Prison," and "Correctional Environments," further present evidence of the value of "person/environment fit" in facilitating both inmate adjustment to prison and longer-term growth. Finally, Hans Toch and J. Douglas Grant's chapter (11), "Noncoping and Maladaptation in the Prison," targets a specific and numerically growing subgroup of prisoners: those who are both emotionally disturbed and aggressive. After outlining the difficulties for staff in managing such inmates, Toch and Grant discuss innovative methods for handling this group of offenders and for providing them with techniques for behavior change.

5. THE PRISON AS A SYSTEM

The chapters in this book, particularly those dealing with rehabilitation, classification, and the response of the prisoner to the prison environment, illustrate that major breakthroughs have been made in correctional research. Individual prisoners can benefit from research findings concerning the "fit" between people and their environment, what treatment programs work for whom, how to classify offenders so they may benefit from a specific program, and how to maximize adjustment and minimize deterioration during incarceration. Research has demonstrated methods that are effective in bringing about positive changes in the prison as a whole as well. An environment that allows for growth and change, staff who view themselves in part as counselors, and objective classification are just a few of the policies reviewed in this volume that have been found to create positive impacts on prison environments.

This type of knowledge, much of it generated within the past 10 years, represents ground-breaking work illustrative of the potential for research to aid corrections practitioners. However, simply knowing what techniques are likely to be most effective does not imply that these methods will automatically be put into place. The authors in this volume are also realistic in their recognition of the limitations of correctional systems to effect change, even if research evidence confirms that change could be accomplished.

Although we have evidence of what "works," in a real-world setting programs often appear to fail. The reason for this failure may be due more to resource limitations than to the inadequacies of program or policy. For example, a program claiming to be based on behavior modification may fail, not because the principles are ineffective but because of factors such as a poorly trained staff, limited time, or low budget.

The authors in this volume recognize that corrections must be viewed as a system and that the components of this system are embedded in a complex network of interrelationships. Rehabilitation requires an environment conducive to growth, and staff are an important component of this environment. If correctional staff are to act as agents of change, they must be given appropriate support and training to succeed in implementing this expanded definition of their job.

Perhaps the most important factor in viewing corrections as a system is the recognition that the system requires resource management. As in any organization, there simply are not enough resources to achieve all objectives or even to attempt to achieve them. Priorities must be set; hard choices must be made as to which objectives take precedence, which goals will be set aside. In considering how to maximize the effective and efficient use of resources, decision makers often must opt against implementing programs demonstrated to be successful. They may claim that the prisoners helped would be too few in number or that the change, although positive, is not positive enough to justify the expense.

The dilemma of maximizing efficiency and effectiveness in an environment of scarce resources is made even more urgent as a result of two problems faced by contemporary prison administrators. The first is overcrowding, discussed by Blumstein, Knapp, and others in this volume. The second is the issue of inmate violence, especially violent inmate gangs, a serious problem in certain prisons that clearly demands much careful study. These problems tax resources and plague the day-to-day lives of prison administrators who have time for little more than staying ahead of the next crisis of violence or inadequate bedspace. Little time, energy, and resources are left for implementing programs that have been demonstrated to be effective or for being committed to principles of equity and justice.

Correctional administrators are confronted with the conflict between commitment to higher-order goals such as prisoner rehabilitation or procedural equity, on the one hand, and the concern for system maintenance, on the other. This conflict is illustrated in several of the chapters contained in this volume. As Knapp discusses, although sentencing guidelines were first established to reduce inequities in the sentencing process, they have received more recent attention solely as a means to control prison crowding. Flanagan's chapter on prison labor and industry reiterates the same tension—viewing prison labor alternatively as a means for cost control or reducing idleness versus the more ambitious objective of producing inmates who are more employable upon release.

The chapters in this volume, with their emphasis on both research and policy, underscore the importance of the system-level focus for both practitioners and researchers. Practitioners must constantly evaluate the cost and effectiveness of their decisions and choose options that make the best use of available resources to benefit the greatest number of people. Scholars and researchers concerned with contemporary corrections must make their research relevant to the concerns of policymakers. The necessary follow-up to the question of "What works for whom?" are the system-level questions such as "How many?" and "At what cost?" Although researchers are best equipped to address the first question, they can also be helpful in providing information about the second and third. The chapters in this volume provide excellent models for the applied corrections researcher.

6. THE FUTURE OF CORRECTIONAL RESEARCH

Considering the current spate of prison construction nationwide, coupled with the projections that prison populations will not decline significantly in the 1990s and beyond, we can anticipate the institution of the prison to be with us well into the twenty-first century. What types of corrections research should we expect to see over the next several decades? As the chapters in this volume attest, the more recent correctional research focuses less on the prisoner and correctional officer from a sociological or social psychological perspective and more on issues of correctional management and policy. In this vein, there are issues missing from this volume that deserve careful attention. In the present climate of the threat of AIDS and the prevalence of inexpensive addictive drugs, the absence of chapters on prison health and the treatment of chemical dependency is noticeable. Moreover, continued systematic attention must be paid to the problems of inmate violence, as some prisons become increasingly populated by gang members.

These areas have become increasingly problematic in recent years and will require some time before systematic research evidence is accumulated about them. Despite these omissions, however, *The American Prison: Issues in Research and Policy*, provides the student of and practitioner in corrections with much material that is useful, to understand what has occurred in the past, to better function in the present, and to develop reasonable expectations for what is to come.

Part I

CORRECTIONS AS A SYSTEM
Contemporary Issues

Chapter 2

AMERICAN PRISONS IN A TIME OF CRISIS

ALFRED BLUMSTEIN

1. INTRODUCTION

Through most of the first three-quarters of this century, the situation in American prisons was remarkably stable. Prison populations were sufficiently stable so that they stimulated a theory of the stability of prison populations (Blumstein and Cohen, 1973), published in 1973. Almost as if by spite, prison populations in 1973 began an astonishing steady climb, from a prison population of under 100,000 in 1969 to almost 600,000 in 1987. In this chapter, I would like to explore some of the factors that contributed to that climb, some prospects for the future, and some policy implications of those trends.

2. THE GROWTH IN PRISON POPULATION

2.1. Prison as Correction

Prior to the early 1970s, the dominant theme of prison management was *rehabilitation*—hence the name *corrections* for the function. This reflected the liberal optimism in the perfectibility of people, or the "medical model" that viewed the offender as somehow damaged, almost cer-

ALFRED BLUMSTEIN • School of Urban and Public Affairs, Carnegie Mellon University, Pittsburgh, Pennsylvania 15213.

tainly as a consequence of his or her deprived social environment. The hope was strong that some reasonable effort on the part of appropriately skilled professionals, perhaps using some reasonable behavioral technology that derived from emerging behavioral science theories, could be applied to the prisoners and that would repair the damage and return them to their appropriate role as responsible members of society.

This structure worked very well to keep prisons and imprisonment policy out of the general view of the public. Rehabilitation was the job of the professionals, and if left in their hands, they would do the job. Also, they were the best ones to decide when any particular inmate was "rehabilitated" and ready to return to society. Thus the dominant sentencing mode was the indeterminate sentence, which in some states provided sufficient leeway to permit sentences that ranged from 1 day to life, with the release date—and hence time served—determined totally by the professionals, typically on the parole board.

This arrangement worked very well for prison management also. If prisons were becoming crowded—and this could occur for many reasons ranging from tougher parole boards to a population bulge in the crime-prone ages (or, more properly, in the prison-prone ages)—then the parole board could accommodate that by lowering the threshold of how rehabilitated an inmate had to be to warrant release.

2.2. The Demise of Rehabilitation

This isolation of prisons from public scrutiny began to change dramatically in the late 1960s. This occurred just as the correctional world was pondering the advice of the President's Commission on Law Enforcement and Administration of Justice (1967) to focus on the "medical model" of corrections—perhaps the last such call. This reflects a presumption that the offender is somehow disabled and merely needs some form of treatment—presumably identifiable and available from some accessible armamentarium of treatments—to attain recovery within a reasonable time.

The weakness of this medical model and its underlying presumptions were highlighted by a variety of evaluations of correctional treatment programs. The most visible upshot of this work was the summary reported by Martinson (1974) (based on the more elaborate report of Lipton, Martinson, and Wilks, 1975) that was widely interpreted as reporting that "nothing works" in rehabilitation. Although that simple summary can reasonably be viewed as an excessive and overly simplistic interpretation of the conclusions, its implications were reasonably consistent with the results of the reported evaluations.

In experimental terms—the methodology that characterized the best of the evaluations—the studies involved a randomly separated treatment group and a control group drawn from some correctional population. The treatment being evaluated was applied to the treatment group and the conventional treatment applied to the control group, and the recidivism of each group was then measured during some follow-up period. The primary outcome of most of these studies was a "null effect" associated with the treatment, that is, the recidivism of the treatment group was no different from that of the control group. Thus, these results do not quite suggest that nothing works (because recidivism in both groups was always appreciably less than a certainty), it does suggest that the novel treatments that were applied and that presumably represented the new and promising technologies did no better than standard practice.

Of course, not all the evaluations were well conducted. Some were designed poorly in the random separation between control group and treatment group (because ethical considerations often inhibited random assignment), and selection biases may have contaminated the results or been poorly controlled. In other cases, the "treatment" was poorly delivered, was delivered in an unskillful way, or was so inherently weak that good professional judgment should have expected no important effect on the relevant population.

Perhaps most fundamentally, the evaluation results highlighted the limitations of the approaches available for inducing significant behavior change in individuals, especially in the absence of any change in the family, peer, and community environments in which offenders function when released from treatment. Furthermore, even if there were a rich array of behavior-change technologies of demonstrated effectiveness, it is not clear how full and ready would be the access to them by the practitioners of the criminal justice system. The concerns articulated in *Clockwork Orange* are by no means absent from the society, even in the current anticrime mood.

Regardless of the ultimate validity of the absolute conclusion that nothing works, it is clear that the perception of that conclusion became widespread by the early 1970s and gave rise to a strong movement to change both the philosophy and control of imprisonment policy. Because it became accepted that the professionals responsible for rehabilitation could not demonstrate effective performance, the cry went out to restrict their authority and autonomy in establishing sentences. Interestingly, the initial assault was from the left, which claimed that because there was no particular evidence that the criminal justice system could rehabilitate, then the level of control should be diminished—intervene less in peoples' lives (e.g., Robison and Smith, 1971).

2.3. The Rise in the Call for Punishment

Of course, that position was unacceptable to the right, which then invoked considerations of general deterrence and incapacitation to argue for more punishment. The left countered with the argument for focusing instead on the retributive purposes of sentencing, arguing that the "desert" was the appropriate issue, presumably with the expectation that they, rather than the political process, would decide how much desert was truly "just" (von Hirsch, 1976, for example).

Perhaps the most striking consequence of this emerging debate resulting from the decline in the faith in rehabilitation was the transfer of the control over sentencing policy. The control was lifted from the rehabilitation professionals and brought into the public arena, directly to the political arena of the legislatures. If the professionals were unable to rehabilitate, then by what right should they have the power to decide on the length of a sentence. (Or, more precisely, on the time served— the effective sentence. It is still the judge who still decides on the literal "sentence." Of course, even that sentence must be consistent with the negotiated charges that are presented to the judge by the prosecutor and the defense attorney.)

As sentencing policy moved into the legislatures, its political attractiveness became irresistible to the political actors who perform there. With the public's growing hostility to crime and with the public's clear identification with the victims and against the offenders, an earlier anxiety about being thought "soft on crime" became replaced by a politically more aggressive stance of being "tough on crime," demanding more vigorous action against criminals, railing at "lenient" judges and parole boards, and acting generally to diminish the validity of current sentencing policies and demanding increasingly more severe ones.

This is particularly evident in the "crime-of-the-month" bills that are regularly introduced into the legislatures to capitalize on the particularly heinous offenses that occur periodically. Immediately following any such offense, particularly if some judge treated that offender leniently for the offense, one can anticipate that some politically entrepreneurial legislator will introduce a bill that requires a mandatory minimum sentence for many variants of that particular offense. Thus the sentence for many versions of the offense gets increased to a level that could be more severe than even the most serious version was dealt with previously.

The principal control over this process is the willingness of the judiciary committees to act to suppress such exploitative legislation. Once such a bill comes to a floor vote, however, no legislator can risk opposing it, and so it sails through.

One response to the politicization of sentencing by the legislature has been the creation of sentencing commissions charged with establishing a sentencing structure that is internally consistent in the sense that more serious offenses should get more serious penalties, that offenders with more serious prior records should get longer sentences. Some of these commissions, most notably the one established in Minnesota, have also adopted the view that the total sentencing structure should be consistent with the overall prison capacity of the state; that is, that the aggregate punishment implied by the commission's sentencing structure should be no greater than the state's available prison capacity.

The initial argument for a sentencing commission also comes from the left, reflecting primarily a concern for the disparity in the sentences received by different offenders who confront different sentencing judges. This was raised as being of particular concern when the two judges preside over the same court jurisdiction. But it is also raised with regard to different jurisdictions within the same state because a rural and an urban prisoner could well be housed in adjoining cells within the same state prison. The greatest disparity could be expected between an urban and a rural jurisdiction, where the higher crime rate of the urban jurisdiction could well be expected to lead to greater inurement to the lesser offenses.

Here, the argument for reducing disparity derives from the proper concern that individuals who committed the same offense and came to the court with the same prior record should receive the same punishment. Of course, two individuals rarely do come with the same record, and two offenses can be crammed into the same named and legal category, but that does not necessarily make them identical.

Thus the legitimate concern for avoiding disparity can become counterproductive by creating groupings that must be treated alike even though the elements within a group may be quite different. Sentencing commissions recognize these problems and so usually permit deviation from the guidelines but impose a burden of explanation on the judges who do deviate. Also, most laws establishing guidelines provide a right to appeal (in some cases, a right granted to both the defense and to the prosecution) sentences that fall outside the guidelines.

Here again, the concerns of the left—disparity—have created an instrument—guidelines—that provide an opportunity for the right to address its concern—judicial leniency. In many cases, once the actual time served is presented in particular terms, it is easy for the political process to find it unreasonably lenient. The public seems much more likely to take as its baseline the extremely long sentence that the press reports a convicted person "faces." That sentence is the sum of the statutory maximum sentences on each of the conviction charges. Of course, no one is ever sentenced for the total time "faced" because most sentences imposed are well below the statutory maximum, and sentences on multiple charges are almost always served concurrently.

The public is further offended when the reported sentence (almost always the maximum sentence in a range of minimum and maximum) is not even served. This is because most people sent to prison are released on parole well before their maximum sentence expires. This makes sense from both a correctional control viewpoint as well as providing the safety-valve function parole has traditionally provided. After several years in a prison environment, it certainly seems reasonable that there be a process of phasing the individual back into the community, first perhaps in a community-based residential program, followed by independent residence in a situation where the parolee has an increased vulnerability to removal in the event that the criminal activity is reinitiated. These are the opportunities provided by a system of parole.

Most actual times served are considerably less than the baseline of sentences "faced" with which the public is generally familiar. This disparity of expectation provides further opportunity for those who wish to claim that a current sentencing structure or a proposed guidelines structure (especially one constrained by available prison capacity) is unreasonably lenient. Furthermore, in the political competition to be "tough on crime," there is a continual process of raising the ante: As each political environment becomes acclimated to the current sentences, it becomes easier to demand still more.

Thus recent years have seen many ways in which there has been significant growth in the politicization of sentencing policy. This has come about primarily through legislatures grabbing control of the sentencing process and using that control to increase the sentencing ranges, to impose a larger number of mandatory minimum sentences, and generally to increase the number of people being sent to prison and the time they serve.

3. THE DEMOGRAPHIC SHIFT

These effects have been exacerbated by the increase in the number of people in the prison-eligible population as a result of the large demographic bulge in the U.S. population known as the "postwar baby boom," those people born between 1947 until the peak years of the early 1960s. The largest cohorts, those of 1960–1962 were 26 to 28 in 1988. This put them just barely past the peak incarceration ages of about 23 to 25. Thus there was in the early to mid-1980s a coincidence of the peak incarceration ages and the peak cohort sizes that further contributed to an increase in the size of the population eligible for imprisonment.

These were factors considered by Blumstein, Cohen, and Miller (1980) in their demographically based forecast of prison populations. Because crime and prison are so strongly related to demographic variables, particularly age, race, and sex, and because the shift in the age composition has been so significant with the coming and passing of the baby boom generation, those projections were shown to be quite accurate in anticipating the peak in crime rates that were found throughout the United States in about 1980.

One of the interesting aspects of those projections was the indication that, even though crime rates were anticipated to peak in 1980, it was projected that commitments to prison would peak in about 1985 and that prison populations would continue to climb throughout the 1980s, reaching a peak in about 1990. That projection was somewhat surprising initially because some intuition would suggest that a peak in prison population ought to come at about the same time as a peak in crime—perhaps somewhat later because of the time for processing the crime through the courts and somewhat longer to reflect the 1 to 3 years of sentence time.

Of course, that consideration would be reasonable if the crime peak were associated with factors other than changing age composition, say, changes in economic conditions. When the changes are associated with age composition, then one must also recognize the difference in the peak ages of crime commission and of incarceration. Crime peaks at about 16 to 18 for most of the index crimes that comprise the bulk of prison populations, whereas incarceration rates peak at about 23 to 25. The difference arises from the rapid rate of termination of criminal careers in the ages just after the crime peak. Thus there are relatively few of these offenders still active into their 20s. Furthermore, very few individuals are imprisoned before passng out of the juvenile years (at age 18 in most states). Even among adults, prison is rarely imposed for the first offense, and most property offenders have several opportunities for conviction before their first imprisonment. The intervals between these missed opportunities for imprisonment add up to several years, and these intervals contribute to the shift in the peak ages from crime to commitment to prison and from commitment to the age of the stock of prisoners reflected in age-specific incarceration rates.

It now appears that even this projection of the peaking of commitments in 1985 based on Pennsylvania is actually occurring. In 1987, there was, for the first time, an actual decline of court commitments to prison. The number of prisoners increased, however, because of the increased number of parole violators sent back to prison. This could well be consistent with the earlier projection of a peak in commitments in 1985 while the total population was increasing. If that pattern is indeed confirmed by continuing into the next year, then there is considerable hope that the population peak will indeed occur in 1990 and that there may begin to be some relief from the growing prison problem of the 1980s.

4. PROSPECTS FOR THE FUTURE

4.1. Continued Politicization

There are some important reasons to be pessimistic about those prospects, however. First, it is important to point out that that projected peak in 1990 was a total of about 12,500 prisoners, and that number was actually passed in about 1983. The current population in 1988 is about 16,000 prisoners; this reflects the stiffening of prison sentences, primarily during the period of the 1980s, thus compounding the demographic and the political aspects of sentencing consequences. As the baby boomers age out of the high imprisonment ages, the demographic effect will turn around, but there is no clear indication that the political one will follow correspondingly.

Indeed, the politicization of the response to the drug problem raises serious doubts about when and how restraint on sentencing will reappear. Most jurisdictions are experiencing calls for stiffer sentences as a response to an admittedly serious social problem. The debate seems to give no consideration to the functional consequences of such an increase. Thus it may be reasonable to expect that any slack provided by the relief from the growing demographic pressure will find many eager political opportunists ready to identify an offense or body of offenders to fill it.

The irrationality in the drug-sentencing policy derives from an inquiry into the objectives that would be achieved through a major increase in the sentences assigned to drug-trafficking offenses, one of the hottest fads of the late 1980s. Drug abuse represents one of the severe social problems faced by American society, and all wish there were some way to get rid of that problem. It is excessively simplistic, however, to think that that can be done merely by increasing prison sentences. Experience with drug-sentencing policies, as well as inquiry into the functions of sentencing, makes it very dubious that increasing sentences for drug dealers will do much to reduce drug trafficking.

The criminal justice system can reduce crime in only three ways: rehabilitation, incapacitation, and deterrence. Prison is not likely to do much for any of these. Although many of the sellers are themselves addicts and users, a prison cell is likely to be even less effective in reducing a drug user's need than any of the many other ways that have been tried in vain. Incapacitation requires that the prisoner take his or her crimes off the street with him or her; that happens with a pathological rapist, but if a drug seller is removed from the street, many replacements will quickly be competing for his or her corner. For deterrence to work, *all* potential sellers would have to find the risk of selling drugs sufficiently great that the supply side of the drug market would dry up. However, profits are so large and the risks of getting convicted are seen as sufficiently small, that no threatened sentence is likely to be sufficient.

4.2. Demographic Prospects

The demographics of the future also fail to provide great optimism that the era of growing prison populations will finally reverse itself dramatically. One of the shifts that is of some consequence is the racial shift and some of the class shifts associated with it. Incarceration rates for blacks are about six to seven times those for whites, and so a relative increase in the black population should be indicative of an increase in the black prisoner population. In the cohorts under 15, blacks comprise about 16% of the U.S. population compared to about 12% of the total population. If the proportion of the black population who engage in crime remains the same, then this suggests both an increase in the prison population and an increase in the black composition of prisons to the point where they comprise the majority of prisoners. In view of the political import associated with the latter shift, it could well be the more serious and the more threatening to the social stability of American society.

These problems are likely to be exacerbated by the socialization environment of the young people in the United States of the 1980s. As many as 22% of the people under 16 were living under the poverty income level in 1984, and in 1986, about 20% of the children born were born to unwed mothers, most of whom were teenagers with considerable demands for organizing their own lives.

The prospects of the future criminal activity of these younger cohorts must give some pause to those concerned with the crime environment and the human capital needs of the United States as it approaches the twenty-first century. It is clear that the demands on schools and other public institutions will be significantly increased, but the efforts at resource allocation and at institutional reform have hardly begun to be addressed. If we fail to address these issues appropriately, the status of prisons and imprisonment in the next century will certainly represent a major time of crisis.

5. SUMMARY

The past two decades have seen major growth in American prison populations, largely as a result of the confluence of important demographic shifts associated with the postwar baby boom and important political shifts that have politicized the decisions regarding who should go to prison and for how long, leading to an increase in general sanction policies. Although there may be some diminution of the demographic shift during the 1990s while the "baby bust" of the late 1960s and 1970s is in the high-incarceration ages, continued politicization seems likely. The arrival into the high-incarceration ages of the "echo boom" generation, with a much larger proportion of its population in lower socioeconomic conditions, makes it likely that—absent other significant changes in either involvement in crime or in sanction policies—there will be major new pressures on prison populations in the early years of the next century.

6. REFERENCES

Blumstein, A., and Cohen, J. A theory of the stability of punishment. *The Journal of Criminal Law & Criminology*, 1973, *64*(2), 198–206.

Blumstein, A., Cohen, J., and Miller, H. Demographically disaggregated projections of prison populations. *Journal of Criminal Justice*, 1980, *8*, 1–26.

Lipton, D., Martinson, R., and Wilks, J. *The effectiveness of correctional treatment: A survey of treatment evaluation studies.* New York: Praeger, 1975.

Martinson, R. What works? Questions and answers about prison reform. *Public Interest*, 1974, *10*, 22–54.

President's Commission on law Enforcement and the Administration of Justice (President's Crime Commission). *The challenge of crime in a free society.* Washington, DC: U.S. Government Printing Office, 1967.

Robison, J. O., and Smith, G. The effectiveness of correctional programs. *Crime & Delinquency*, 1971, *17*, 67–80.

von Hirsch, A. *Doing justice: The choice of punishments.* New York: Hill and Wang, 1976.

Chapter 3

THE EFFECTIVENESS OF CORRECTIONAL REHABILITATION
Reconsidering the "Nothing Works" Debate

FRANCIS T. CULLEN and PAUL GENDREAU

> *Big time, no rehabilitation, lock 'em up like animals—*
> *then let them out on society crazed and angry. Shit don't*
> *make no sense but the people cry for punishment and*
> *the politicians abide them—can they really be so blind?*
> Robby Wideman, in *Brothers and Keepers*
> (1984:243)

From its inception in the 1820s, the American prison was meant to be more than a sturdy cage of high, thick, stone walls in which the wayward could be restrained. The prison's founders called their invention a "penitentiary," a label that embodied their optimism that this carefully planned social institution had the power to reform even the most wicked spirit (Rothman, 1971).

For much of the past century and a half, faith in the prison's curative powers showed a remarkable durability. To be sure, the bleak, if not inhumane, realities of institutional life often made it difficult to believe that existing prisons were improving their charges. Even so, most "en-

FRANCIS T. CULLEN • Department of Criminal Justice, University of Cincinnati, Cincinnati, Ohio 45221-0108. PAUL GENDREAU • Centracare Saint John Inc., Saint John, New Brunswick E2M 4H7, Canada.

lightened" commentators agreed that rehabilitation *should* be the overriding goal of incarceration. Toby's 1964 review of leading criminology texts, for example, led him to conclude that "students reading these textbooks might infer that punishment is a vestigial carryover of a barbaric past and will disappear as humanitarianism and rationality spread" (1964: 332). Other commentators echoed this observation in 1971, when they noted that "the treatment approach receives nearly unanimous support from those working in the field of criminal justice" (American Friends Service Committee Working Party, 1971:83).

By the end of the 1970s, however, this consensus on the purpose of imprisonment had shattered. Suddenly, it seemed, many within the criminological community—scholars, policymakers, and even some practitioners—changed their minds: It was now fashionable to reject the idea that prisons could transform lawbreakers into lawabiders. This reversal of sentiments has its underlying causes (as we shall see), but on the surface it was ostensibly based on good scientific reasoning: Evaluation studies showed that correctional treatment did not work. "In the absence of any strong evidence in favor of the success of rehabilitative programs," Conrad (1973:209) concluded, "it is not possible to continue the justification of policy decisions in corrections on the supposition that such programs achieve rehabilitative objectives."

Although not willing to dismiss fully the criticisms leveled at correctional treatment, we argue for a reconsideration of this pervasive belief among criminologists that "rehabilitation doesn't work." We begin by suggesting that the rejection of rehabilitation has less to do with a careful reading of the empirical literature and more to do with changes in the social fabric that triggered a corresponding shift in thinking about corrections. We then turn to the growing body of research demonstrating the effectiveness of correctional programs and highlight the most prominent characteristics of successful intervention strategies. This discussion is followed by an assessment of the widely held assumption that citizens endorse a purely punitive or "get tough" approach to corrections. Contrary to what most commentators have declared, the data show, we believe, that the prevailing ideological context is favorable to the implementation of effective treatment programs.

1. THE "NOTHING WORKS" DEBATE

1.1. The Martinson Phenomenon

In 1974, Robert Martinson published in *The Public Interest* "What Works?—Questions and Answers About Prison Reform"—an article that readily captured the keen interest of the criminal justice community. Distilled from a larger coauthored research report (Lipton, Martinson, and Wilks, 1975), Martinson's essay presented the results of his research team's assessment of 231 evaluation studies of treatment programs conducted between 1945 and 1967. He then offered a disquieting indictment of correctional treatment. "With few and isolated exceptions," he (1974: 25) concluded, "the rehabilitative efforts that have been reported so far have had no appreciable effect on recidivism."

At the article's end, Martinson (1974:48–50) paused to raise a fundamental policy question, "Does nothing work?" He was careful to note that the failure to find treatment successes may have been the result of factors such as the inability of studies to detect when programs are effective and the use of rehabilitation programs weakened by a lack of commitment and therapeutic expertise. These caveats aside, however, he offered little room for optimism. "It may be," he cautioned, "that there is a more radical flaw in our present strategies—that education at its best, or that psychotherapy at its best, cannot overcome, or even appreciably reduce, the powerful tendencies of offenders to continue in criminal behavior" (1974:49).

Most onlookers paid little heed to Martinson's caveats, finding more persuasive his suggestion that correctional treatment was an inherently flawed enterprise. "The phrase 'nothing works,'" observes Walker (1985: 168), "became an instant cliché and exerted an enormous influence on both popular and professional thinking." Moreover, the nothing works doctrine continues to inform commentary on American corrections. While Attorney General Edwin Meese, for example, referred to the "substantially discredited theory of rehabilitation" (*Criminal Justice Newsletter*, 1987:3). Alfred Regnery (1985:3), at the time the administrator of the Office of Juvenile Justice and Delinquency Prevention—"the federal agency charged with reducing crime by juveniles"—offered a balder statement on the "folly of rehabilitation":

> Rehabilitation has been the premise of the juvenile court system throughout the 20th century, but it has failed miserably. . . . Martinson did his review in the late 1960s; since that time, rehabilitation has sunk further in esteem, both in the eyes of the public and the professionals. The criminal justice system has all but given up on the concept. Virtually no successful juvenile programs—those that reduce recidivism to an appreciable degree—rely on rehabilitation.

At first glance, then, Martinson's research appears to have given rise to the sensible rejection of correctional treatment: Because nothing works, why continue futile efforts to reform the wicked? In this view, the tarnishing of the rehabilitative ideal is simply a matter of good science; the data have spoken, and the issue is closed. As Walker (1985:

192) has concluded from his review of the debate sparked by Martinson, "It is wishful thinking to believe that additional research is going to uncover a magic key that has somehow been overlooked for 150 years."

But this reasoning fails to solve the puzzle of rehabilitation's apparent decline, for two matters are left unexplained. On one hand, Martinson was far from the first researcher to report that treatment programs were apparently not reducing rates of recidivism (Allen, 1981:57). In 1959, Wootton's (1959:334) review of existing studies prompted her conclusion that "as to the effectiveness of the comparatively humane methods now in use, surprisingly little evidence is available." Others reported similar conclusions (cf. Cressey, 1958; Gold, 1974; Robison and Smith, 1971). One wonders why Martinson's study garnered so much attention (including his appearance on CBS television's "60 Minutes"), whereas these earlier studies fell largely on deaf ears.

On the other hand, reviews of evaluation studies published after Martinson's essay indicate that substantial research exists demonstrating the effectiveness of correctional treatment (Gendreau, 1981; Gendreau and Ross, 1979, 1981, 1987; Greenwood and Zimring, 1985; Halleck and Witte, 1977; Palmer, 1983; Van Voorhis, 1987). Even so, this growing body of work is frequently overlooked by critics who proclaim so confidently rehabilitation's demise. Another twist in the saga remains, however. Based on a review of more recent studies, Martinson (1979:244, 252) took pains to recant his earlier conclusions:

> Contrary to my previous position, some treatment programs do have an appreciable effect on recidivism. . . . Some programs are indeed beneficial. New evidence from our current study leads me to reject my original conclusion. . . . I have hesitated up to now, but the evidence in our surveys is simply too overwhelming to ignore.

It is ironic, but instructive, that whereas Martinson's 1974 nothing works article is among the most cited of criminological writings, his revisionist 1979 essay earned scant attention.

These considerations cast doubt on an explanation that sees the attack on rehabilitation as simply a case of the prudent reading of existing scientific evidence. It seems inescapable that the studies were paid attention to selectively and, for most people, were used to justify, not to form, opinions about correctional treatment. As Gould (1981) reminds us, not only citizens but also scientists—including those studying crime—are embedded within a social context that shapes, often unconsciously, what evidence they attend to and what evidence they overlook. This insight leads us to suggest that Martinson's article became a phenomenon not on the basis of the sheer force of the intellectual argument—however much this was—but because it had the good fortune of appearing in a social context that had become receptive to its message.

Currie (1985:237) reaches a similar conclusion, observing that the enthusiastic reception accorded Martinson's nothing works idea "had at least as much to do with ideology as with evidence." Allen's (1981:10) words are equally instructive:

> The decline of the rehabilitative ideal in the 1970s cannot be explained satisfactorily as the consequence of the rational cases arrayed against it. . . . The very diversity of the attacks on the rehabilitative ideal, their conflicting assumptions and motivations, and the suddenness of the decline suggest that *broader social and cultural influences* are involved. (emphasis added)

We explore this theme in more detail later.

1.2. The "Nothing Works" Doctrine in Context

What was taking place in this broader environment that might account more adequately for the popularity of the nothing works doctrine and, more generally, for the full-scale attack on rehabilitation? As Rothman's (1971, 1980) historical analyses reveal, times of disorder and change provide fertile ground for the sprouting of correctional reform. People are suddenly thrust into new social circumstances, and these experiences create the potential for them to view the world differently or perhaps with a greater sense of urgency. The decade of social turbulence preceding the publication of Martinson's 1974 article profoundly affected many Americans, including criminologists and criminal justice policymakers. Inequitable arrangements—including racial, class, and patriarchal hierarchies of dominance—had been exposed and challenged in the courts and in the streets. Protest seemed ubiquitous, first over issues of civil rights and then over Vietnam. Riots and bombings rocked cities and campuses; crime rose at an alarming rate, while Harvard professors talked about the benefits of drugs. And a lengthy roster of events captured national attention and shook, if not split, the nation's citizenry: names such as Kent State, Attica, and Watergate became etched in the public mind.

This unusual coalescence of events, we contend, underlies the antagonism thrust at correctional treatment from commentators located on both sides of the political spectrum. Conservatives, of course, had long blamed rehabilitation for robbing the correctional system of its crime control powers. In this view, discretionary decisions in the name of individualized treatment allow offenders to escape imprisonment or, if incarcerated, to earn early release. The lasting lesson taught is that the bark of the justice system is louder than its bite; crime, it seems, is not so costly an enterprise, particularly when the profits it offers are included in the utilitarian calculus.

Even with this tradition of favoring a punitive response to crime, in the late 1960s, conservatives became especially vociferous in advocating the need to "get tough" with the lawlessness gripping the nation. What might explain the special attention they paid to the crime problem? Part of the answer lies in escalating offense rates, which could be pointed to as evidence of the need for stringent control measures. But as Finckenauer (1978:15) reveals, it was "not crime per se that became an issue in the 1960s, but rather 'law and order'." The turbulent events of the day had fostered anxiety that social and political collapse was imminent. In this context, lawlessness symbolized, in Quinney's (1977:13) words, "the ultimate crack in the armor of the existing social order." It seemed that nothing short of a "war on crime" was needed to preserve a social fabric coming apart at its seams.

Martinson's study, published in the midst of this campaign to insure social order, was welcome news to conservatives. Often accused of harboring a repressive ideology, they could now point to hard, objective data showing that correctional treatment programs were ineffective. Science, they claimed, had proven their vision of criminal justice correct. Accordingly, they seemed on solid footing in insisting that a realistic crime control agenda would involve curtailing discretionary decision making by passing laws that mandated incarceration, made prison sentences determinate, abolished parole boards, and selectively incapacitated the worst offenders (Wilson, 1975).

More perplexing, however, is that the rehabilitative ideal was also criticized fervently by liberals. Indeed, their disenchantment was instrumental in weakening treatment's appeal, for it meant that the ranks had thinned of those who had traditionally defended rehabilitation against attacks from the right. "The subsequent turn against rehabilitation cannot be explained primarily as a conservative reaction to rising crime rates," Plattner (1976:105) observed. "It was made possible only by a discrediting of rehabilitation by the left."

Why would the political left abandon correctional rehabilitation at this particular historical juncture? Liberals, like conservatives, lived through the turmoil of the decade preceding Martinson's article, but they saw the period's events through different lenses. Everywhere conservatives looked, they saw signs of disorder and social decay; in contrast, liberals saw evidence of a corrupt social and political order. In particular, they developed a deep suspicion of the motives of state officials. The beatings suffered by civil rights protesters, the shooting of students at Kent State, the stunning death toll of the Attica prison riot, the carnage in Vietnam, and the Watergate scandal—to list only some of the more poignant events—furnished ample evidence that the state was prepared to use any means to protect its interests. "Liberal assumptions about the benevolence of the state," Greenberg and Humphries (1980:209) observed, "could no longer be sustained."

As America turned into the 1960s, feelings had been quite different. The decade had begun with promises that a new frontier would be traversed and a more equitable order achieved; a "Great Society" seemed within reach. By the decade's end, this optimism had declined markedly, often turning into the despairing realization that the state could not be trusted to do social good (Allen, 1981; Bayer, 1981; Empey, 1979; Friedrichs, 1979; Rothman, 1978). The fallout of this thinking for correctional treatment was immense, for inherent in the rehabilitative ideal was the belief that state criminal justice officials could be relied upon to reform offenders. "Individualized treatment," the correctional model handed down by progressive reformers, granted officials wide discretion to fit the treatment to the offender's unique set of needs (Rothman, 1980: 43–81). Close scrutiny of this system in operation, liberals now contended, disclosed its disturbing ramifications: Unbridled discretion created not the opportunity for doing good but for abuse. Thus judicial discretion often resulted in preferential sentences for the advantaged, whereas correctional/parole officials used the indeterminate sentence and their powers to regulate release not as a carrot to motivate inmate personal growth but as a stick to coerce inmate conformity.

In this context, Martinson's (1974) report that treatment programs have "no appreciable effect on recidivism" confirmed what many liberals had already concluded. After all, how could one expect a coercive therapeutic regime enforced by state power to work? With thoughts of *A Clockwork Orange* and *One Flew Over the Cuckoo's Nest* fresh in mind, it seemed more prudent to forfeit hopes of bettering inmates and to get on with the more urgent task of protecting them against the abuse of state power (Rothman, 1978).

Liberals thus embraced what is commonly called the "justice model" of corrections (Fogel, 1979; von Hirsch, 1976). The goal of this scheme was to limit the largely unfettered powers enjoyed by state officials. Accordingly, they took special aim at the "indeterminate sentence," the linchpin of the progressive design of individualized treatment. They called for determinacy in sentencing, believing that criminal codes prescribing set sanctions for each offense would purge the system of discretion. Judges would no longer have the freedom to select a sanction from a wide range of alternatives, but regardless of the offender's race, class, gender, or circumstance would assign the penalty listed in the statute. Because prison terms would be set in law and known at the time of sentencing, parole boards would be abolished. In this scheme, offenders would receive equal treatment before the law; they would receive punishment commensurate with the seriousness of their crimes.

Just deserts, not individualized treatment, would be the guiding principle of the correctional process.

Thus the social context that made liberals anxious about state power and conservatives anxious about social disorder served to undermine confidence in and to fuel an attack on the rehabilitative ideal. Martinson's study assumed such a lasting significance not on the basis of its empirical merits but because it gave scientific legitimacy to existing, deeply felt sentiments. Caught up in larger sociohistorical circumstances, his study took on the status of the final word on the effectiveness of correctional treatment. As such, the doctrine of nothing works is best seen not as an established scientific truth but as a socially constructed reality.

1.3. Nothing Works? A Time for Reassessment

Our comments are not meant to imply that no benefits accrued from the sustained critical attention given to correctional rehabilitation. This scrutiny illuminated very real problems that too often accompany enforced therapy, raised issues of accountability in criminal justice decision making, and ended naive talk of treatment as a panacea for the crime problem. Even so, we are troubled by what Allen (1981:57) calls a "new orthodoxy," the conviction that "rehabilitative objectives are largely unattainable and that rehabilitative programs and research are dubious and misdirected." This orthodoxy, as Allen (1981:9) notes, is especially prevalent among academic criminologists who have jumped in large numbers upon the antitreatment bandwagon. Key policymakers in a variety of states also have come to assume that rehabilitation is a failed agenda. This conclusion gains credence, when we consider that a growing proportion of states have rejected the notion of individualized treatment and introduced determinacy and punishment as the guiding principles of adult and juvenile systems of justice (Cullen and Gilbert, 1982; Goodstein and Hepburn, 1985; Serrill, 1980).

The risk exists, therefore, that much of the criminal justice community will continue to assume uncritically that the treatment effectiveness issue has been settled. Ironically, as we will see next, this lack of skepticism toward the nothing works doctrine is occurring at precisely the time when evidence is accumulating as to what does, and does not, work.

We take some solace, however, that despite the sustained attack against it, the appeal of the rehabilitative ideal has proven fairly robust, especially among citizens, the group often said to be most opposed to offering human services to inmates. Somewhat paradoxically, moreover, research on treatment effectiveness has grown. Some of this research has been produced by crime scholars who have remained committed to rehabilitative thinking, but many other studies have been produced by those in other disciplines who have not been exposed to and deterred by the criminologists' occupational ideology that "nothing works." Further, many other studies have been a product of the great increase throughout criminal justice over the past two decades in the belief in and requirements for program evaluation. These evaluations have expanded the knowledge base and provided valuable information on what works in corrections.

Finally, even though faith in correctional treatment has declined in meaningful ways, it is noteworthy that rehabilitation programs continue to be a ubiquitous feature of prison life (Goodstein and Hepburn, 1985: 152–155). The programs' existence is less an expression of ideological commitment than of the reality that institutional programming fulfills such useful functions as reducing idleness and contributing to inmate adjustment (Lipton *et al.*, 1975: 532–558). Given that treatment programs—for whatever reason—will continue to be part of the prison fabric, it would seem misguided to embrace a nothing works stance and forfeit the opportunity to learn more about how these resources can be employed in the most judicious way possible. In this light, the next section considers the empirical base of support for rehabilitation and the factors that contribute to effective correctional interventions.

2. EFFECTIVE CORRECTIONAL TREATMENT: PROSPECTS AND PRINCIPLES

Even though Martinson's review was supposed to have signaled the end of experimental attempts at demonstrating the value of rehabilitation, in fact, the converse occurred. Quite literally, about 200 studies appeared in the literature for the 1973–1987 period. There have been five extensive reviews of the rehabilitation literature covering this period (Gendreau and Ross, 1979, 1981, 1987; Ross and Gendreau, 1980; Ross and Fabiano, 1985). These reviews summarized studies that had at least quasi-experimental designs, community-based follow-up outcome measures ranging from rearrest to reincarceration, and were published in edited journals/texts. The literature is more extensive when other sources (e.g., government documents) are considered. A forthcoming meta-analysis by Lipsey (see Gendreau and Ross, 1987:394) includes several hundred reports.

For the purposes of this chapter, we will summarize this voluminous literature by referring to the conclusions drawn from the Gendreau and Ross reviews. First, many of the studies reviewed reported reductions of offenders' law-violating behavior as a result of intervention. Reductions, expressed in percentage terms, were frequently in the order of 10% to 30%, with instances of reduced rates in the 50% to 80% range. Approximately one-third of the studies were randomized experiments, whereas about half employed baseline comparisons and matched/comparison group designs. The follow-up periods were not trivial, frequently lasting 1 to 2 years and, in some studies, 5 to 15 years. Moreover, the studies that reported reductions did not come from one or two specific areas. The family therapy, early intervention, probation, diversion, substance abuse, and sexual deviation literatures all contributed significantly.

Therein rests an important point. If there is, as it certainly appears, an extensive literature attesting to the fact that rehabilitation programs can "work" and work in several areas for a variety of offenders, then it would be reasonable to assume that a set of underlying principles can be derived that are predictive of successful programs. In no uncertain terms, this has turned out to be the case: Several reviews of literature have concluded that successful programs can be distinguished from unsuccessful ones on the basis of theory, practice, and therapeutic integrity (Andrews, 1979, 1980; Andrews and Kiessling, 1980; Gendreau and Ross, 1981, 1984). Thus, in contrast to past assessments that have addressed the global question of whether treatment works (Lab and Whitehead, 1988; Martinson, 1974), it seems prudent that we look now into the "black box" of treatment programs to examine their theoretical underpinnings, what therapeutic strategies were employed, and the programs' therapeutic integrity. Following this reasoning, we discuss the characteristics of successful programs before turning to a review of recent research on treatment effectiveness.

2.1. Principles of Effective Correctional Intervention

The principles of effective correctional intervention, which are summarized in Table 1, are not inviolate and no doubt will be extended and modified in the future. Even so, they merit attention, for it would be difficult to uncover a study that did not include some or most of the criteria depicted in Table 1.

Space does not permit a detailed elucidation of Table 1, but a few explanatory comments on what seem to be a relatively straightforward set of principles is in order. First, the theories that have formed the underpinnings of successful correctional interventions all overlap, not surprisingly, to some extent. For interested readers, some key references for the theories noted are Alexander and Parsons (1982), Andrews

TABLE 1. Principles of Effective Intervention: Theories and Strategies

Theories associated with effective intervention	Intervention strategies	
	Effective	Ineffective
Social learning	Anticriminal modeling	Nondirective
Cognitive models	Problem solving	Behavior modification that
Skills training	Utilize community	focuses on incorrect
Differential association	resources	targets, is imposed,
Behavioral—systems	Quality interpersonal	emphasizes punishment,
family therapy	relationships	fails to utilize peer groups
	Authority	Deterrence
	Relapse prevention/self-efficacy	"Medical model" approaches

(1980), Bandura (1977, 1986), Goldstein (1986), Platt, Prout, and Metzger (1986), and Ross and Fabiano (1985).

Second, the first five effective strategies listed in Table 1 are from Andrews and Kiessling (1980:446). Essentially, they demand of the counselor to promote, as frequently as possible, the acquisition of pro-social attitudes and behavior on the part of the offender, to problem-solve those behaviors that will aid and reward the offender for noncriminal pursuits, and to utilize community resources that provide services suitable and relevant to the offender's needs. In addition, the services provided should be presented in a manner that ensures a just, honest, and empathetic relationship, yet that sees to it that the offender is aware that he or she must abide by reasonable program contingencies spelled out, for example, by the probation order or the requirements of the therapeutic contract.

Third, relapse prevention and self-efficacy notions, developed primarily in the addictions field, refer to the idea that one should focus interventions on the reasons why interventions fail to maintain positive changes after they demonstrated success during treatment. As well, the client must be taught coping skills that allow for a graduated mastery of high-risk situations that signal relapse.

Ineffective intervention strategies, which Table 1 also lists, require some clarification. First, nondirective counseling approaches have traditionally been those that promoted a "good" relationship between the counselor and the offender at the expense of ignoring the five key elements outlined by Andrews and Kiessling (1980). Second, we must emphasize that behavior modification techniques (e.g., token economies, behavioral contracting) can be effective; it depends on how they are carried out. Table 1 denotes just those ways of administering behavior modification programs that usually lead to negative consequences. Obviously, a wise clinician could reverse the processes listed. Third, the deterrence literature, in all its forms, has been reviewed elsewhere (Gendreau and Ross, 1981, 1987: 367–370) and has been found sadly wanting in contrast to therapeutic procedures that do not attempt only to punish offenders. Finally, "medical model" treatments are those that operate from a disease conceptualization of delinquency and rely on pharmacological and nutritional therapies, to name two such examples.

Although not included in Table 1, there is one other principle, noted previously, that applies to all conceivable aspects of service delivery to offenders. It is "therapeutic integrity," or as Gendreau and Ross (1979: 467) put it:

> To what extent do treatment personnel actually adhere to the theoretical principles and employ the techniques of the therapy they purport to provide? To what extent are the treatment staff competent? How hard do they work? How much is treatment diluted in the correctional environment so that it becomes treatment in name only?

It is virtually impossible to find a successful intervention study that cannot answer the previous questions by documenting staff and program quality. In this regard, an excellent example of therapeutic integrity in practice is the recent diversion program of Davidson, Redner, Blakely, Mitchell, and Emshoff (1987).

2.2. Recent Research: Further Reason for Optimism

In closing, we provide further testimony to the viability of a vigorous rehabilitation agenda. In order to determine whether the evidence supporting rehabilitation continues to appear in the literature at the same impressive rate as witnessed in the most recent review (Gendreau and Ross, 1987, which was completed in September of 1987), we conducted another examination of the literature for the period extending to February 1988. Simply put, there have been more significant gains from the perspectives of theory development, clinical practice, treatment outcome literature, and policy development.

In terms of theory, Eron (1987) and Peele (1987), respectively, have made important contributions to our knowledge about the development of aggressive behavior and substance abuse dependency. Rowe (1987) has advanced our understanding of how people and situations interact that will lead to more sophisticated conceptualizations of criminal behavior. And Izzo and Ross's (1987) meta-analysis of treatment programs for juvenile delinquents further reinforces the notion (cf. Garrett, 1985) that cognitive-based theories of behavioral change are among the most effective.

Clinicians' knowledge as to the *hows* of effective intervention has been augmented by Stumphauzer's (1987) invaluable documentation of useful treatment techniques for a wide cross-section of delinquents. Platt and his colleagues (e.g., Platt, Taube, Metzger, and Duome, in press) have done likewise for cognitive interpersonal problem-solving procedures. Annis and Davis (1988a,b) provide a wealth of clinical information on the application of relapse prevention and self-efficacy strategies to the treatment of alcohol abuse. Pithers, Kashima, Cumming, Beal, and Buell (1987) also have adapted relapse prevention components for their treatment of sexual offenders. In our view, their methodologies are quite applicable to the design of community-based interventions for those offenders who do not have a serious addiction or sexual problems.

The outcome literature persists in demonstrating at least modest gains in the reduction of future offending behavior in the areas of work programs (Rauma and Berk, 1987), restitution (Schneider, 1986), school-based interventions (Gottfredson, 1986), treatment for adolescent and adult sex offenders (Davis and Leitenberg, 1987; Pithers *et al.*, 1987), substance abuse treatment (Platt and Metzger, 1987), early intervention programs (Hawkins, Catalano, Jones, and Fine, 1987; Lally, 1986; Tolan, Perry, and Jones, 1987), and intensive probation supervision (Pearson, 1987). Indeed, two studies have reported rather impressive results. Documentation on the famous Perry Preschool study (Schweinhart, 1987) indicated dramatic reductions (almost 100%) in arrest rates per person in favor of the experimental group. Follow-up periods extended up to 15 years. In a long-term evaluation—follow-up periods were 1 to 11 years—of a cognitive-behavioral treatment program for child molesters, Marshall and Barbaree (1988) reported reductions in recidivism of up to 30%, depending upon the comparisons made.

Finally, the rehabilitation literature is offering a number of helpful policy recommendations for service delivery systems. They are to be found in the early intervention area (Loeber, 1987; Schweinhart, 1987; Wilson, 1987; Zigler and Hall, 1987), the field of alcohol treatment (Miller, 1987), and offender classification (Clear, 1988). Also, the analyses of the absence or presence of therapeutic integrity of programs in such diverse areas as intensive probation supervision (Latessa, 1987) and shock incarceration (MacKenzie, Gould, Riechers, and Shaw, 1988) will no doubt foster sound program policies in the future.

3. THE TENACITY OF REHABILITATIVE IDEOLOGY

A close reading of the data, therefore, suggests that much progress has been made in determining the principles of effective correctional intervention. Even so, the question remains as to whether sufficient citizen support exists to back such efforts. The public is often portrayed as oppositional to treating criminals and as clamoring for vengeance and more stringent crime control measures (Cullen, Clark, and Wozniak, 1985; Cullen, Cullen, and Wozniak, 1988; Scheingold, 1984; Thomson and Ragona, 1987). A survey of policymakers in Michigan, for example, reported that only 12% believed that citizens supported rehabilitation as the "purpose of criminal justice" (Michigan Prison and Jail Over-crowding Project, 1985). In this context, can much hope be marshaled that rehabilitative ideology retains its legitimacy?

Several conclusions can be offered. *First, the American public is punitive toward crime.* Much evidence exists that citizens support getting tough with lawbreakers (Stinchcombe *et al.*, 1980; Zimmerman, van Alstyne, and Dunn, 1988). Since the mid-1960s, the percentage of the public favoring capital punishment has risen from slightly more than 40% to over 70% (*Public Opinion*, 1987: 26; Rankin, 1979). A 1987 NORC survey found that 84% of those sampled felt that the courts do "not deal harshly enough with criminals" (*Public Opinion*, 1987: 26). Similarly, a 1986 poll discovered that only 15.7% of Cincinnati respondents and 10% of Columbus respondents favored "shortening sentences to reduce overcrowding" (Skovron, Scott, and Cullen, 1988:158).

Second, since the late 1960s, support for rehabilitation has declined. National polls suggest that there has been a jump in punitiveness and a commensurate decline in support for treatment. The concerted attacks on rehabilitation appear to have taken a toll. Thus, when asked what should be the main purpose of imprisonment, 73% of the respondents in a 1968 Harris poll answered rehabilitation; by 1982 this percentage had dropped precipitously to 44% (Flanagan and Caulfield, 1984:42).

Third, despite these trends, support for rehabilitation remains surprisingly strong. Indeed, in the face of criticism from all sides, one might have anticipated that confidence in correctional treatment would have been eroded fully. But this does not appear to have taken place. Just above, we noted that a longitudinal analysis of Harris polls indicated a sharp decline in support for treatment. Even so, it is instructive that respondents in the 1982 poll still favored as the "main emphasis of prisons" rehabilitation (44%) more than the other choices of "protect society" (32%) and "punishment" (19%). And this is not an isolated finding: Similar results have been found in a series of national and state surveys (Cullen, Clark, and Wozniak, 1985; Cullen, Skovron, Scott, and Burton, in press; Cullen and Gilbert, 1982; Duffee and Ritti, 1977; *Gallup Report*, 1982; Gottfredson and Taylor, 1983; Public Opinion Research, 1986; Skovron *et al.*, 1988; Thomson and Ragona, 1987).

It does not appear, moreover, that such support for rehabilitation is merely an artifact of using surveys that tap only weakly held values or perhaps elicit the socially desirable, "humanitarian" response that we should do more than warehouse offenders. This conclusion gains credence from the results of a 1986 study commissioned by the Edna McConnell Clark Foundation. Groups of 12 citizens in 10 metropolitan areas were brought together for in-depth "discussions on crime and corrections." Each meeting comprised a "focus group," which by design is intended "to investigate why people hold the views they do and to get beyond the 'top of the head' responses given in most public opinion polls" (Public Agenda Foundation, 1987:9). The researchers "had assumed that a fierce desire for retribution lay at the heart of public support for harsher punishments" and that "public support for rehabilitation was dead." They discovered instead that citizens "want assurances of safety much more than they want assurances of punishment," and they "want prisons to promote rehabilitation as a long-term means of controlling crime" (Public Agenda Foundation, 1987:5).

All this is not to assert that public opinion is about to fuel a campaign to transform prisons into therapeutic communities; it seems that citizens are more likely to take umbrage when offenders avoid imprisonment than when they are not afforded treatment services. But little evidence exists that the public opposes correctional programs or sees punishment and rehabilitation as mutually exclusive goals (Cullen et al., 1988; Duffee, 1980:194; Duffee and Ritti, 1977). Thus, although they favor sending felons to prison, often for lengthy terms, they also endorse interventions that hold the promise of returning offenders to society as better people.

Part of the reason for the resilience of support for treatment can be found in our fourth conclusion: *The majority of the public rejects the nothing works doctrine.* Despite the widespread belief among criminologists that rehabilitation is a failed penal policy (von Hirsch, 1985:4), citizens have not embraced the view that offenders, particularly young lawbreakers, are beyond reform. A 1982 Illinois survey, for example, found that only 43.2% agreed that "rehabilitation has proven to be a failure" and less than 24% agreed that the "rehabilitation of adult criminals just does not work" (Cullen et al., 1988; see also Cullen, Golden, and Cullen, 1983). A more recent survey in Ohio, moreover, reported similar results: Approximately 60% of the respondents agreed that rehabilitation would be "helpful to adult offenders," whereas over three-fourths stated that such programs would be "helpful to juvenile offenders" (Cullen et al., in press).

In short, the public favors the inclusion of rehabilitation as a central purpose of imprisonment and retains faith in the potential effectiveness of correctional interventions. The context thus seems favorable for calls to reaffirm rehabilitation. Still, a major barrier exists to initiating such an agenda, as our final point indicates: *Legislators and other criminal justice policymakers overestimate the public's punitiveness and underestimate the public's support of rehabilitation.* On a personal level, policymaker attitudes on corrections are multifaceted: They place a primacy on social protection but also endorse expanding rehabilitation programs and even tend to reject the idea that nothing works (Berk and Rossi, 1977; Bynum, Greene, and Cullen, 1986; Cullen, Bynum, Garrett, and Greene, 1985; Flanagan and McGarrell, 1986; Gottfredson and Taylor, 1983; Hamm, 1986; McGarrell and Flanagan, 1987). On a political level, however, most policymakers interpret the public will as demanding harsher sanctions for those that threaten the communal order; in turn, they misperceive the openness of citizens to a more diverse, progressive approach to corrections (Gottfredson and Taylor, 1983; Riley and Rose, 1980). Recall, for example, the Michigan study cited in the first part of this section, where only 12% of the policymakers perceived the public as supporting rehabilitation; in reality, nearly two-thirds of Michigan citizens sampled endorsed treatment as a goal of corrections (Michigan Prison and Jail Overcrowding Project, 1987:5).

Results such as these provide reason for both concern and hope for those who believe that rehabilitation should be reaffirmed. A reality has been constructed and legitimized by many criminologists that rehabilitation is a failed policy that the public will no longer tolerate. Belief in this vision of public sentiments furnishes little incentive for endorsing reforms aimed at improving the integrity of intervention programs. Yet these findings also suggest a starting point for social action. It seems reasonable to assume that the prospects for improving prison rehabilitation would be enhanced should policymakers be given fuller access to data on the structure of public attitudes and on the effectiveness of correctional treatment. Information campaigns, of course, are hardly a panacea for resistance to initiating substantive reform, but it appears a necessary first step if the ideological decline of the rehabilitative ideal is to be meaningfully reversed.

4. CONCLUSION

The occasion of Robert Martinson's article signified and encouraged an important turning point in American correctional thinking. Although his attack on offender therapy had the benefit of illustrating the considerable gap between the humane promises of the rehabilitative ideal and the actual services provided offenders, it also had the unfortunate consequence of establishing the nothing works doctrine as an accepted criminological truth. Even today, one does not have to look hard to still see examples of criminologists citing Martinson's piece and then smugly concluding that the issue of rehabilitation has been settled.

In the end, our essay is meant as a cautionary tale. We do not claim that correctional rehabilitation is without problems or that it offers a panacea to the crime problem, but we are firm in the belief that the nothing works doctrine is a socially constructed reality that lacks an empirical base. A growing body of data suggests not only that many interventions are successful but also that it is becoming increasingly possible to decipher the principles of effective correctional treatment. And as just reveiwed, it appears that despite treatment's persistent criticism over the past decade, much of the American public continues to believe that rehabilitation should be an integral goal of the correctional process.

It is sobering to contemplate that the tarnishing of the rehabilitative ideal has not ushered in a new era of crime control and justice but an era in which unprecedented incarceration rates are leaving most prison systems crowded and in crisis. If nothing else, this observation should prompt criminologists to review their easy rejection of treatment and to weigh the practical and moral value of a vibrant rehabilitative ideal.

5. REFERENCES

Alexander, J. F., and Parsons, B. V. *Functional family therapy.* Monterrey, CA: Brooks/Cole, 1982.

Allen, F. A. *The decline of the rehabilitative ideal: Penal policy and social purpose.* New Haven: Yale University Press, 1981.

American Friends Service Committee Working Party. *Struggle for justice: A report on crime and punishment in America.* New York: Hill and Wang, 1971.

Andrews, D. A. *The friendship model of voluntary action and controlled evaluations of correctional practices: Notes on relationships with behavior theory and criminology.* Toronto: Ontario Ministry of Correctional Services, 179.

Andrews, D. A. Some experimental investigations of the principles of differential association through deliberate manipulations of the structure of service systems. *American Sociological Review,* 1980, 45, 448–462.

Andrews, D. A., and Kiessling, J. J. Program structure and effective correctional practices. A summary of the CAVIL research. In R. R. Ross and P. Gendreau (Eds.), *Effective correctional treatment.* Toronto: Butterworths, 1980.

Annis, H., and Davis, C. S. Assessment of expectancies in alcohol dependent clients. In G. A. Marlatt and D. M. Donovan (Eds.), *Assessment of addictive behaviors.* New York: Guilford, 1988a.

Annis, H. M., and Davis, C. S. Relapse prevention. In R. K. Hester and W. R. Miller (Eds.), *Handbook of alcoholism treatment approaches.* New York: Pergamon Press, 1988b.

Bandura, A. Self-efficacy: Toward a unifying theory of behavioral change. *Psychological Review,* 1977, 84, 191–215.

Bandura, A. *Social foundations of thought and action: A social cognitive theory.* Englewood Cliffs, NJ: Prentice-Hall, 1986.

Bayer, R. Crime, punishment and the decline of liberal optimism. *Crime and Delinquency,* 1981, *27,* 169–290.

Berk, R. A., and Rossi, P. H. *Prison reform and state elites.* Cambridge, MA: Ballinger, 1977.

Bynum, T. S., Greene, J. R., and Cullen, F. T. Correlates of legislative crime control ideology. *Criminal Justice Policy Review,* 1986, *3,* 253–267.

Clear, T. Statistical prediction in corrections. *Research in Corrections,* 1988, *1,* 1–39.

Conrad, J. P. Corrections and simple justice. *Journal of Criminal Law and Criminology, 1973, 64,* 208–217.

Cressey, D. R. The nature and effectiveness of correctional techniques. *Law and Contemporary Problems,* 1958, *23,* 754–771.

Criminal Justice Newsletter "Election-year politics could mar sentencing reform, Meese warns," 1987, June 15, p. 3.

Cullen, F. T., and Gilbert, K. E. *Reaffirming rehabilitation.* Cincinnati: Anderson Publishing Company, 1982.

Cullen, F. T., Golden, K. M., and Cullen, J. B. Is child saving dead? Attitudes toward juvenile rehabilitation in Illinois. *Journal of Criminal Justice,* 1983, *11,* 1–13.

Cullen, F. T., Bynum, T. S., Garrett, K. M., and Greene, J. R. Legislative ideology and criminal justice policy; Implications from Illinois. In E. Fairchild and V. J. Webb (Eds.), *The politics of crime and criminal justice.* Beverly Hills: Sage, 1985.

Cullen, F. T., Clark, G. A., and Wozniak, J. F. Explaining the get tough movement: Can the public be blamed? *Federal Probation,* 1985, *49,* 16–24.

Cullen, F. T., Cullen, J. B., and Wozniak, J. F. Is rehabilitation dead: The myth of the punitive public. *Journal of Criminal Justice,* 1988, *16,* 303–317.

Cullen, F. T., Skovron, S. E., Scott, J. E., and Burton, V. S., Jr. Public support for correctional treatment: The tenacity of rehabilitative ideology. *Criminal Justice and Behavior,* in press.

Currie, E. *Confronting crime: An American challenge.* New York: Pantheon Books, 1985.

Davidson, W. S., Redner, R., Blakely, C., Mitchell, C., and Emshoff, J. Diversion of juvenile offenders: An experimental comparison. *Journal of Consulting and Clinical Psychology,* 1987, *55,* 68–75.

Davis, G. E., and Leitenberg, H. Adolescent sex offenders. *Psychological Bulletin,* 1987, *101,* 417–427.

Duffee, D. E. *Explaining criminal justice: Community theory and criminal justice reform.* Cambridge, MA: Oelgeschlager, Gunn, and Hain, 1980.

Duffee, D. E., and Ritti, R. R. Correctional policy and public values. *Criminology,* 1977, *14,* 449–459.

Empey, L. T. Foreword—From optimism to despair: New doctrines in juvenile justice. In C. A. Murray and L. A. Cox, Jr., *Beyond probation: Juvenile corrections and the chronic delinquent.* Beverly Hills: Sage, 1979.

Eron, L. D. The development of aggressive behavior from the perspective of a developing behaviorism. *American Psychologist,* 1987, *42,* 435–442.

Finckenauer, J. O. Crime as a national political issue: 1964–76—from law and order to domestic tranquility. *Crime and Delinquency,* 1978, *24,* 13–27.

Flanagan, T. J., and Caulfield, S. L. Public opinion and prison policy: A review. *Prison Journal,* 1984, *64,* 31–46.

Flanagan, T. J., and McGarrell, E. F. *Attitudes of New York legislators toward crime and criminal justice: A report of the state legislator survey—1985.* Albany: Hindelang Criminal Justice Research Center, 1986.

Fogel, D. *"We are the living proof": The justice model for corrections.* Second edition. Cincinnati: Anderson Publishing Company, 1979.

Friedrichs, D. O. The law and the legitimacy crisis: A critical issue for criminal justice. In

R. G. Iacovetta and D. H. Chang (Eds.), *Critical issues in criminal Justice*. Durham: Carolina Academic Press, 1979.

Gallup Report. Public backs wholesale prison reform. 1982, *22*, pp. 3–16.

Garrett, C. J. Effects of residential treatment on adjudicated delinquents: A meta-analysis. *Journal of Research in Crime and Delinquency*, 1985, *22*, 287–308.

Gendreau, P. Treatment in corrections: Martinson was wrong! *Canadian Psychology*, 1981, *22*, 332–338.

Gendreau, P., and Ross, R. R. Effective correctional treatment. Bibliotherapy for cynics. *Crime and Delinquency*, 1979, *25*, 463–489.

Gendreau, P., and Ross, R. R. Correctional potency: Treatment and deterrence on trial. In R. Roesch and R. R. Corrado (Eds.), *Evaluation in criminal justice policy*. Beverly Hills: Sage, 1981.

Gendreau, P., and Ross, R. R. Correctional treatment. Some recommendations for successful intervention. *Juvenile and Family Court Journal*, 1984, *34*, 31–40.

Gendreau, P., and Ross, R. R. Revivification of rehabilitation: Evidence from the 1980s. *Justice Quarterly*, 1987, *4*, 349–408.

Gold, M. A time for skepticism. *Crime and Delinquency*, 1974, *20*, 20–24.

Goldstein, A. P. Psychological skill training and the aggressive adolescent. In S. Apter and B. Harootunian (Eds.), *Youth violence: Program and prospects*. New York: Pergamon, 1986.

Goodstein, L., and Hepburn, J. *Determinate sentencing and imprisonment: A failure of reform*. Cincinnati: Anderson Publishing Company, 1985.

Gottfredson, D. C. An empirical test of school-based environmental and individual interventions to reduce the risk of delinquent behavior. *Criminology*, 1986, *24*, 705–731.

Gottfredson, S. D., and Taylor, R. B. *The correctional crisis: Prison populations and public policy*. Washington, DC: Department of Justice, 1983.

Gould, S. J. *The mismeasure of man*. New York: W. W. Norton, 1981.

Greenberg, D. F., and Humphries, D. The co-optation of fixed sentencing reform. *Crime and Delinquency*, 1980, *26*, 206–225.

Greenwood, P. W., and Zimring, F. E. *One more chance: The pursuit of promising intervention strategies for chronic juvenile offenders*. Santa Monica: Rand, 1985.

Halleck, S. L., and Witte, A. D. Is rehabilitation dead? *Crime and Delinquency*, 1977, *23*, 372–382.

Hamm, M. S. *Attitudes of Indiana legislators toward crime and criminal justice: A Report of the state legislator survey—1986*. Terre Haute: Department of Criminology, Indiana State University, 1986.

Hawkins, J. D., Catalano, R. F., Jones, G., and Fine, D. Delinquency prevention through parent training: Results and issues from work in progress. In J. Q. Wilson and G. C. Loury (Eds.), *From children to citizens*. New York: Springer-Verlag, 1987.

Izzo, R., and Ross, R. *Meta-analysis of correctional treatment programs for juvenile delinquents*. Ottawa: Department of Criminology, University of Ottawa, 1987.

Lab, S. P., and Whitehead, J. T. An analysis of juvenile correctional treatment. *Crime and Delinquency*, 1988, *34*, 60–83.

Lally, R. *Family development research program: Brief summary of incidence, severity, and cost of juvenile delinquency in program and control children*. Paper presented at National Association for the Education of Young Children, Washington, DC: 1986.

Latessa, E. J. The effectiveness of intensive supervision with high risk probationers. In B. R. McCarthy (Ed.), *Intermediate punishments: Intensive supervision, home confinement, and electronic surveillance*. Monsey, NJ: Criminal Justice Press, 1987.

Lipton, D., Martinson, R., and Wilks, J. *The effectiveness of correctional treatment: A survey of treatment evaluation studies*. New York: Praeger, 1975.

Loeber, R. What policy-makers and practitioners can learn from family studies of juvenile conduct problems and delinquency. In J. Q. Wilson and G. C. Loury (Eds.), *From children to citizens*. New York: Springer-Verlag, 1987.

MacKenzie, D. L., Gould, L. S., Riechers, L. M., and Shaw, J. *Evaluating shock incarceration in Louisiana: A review of the first year*. Baton Rouge: Department of Criminal Justice and Experimental Statistics, Louisiana State University, 1988.

Marshall, W. L., and Barbaree, H. E. The long-term evaluation of a cognitive-behavioral treatment program for child molesters. *Behavior Research and Therapy*, 1988, *26*, 499–511.

Martinson, R. What works?—Questions and answers about prison reform. *Public Interest*, 1974, *35*, 22–54.

Martinson, R. New findings, new views: A note of caution regarding sentencing reform. *Hofstra Law Review*, 1979, *7*, 243–258.

McGarrell, E. F., and Flanagan, T. J. Measuring and explaining legislator crime control ideology. *Journal of Research in Crime and Delinquency*, 1987, *24*, 102–118.

Michigan Prison and Jail Overcrowding Project. *Perceptions of criminal justice surveys: Executive summary*. Traverse City: Michigan Prison and Jail Overcrowding Project Inc., 1985.

Miller, W. R. Behavioral alcohol treatment research advances: Barriers to utilization. *Advances in Behavior Research and Therapy*, 1987, *9*, 165–171.

Palmer, T. The "effectiveness" issue today: An overview. *Federal Probation*, 1983, *46*, 3–10.

Pearson, F. S. *Final report of research on New Jersey's Intensive Supervision Program*. New Brunswick, NJ: Institute for Criminological Research, Department of Sociology, Rutgers University, 1987.

Peele, S. A moral vision of addiction: How people's values determine whether they become and remain addicts. *Journal of Drug Issues*, 1987, *17*, 187–215.

Pithers, W. D., Kashima, K. M., Cumming, G. F., Beal, L. S., and Buell, M. M. *Relapse prevention of sexual aggression*. South Burlington: Vermont Department of Corrections, 1987.

Platt, J. J., and Metzger, D. S. Cognitive interpersonal problem-solving skills and the maintenance of treatment success in heroin addicts. *Psychology of Addictive Behaviors*, 1987, *1*, 5–13.

Platt, J. J., Prout, M. F., and Metzger, D. S. Interpersonal cognitive problem-solving therapy (ICPS). In W. Dryden and W. Golden (Eds.), *Cognitive behavioral approaches to psychotherapy*. London: Harper & Row, 1986.

Platt, J. J., Taube, D. O., Metzger, D. S., and Duome, M. Training in interpersonal cognitive problem-solving (TIPS). *Journal of Cognitive Psychotherapy*. Forthcoming.

Plattner, M. F. The rehabilitation of punishment. *Public Interest*, 1976, *44*, 104–114.

Public Agenda Foundation. *Crime and Punishment: The Public's view*. New York: Edna McConnell Clark Foundation, 1987.

Public Opinion Opinion roundup: Crime and punishment. 1987, *10*, 26.

Public Opinion Research. *Confidential analytical report prepared for North Carolina Center on Crime and Punishment*. Washington, DC: Public Opinion Research, 1986.

Quinney, R. *Class, state, and crime: On the theory and practice of criminal justice*. New York: David McKay Co., 1977.

Rankin, J. H. Changing attitudes toward capital punishment. *Social Forces*, 1979, *58*, 194–211.

Rauma, D., and Berk, R. A. Remuneration and recidivism: The long-term impact of unemployment compensation on *ex*-offenders. *Journal of Quantitative Criminology*, 1987, *3*, 3–28.

Regnery, A. S. Getting away with murder: Why the justice system needs an overhaul. *Policy Review*, 1985, *34*, 1–4.

Riley, P. J., and Rose, V. M. Public and elite opinion concerning correctional reform: Implications for social policy. *Journal of Criminal Justice*, 1980, *8*, 345–356.

Robison, J., and Smith, G. The effectiveness of correctional programs. *Crime and Delinquency*, 1971, *17*, 67–80.

Ross, R. R., and Fabiano, E. A. *Time to think: A cognitive model of delinquency prevention and offender rehabilitation*. Johnson City, TN: Institute of Social Science and Arts, 1985.

Ross, R. R., and Gendreau, P. *Effective correctional treatment*. Toronto: Butterworths, 1980.

Rothman, D. J. *The discovery of the asylum: Social order and disorder in the new republic*. Boston: Little, Brown, 1971.

Rothman, D. J. The state as parent: Social policy in the progressive era. In W. Gaylin, I. Glassner, S. Marcus, and D. Rothman, *Doing good: The limits of benevolence*. New York: Pantheon, 1978.

Rothman, D. J. *Conscience and convenience: The asylum and its alternatives in progressive America*. Boston: Little, Brown, 1980.

Rowe, D. C. Resolving the person-situation debate. *American Psychologist*, 1987, *42*, 218–227.

Scheingold, S. A. *The politics of law and order: Street crime and public policy*. New York: Longman, 1984.

Schneider, A. L. Restitution and recidivism rates of juvenile offenders: Results from four experimental studies. *Criminology*, 1986, *24*, 533–552.

Schweinhart, L. Can preschool programs help prevent delinquency? In J. Q. Wilson and G. C. Loury (Eds.), *From children to citizens*. New York: Springer-Verlag, 1987.

Serrill, M. S. Washington's new juvenile code. *Correctional Magazine*, 1980, *6*, 36–41.

Skovron, S. E., Scott, J. E., and Cullen, F. T. Prison crowding: Public attitudes toward strategies of population control. *Journal of Research in Crime and Delinquency*, 1988, *25*, 150–169.

Stinchcombe, A. L., Adams, R., Heimer, C. A., Scheppele, K. L., Smith, T. W., and Taylor, D. G. *Crime and punishment: Changing attitudes in America*. San Francisco: Jossey-Bass, 1980.

Stumphauzer, J. *Helping delinquents change: A treatment manual of social learning approaches*. New York: Haworth, 1987.

Thomson, D. R., and Ragona, A. J. Popular moderation versus governmental authoritarianism: An interactionist view of public sentiments toward criminal sanctions. *Crime and Delinquency*, 1987, *33*, 337–357.

Toby, J. Is punishment necessary? *Journal of Criminal Law, Criminology, and Police Science*, 1964, *55*, 332–337.

Tolan, P. H., Perry, M. S., and Jones, T. Delinquency prevention: An example of consultation in rural community mental health. *Journal of Community Psychology*, 1987, *15*, 43–50.

Van Voorhis, P. Correctional effectiveness: The high cost of ignoring success. *Federal Probation*, 1987, *51*, 56–62.

von Hirsch, A. *Doing justice: The choice of punishments*. New York: Hill and Wang, 1976.

von Hirsch, A. *Past or future crimes: Deservedness and dangerousness in the sentencing of criminals*. New Brunswick, NJ: Rutgers University Press, 1985.

Walker, S. *Sense and nonsense about crime: A policy guide*. Monterey, CA: Brooks/Cole, 1985.

Wideman, J. E. *Brothers and keepers*. New York: Holt, Rinehart & Winston, 1984.

Wilson, J. Q. *Thinking about crime*. New York: Vintage Books, 1975.

Wilson, J. Q. Strategic opportunities for delinquency prevention. In J. Q. Wilson and G. C. Loury (Eds.), *From children to citizens*. New York: Springer-Verlag, 1987.

Wootton, B. *Social science and social pathology*. London: George Allen & Unwin, 1959.

Zigler, E., and Hall, N. W. The implication of early intervention efforts for the primary prevention of juvenile delinqency. In J. Q. Wilson and G. C. Loury (Eds.), *From children to citizens*. New York: Springer-Verlag, 1987.

Zimmerman, S. E., van Alstyne, D. J., and Dunn, C. S. The national punishment survey and public policy consequences. *Journal of Research in Crime and Delinquency*, 1988, *25*, 120–149.

Chapter 4

PROPRIETARY PRISONS

CHARLES H. LOGAN

The concept of hiring private contractors to manage prisons can be traced back at least as far as Jeremy Bentham (Roper, 1986: 85–88). More broadly defined, the private administration of punishment goes back, of course, much further. The notion that punishing criminals is the exclusive prerogative of the state is an invention of the state. That is, its origins are not ancient but coincident with the development of modern nation-states. Private involvement in punishment, however, continued even after the rise of the state. In the early years of this nation, many functions that are now widely regarded as public (i.e., state or government) responsibilities were then provided by private agencies and organizations, both communal and proprietary. Examples would include education, highways, police and fire protection, dispute resolution, and at least some kinds of punishment. Also, the nineteenth-century practice, more common in southern states, of contracting out the labor of prisoners to private employers, is often cited as historical precedent for the contemporary privatization of corrections.

More currently, private, low-security facilities have served the juvenile justice system in America throughout this century, and in some jurisdictions private contractors now provide the majority of adult community correctional programs, including all those for the federal prison system. In addition, virtually all the individual components of correc-

CHARLES H. LOGAN • University of Connecticut, Storrs, Connecticut 06268. This chapter was written during a Visiting Fellowship (86-IJ-CX-0062) at the National Institute of Justice. The views are those of the author and do not necessarily reflect Department of Justice policy.

tions (food services, medical services and counseling, educational and vocational training, recreation, maintenance, security, industrial programs, etc.) have been provided separately by private contractors.

However, all such claims of historical continuity and contemporary parallels notwithstanding, something new has emerged in the field of corrections in the 1980s. Modern prisons are very different from early English and American jails, and managing an entire institution has little in common with the leasing of convict labor or the contractual provision of particular services. Private entrepreneurs now manage, under contract to government, total institutions of penal or correctional confinement.

These are not primarily residential facilities, like foster homes, group homes, halfway houses, or community treatment centers. They are places of incarceration. They are privately owned or managed—that is, "proprietary"[1]—prisons, detention centers, jails, reformatories, and other correctional or penal institutions.

1. THE RECENT INTEREST IN PRIVATIZATION

Why are these institutions developing now? The usual explanations emphasize rising crime, tougher responses to crime, increased prison crowding, spiraling costs, and disillusionment with the government's ability to run its own prisons effectively and efficiently. However, the movement in corrections is part of a much broader trend toward privatization and reflects a rather general disenchantment with government. From the late 1950s to the mid-1970s, trust in government declined from almost 80% to about 33% (Savas, 1982: 1). This was part of a general lowering of public confidence in American institutions and leadership (Lipset and Schneider, 1983). Much of that decline could be accounted for by adverse economic conditions. However, rising employment and declining inflation in the early 1980s were "accompanied by the largest increase in confidence in any two-year period since the polls began to query Americans on the subject" (Lipset, 1985: 9). This was also the period of Reagan's popular emphasis of "getting the government off our backs" and the time during which *privatization* became a prevalent, if somewhat awkward, buzzword.

---

[1] In this chapter, the terms *private, proprietary,* and *contracted* (prisons) may be taken as synonymous. *Proprietary* implies private ownership, at least of the company, if not of the prison buildings and grounds. They are sometimes called "commercial" prisons or "prisons for profit," but a private company may be organized on a not-for-profit basis and still be regarded as "proprietary."

Private correctional institutions were not a direct result of any specific Reagan administration policies. The earliest facility described here (Weaversville, established in 1975) preceded his administration by a number of years, though most have been established after his election. Still, the emergence of private enterprise prisons and, even more, their identification as potential solutions to a problem, were undoubtedly aided by popular support for Reagan's ideological commitment to strengthening the private sector and weakening the governmental one.

Americans tend to distrust big business as well as big government and to favor competition and free enterprise (Lipset, 1985: 7). If and when private prisons become identified as big business, some of their current supporters may rethink their positions. For now, however, many see them as innovative and competitive responses to problems created under government monopoly (Logan and Rausch, 1985).

2. THE EARLY CONTRACTS

As of 1987, private companies in at least nine states were running confinement institutions—such as jails, detention centers, training schools, ranches, and prisons—under contract to federal, state, or local levels of government. A list of these facilities is presented in Table 1.

All of these facilities, totaling over 3,000 beds, are run by private firms under contracts to agencies of government. Some of the facilities are owned by the jurisdiction letting the contract, others by the private company. Some are newly constructed or converted from other uses by the company. Others were existing facilities previously run by the government; often, such takeover facilities are renovated by the company.

In takeover cases, the company generally hires the previous public employees. In one case (Butler County Prison), a private company ended up managing a work force of unionized county employees. They were kept on the county payroll when a last-minute court order blocked the original plan to replace them.

Although no medium or maximum security state or federal prison is managed yet under private contract, the jail contracts do include some maximum security wings. Most of the contracts so far, however, have been for relatively low security, typified by close supervision, locked doors and windows, and perimeter fencing, often with razor wire. Most of the adult contracts are designed for low-risk inmates. The jails, however, generally must take the full range of pretrial suspects, and some of the juvenile institutions are intended for serious, including violent, offenders. Detention time has tended to be short in private prisons so

TABLE 1. Proprietary Prisons as of Summer, 1987

Juvenile facilities

1. Weaversville, a high-security institution for 22 serious juvenile offenders in Pennsylvania.
2. The former Florida School for Boys at Okeechobee, a 425-bed, fenced-in facility holding predominantly serious felony delinquents.
3. Shelby (County) Training Center, a secure institution in Memphis, Tennessee, for delinquent boys who would otherwise be placed in state institutions. The state pays the county to confine them locally; the county contracts. Capacity, 150; average population, 110.
4. Artesian Oaks, a fenced-in campus for 100 juvenile parole violators in Saugas, California

Adult facilities—Federal contracts

5. Over half a dozen minimum or medium security centers for the detention of illegal aliens awaiting deportation by the Immigration and Naturalization Service; total, over 1,000 beds.
6. Hidden Valley Ranch (federal), a fenced-in campus at LaHonda, California, holding about 60 young federal offenders for the Bureau of Prisons under the Youth Corrections Act.

Adult facilities—State contracts

7. Hidden Valley Ranch (state), up to 80 adult, low-risk parole violators held for the State of California, at LaHonda.
8. Marion Adjustment Center, a minimum security prison for about 200 Kentucky state prisoners nearing their parole eligibility dates.

Adult facilities—Local contracts

9. Bay County (Florida) Jail and Jail Annex, with a total of 370 beds and a combined rated capacity of 404, holding every type of offender, from minimum to maximum security, with separate facilities for females and juveniles.
10. Silverdale, a minimum to medium security prison for Hamilton County, Tennessee, at Chattanooga; about 364 adult males and females (rated capacity, 400); convicted county misdemeanants and state felons.
11. Butler County Prison in Pennsylvania, a high-security prison and jail (100 beds) plus work release center (16 beds).
12. Santa Fe (County, New Mexico) Detention Facility, a 133-bed jail (rated capacity 188), with separate cells for juveniles.
13. Volunteers of America Regional Corrections Center in Roseville, Minnesota, a 40-bed postconviction jail for women sentenced by county, state, and federal courts.

far, ranging from just days for the INS facilities to a maximum of 6 years (but an average of 45 days) at Silverdale.

There have been escapes from private prisons, as there are from others. During the first 7 months of operation at the Marion Adjustment Center, there were four walk-aways, three of whom were recaptured within 24 hours. In a comparison state facility, walk-aways averaged 1.5 per week (Commonwealth of Virginia, 1986: 57–58).[2] At the Okeechobee School for Boys, the escape rate was 25.6, 27.6, and 25.6 per 100 inmates in the years before, during, and after transfer from government to private hands. This is essentially no change, in spite of a difficult transition year with extremely high turnover among the cottage counselors (American Correctional Association, 1985: 58).[3]

Guns are not carried in any of these facilities. Some have guns available outside, with employees who are authorized to carry them. One serious incident occurred when an illegal alien detained by a private contractor for the INS was accidentally killed with a shotgun during an escape attempt.[4] The contractor was sued, paid damages, and is no longer in business.

All private facilities are required to adhere to local, state, and federal standards. In addition, some abide by the standards of the American Correctional Association; a few have received accreditation by the Commission on Accreditation for Corrections. (Most governmental correctional facilities, outside the Federal Bureau of Prisons, are not accredited.) Officers of several of these companies have had long careers in federal and state corrections.

Contracts generally include provisions for monitoring by the relevant government agency. Often, the monitor's duties include either making or reviewing disciplinary decisions that effect the date of release, such as allocation of "good time" or "gain time."

No contract can absolve the government of responsibility for imprisonment or make it immune to lawsuits. Government remains liable. However, contractors generally carry large insurance policies, and contracts may include indemnification clauses requiring the company to protect the government against litigation costs and legal damages.

The contracts run from 1 year to 32 years. All contracts have provisions for termination, and the longer contracts have provisions for periodic renewal and renegotiation. Fees may be renegotiated annually, or every few years, or indexed to inflation. They may be fixed at a flat,

---

[2] Differential selectivity of admission at these two facilities, however, makes this comparison not too useful.
[3] At Dozier School for Boys, a "comparison" (but not truly comparable) state-run facility, the escape rates for those 3 years were 10.6, 8.0, and 6.3 per 100.
[4] See *Medina v. O'Neill* (589 F. Supp. 1028 1984).

per prisoner, per diem rate or they may be set on a sliding scale. A sliding scale charges lower rates for prisoners above specified population breakpoints, to take advantage of economies of scale. Some contracts also allow the company to fill unused space with prisoners from other jurisdictions. This also promotes economies of scale. Any excess in the fee charged to the other jurisdiction is split between the company and the primary jurisdiction. Profit margins from 5% to 8% of revenues have been reported, but some companies also have operated at a loss during the early years of a contract.

3. PRIVATE PRISON ISSUES: PROS AND CONS

Privately contracted prisons raise many philosophical, empirical, and policy issues. Far from having established answers, we are still in the stage of identifying the relevant questions. Hypotheses to test, policy options to evaluate, issues and questions to debate, and arguments to analyze are still emerging rapidly. They cover at least the following range of issues:

1.	Propriety	6.	Security
2.	Cost	7.	Liability
3.	Quality	8.	Accountability
4.	Quantity	9.	Corruption
5.	Flexibility	10.	Dependency

1. Questions of *propriety* may be philosophical, political, or legal. Is it proper for imprisonment to be administered by anyone other than officials and employees of government? How might private delegation of authority affect its legitimation in the eyes of prisoners or the public? Is the "profit motive" more or less compatible with doing justice than the motives to be found within state bureaucracies, employee unions, or nonprofit agencies? Should private prison contracts permit the private exercise of quasi-judicial authority (e.g., classification, discipline, allocation of gain time)?

2. Is *cost* as likely to be reduced with the privatization of corrections as it has with some other public services? Or does experience with privatization in other areas suggest that the net costs may actually be higher in the long run, as a result of "low-balling" or due to the added costs of supervision and of the contracting process itself? Can the process of contracting help clarify the true costs of both public and private service delivery in corrections?

3. Will privatization increase the *quality* of imprisonment due to innovations by private companies? Or will commercial companies cut corners to save costs and thereby lower quality? What are the advantages and disadvantages of government control versus competition as a quality control mechanism? Can the advantages of competition be obtained without involvement of the private sector? How can the contracting process be used to specify and clarify standards?

4. How might privatization affect the *quantity* of imprisonment? Will it merely help meet an independently determined demand, or will commercial companies lobby to increase the demand?

5. Will private contracts bring with them the greater *flexibility* of small businesses and entrepreneurs? Do they reduce red tape and avoid the perpetuation of agencies and programs commonly found in government? Can the private sector more accurately anticipate and more rapidly respond to the correctional needs of government? Or will contracts bring with them their own form of rigidity, as restrictions on what can be expected or demanded? Do contracts encourage short-term, over long-term, planning?

6. Can *security* be ensured in private prisons? What are the legal limits to the delegation of authority to use deadly force? How does the training of government correctional personnel compare to that of the staff of private companies? What steps can be taken to prevent, insure against, or deal with a possible disruption of private prison operations due to strikes or bankruptcy?

7. Does a private prison contract simply extend and add to the *liability* of government, or does it defray and reduce liability costs, through insurance and increased incentives to avoid expensive lawsuits?

8. Is *accountability* decreased because private prisons are less accessible to public scrutiny, or increased because the private sector is more vulnerable to legal controls than is the state? Do contracts diffuse responsibility, or do they increase it, by providing another mechanism of control over prison managers? How accountable are correctional institutions and personnel under current arrangements?

9. Would the potential for *corruption* in running prisons be higher, lower, or merely different in form under contractual arrangements? Can close monitoring, along with competition and market processes keep the bidding for and the granting of contracts honest, or is collusion

inevitable? How do the possible forms of corruption under public–private management differ from those under purely public systems? Which forms are easier to control?

10. How can government protect itself from becoming *dependent* on a private provider, merely substituting a private monopoly for a public monopoly? Should it retain some correctional capacity in its own hands? Should it contract only to multiple providers? Or does the possibility of future competition limit the potential for abuse of position by a solitary contractor?

Of the issues identified here, I will address the two that are probably the most salient: propriety and cost.

4. THE PROPRIETY OF PROPRIETARY PRISONS[5]

The most fundamental objection to private prisons is often stated as a matter of principle: the claim that imprisonment is an inherently and exclusively governmental function and therefore should not be performed by the private sector at all, even under contract to the government. This is often phrased in such a way as to make the idea sound frightening, and it derives some popular support from the fact that private prisons are an unfamiliar concept.

Even to raise the issue, however, is to concede an important point. To question the propriety of private prisons is to recognize that propriety is an issue in imprisonment by anyone, including by the state. It is not just a question of power but of authority. Where does the state's authority to imprison come from?

In the Lockean, classical liberal (or in modern terms, libertarian) tradition on which the American system of government is founded, all rights are individual, not collective. The state is artificial and has no authority, legitimate power, or rights of its own, other than those transferred to it by individuals.

John Locke argued that individuals in the state of nature have the right to punish those who aggress against them. When they contract to form a state, they turn over to it their power to punish. Thus the power and authority to imprison do not originate with the state and do not attach inherently or uniquely to it. Rather, they are delegated to gov-

---

[5] This section is drawn from a longer discussion (Logan, 1987), in which I also discuss the question of public-sector versus private-sector motives.

>wer ID:	21111123978116
Date:	10/03/2009
Time:	4:20 pm

t everyone in Britain should know about
and punishment /

1009899921

Date:	24/03/2009 23:59

American prison :
1009209527

Date:	31/03/2009 23:59

g research on crime and justice.
1011633078

Date:	24/03/2009 23:59

al policy /
1011637830

Date:	31/03/2009 23:59

ernment by the people and can, with the consent of citizens, be further delegated by the state, in turn, to private agencies.

The state does not *own* the right to punish. It merely *administers* it in trust, on behalf of the people. There is no reason why subsidiary trustees cannot be designated, as long as they, too, are ultimately accountable to the people and subject to the same provisions of law that direct the state. The authority to imprison is not *state* authority but *legal* authority and will be subject to the rule of law whether it is exercised by salaried employees or by contracted agents.

In any prison, someone will need authority to use force, including potentially deadly force in emergencies. In a system characterized by rule of law, state agencies and private agencies alike are bound by the law. For actors within either type of agency, it is the law, not the civil status of the actor, that determines whether any particular exercise of force is legitimate.

Consider the case of state-employed prison guards who engage in clear-cut and extreme brutality. We do not say that their actions are authorized or legitimate, or even that they are acting at that moment as agents of the state. In fact, we deny it, in spite of their uniforms and all the other trappings of their position. We say that they have overstepped their authority and behaved in an unauthorized and unlawful fashion. The state may or may not accept some accountability or liability for their acts but that is a separate issue.

There is, in effect, an implicit contract between a state and its agents that makes the authority of the latter conditional on the proper performance of their roles. This conditional authority can be bestowed on explicitly contracted agents of the state just as it is on those who are salaried. The boundaries of authority for contracted state agents should be no less clear than those for state employees, and they could be even clearer, if they are spelled out in the conditions of the contract.

What about perceptions of authority inside the prison itself? Would private prisons lack authority in the eyes of inmates?

Prisoners are mainly concerned about practical, not symbolic, distinctions. They care more about how guards treat them than about what insignia grace their uniforms. Real authority is not simply titular; it must be established and maintained—earned—whether in a private or a government prison. To the extent that they are treated with fairness and justice, as well as strictly and firmly, inmates will be more inclined to legitimate their keepers' authority and to cooperate with them.

This is especially important to a private prison. The exercise of naked power is extremely costly; cooperation is much more cost-effective than is coercion. Commercial prisons, unlike the state, cannot indefinitely absorb or pass along to taxpayers the cost of riots, high insurance rates, extensive litigation by maltreated prisoners, cancellations of poorly performed or controversial contracts, or even just too much adverse publicity.

Legitimation constitutes one of the most effective methods of cutting the cost of power in all forms of social organization; prisons are no exception. Because legitimation is generally granted in exchange for the fair exercise of power, a profit-seeking prison has a vested interest in being perceived by inmates as just and impartial in the application of rules.

Moreover, the state is more likely to renew a contract with an organization that has a good record of governance than with a contractor who generates numerous complaints and appeals from inmates. Thus, economic self-interest can motivate good governance as well as good management.

At the least, there is no inherent incompatibility between the making of profit and the pursuit of justice. The two may sometimes conflict, just as the internal motives and needs of government agencies may sometimes conflict with their official missions. The remedy in either case is to structure incentives so as to reward proper performance.

5. PUBLIC AND PRIVATE PRISON COSTS

The question that is probably foremost in the public mind is the issue of cost. How do the costs of proprietary prisons compare to those of government-run prisons? Elsewhere (Logan and Rausch, 1985), I have discussed theoretical reasons for anticipating savings as a result of private prison contracting. Here I try to answer the question a little more empirically.

Unfortunately, there is no published or otherwise easily available study that compares the costs of private and governmental prisons in adequate detail. In an extensive search of news stories, research reports, government documents, and other literature on private prisons, I found several comparisons of per diem operating costs that favored government prisons and a much larger number that favored private prisons. Most of these simple comparisons, however, are almost useless. In no case was enough information given to determine the thoroughness and accuracy of the cost figures or the appropriateness of the comparison.

One cannot take at face value those frequently reported comparisons between the costs of contracted facilities (or proposed contracts) and costs at "comparable government facilities." Facilities differ on many variables that relate to cost: location, age, design, security level and custody needs, population size and homogeneity, sentence lengths and turnover, variety and types of programs, and details of capital financing. Casual matching of facilities on one or two obvious characteristics, like type and size, may not be enough to allow a valid comparison.

Before-and-after comparisons might seem, at first glance, to avoid some of the problems of cross-facility comparisons. However, many things relevant to cost may still change—indeed, it is frequently one of the goals of privatization to bring about these changes. The private company may renovate or build to increase capacity. It may introduce new programs. It is likely to be required to seek accreditation and thus to meet standards not previously met. Monitoring, which may be included in the cost of the contract, also adds a dimension that makes the operation different from before.

In short, even a before-and-after analysis does not compare the "same" facility under two different forms of management, although it may come closer to it than a cross-facility comparison does.

Whether it is through time or across facilities, however, to compare a contractor's fee with a figure taken directly from the budget of its governmental "counterpart" is to compare a close calculation with an underestimate. A contractor's fee will generally tend to capture all of the contractor's costs of running a prison and to clarify (through the contracting process) what costs remain with the government. In contrast, most available figures on what it costs the government to run a prison are much less complete. These figures, taken as they usually are directly from the operating budget of an institution or its parent agency, often greatly understate total government costs (Camp and Camp, 1985).

5.1. The "Hidden Costs" of Corrections

Correctional agencies vary a great deal in terms of what components they include in their official budgets. It is probably fair to say, however, that no agency budget shows all of the direct and indirect costs of corrections. Costs that do not appear in an agency's budget are sometimes referred to as "hidden costs." This does not imply that they are deliberately concealed, only that they are not readily apparent or easily discernable. Most will come from the budgets of other government agencies and hence are not easily identified as expenditures on corrections. For example, litigation and liability costs are generally taken from the budget of the state or county attorney, not the corrections department or the individual institution. Fringe benefits and pensions often come out of some general fund rather than the budgets of particular agencies or facilities. Services provided by other agencies should be (but rarely are) prorated into the budgets of correctional agencies, and services provided centrally by a correctional agency should be prorated into the budgets of individual facilities. Facility budgets commonly list only operating costs, omitting land purchase, construction, financing, depreciation, and other capital costs.

An adequate cost comparison requires that all the specific cost components of a facility and its operation be taken into account—including construction, depreciation, debt servicing, rent or its equivalent, taxes paid or foregone, salaries, pensions, benefits, staff training costs, other general personnel costs, food, clothing, equipment, supplies, health care, education, counseling, other treatment costs, legal services, insurance and other liability costs, utilities, maintenance, garbage collection, transportation, administration overhead, external oversight, and other interagency or indirect costs.

A thorough cost analysis comparing private and government prisons would attempt to include as many of these cost components as possible. Although there have been some cost analyses of government prisons, none has been published that includes a comparison to a contractor's fee for running the same or a similar facility. The closest I have seen to such an analysis is a set of unpublished figures calculated by Bill McGriff, county auditor for Hamilton County, Tennessee, site of the Silverdale Detention Center.[6]

5.2. Hamilton County: A Relatively Complete Cost Analysis

Hamilton County has both a jail, for pretrial cases, and a prison, holding county misdemeanants and felons convicted by state courts. The county prison, Silverdale, is run under contract by Corrections Corporation of America. The fee charged by CCA is renegotiated with the county every year. Bill McGriff, the county auditor, each year prepares an analysis comparing the total cost to the county of running the prison under contract to CCA with what it would cost the county to resume direct management of the facility itself.

To compute the cost of operating the prison under county management, McGriff has taken pains to identify as many as possible of the indirect and interagency (the "hidden") costs referred to before. The components he has identified are listed in Table 2.

The costs listed in the column on the left are those that would ordinarily be found in any prison budget. The costs listed on the right, however, are charged to other budgets and not accounted for in the same budget as the prison. As county auditor, however, McGriff was in a position to identify these indirect and interagency costs.

---

[6] For further analysis of these figures, see Charles H. Logan and Bill W. McGriff, "Comparing Costs of Public and Private Prisons—A Case Study," National Institute of Justice, *Research in Action* (Washington, DC: U.S. Department of Justice, 1989).

TABLE 2. Hamilton County Penal Farm Component Costs

Salaries and wages	Maintenance and garbage
Fringe benefits	Workhouse records clerk
Consumable maintenance supplies	County hospital care
Utilities	Insurance
Medicine and personal care	Interest expense
Food and kitchen supplies	Depreciation
Uniforms	Other direct costs[a]
Capital outlay (equipment)	Other indirect costs[b]
Other operating expenses	

[a] Other direct costs: personnel, accounting, financial management, data processing, purchasing, county physician, human services administrator.
[b] Other indirect costs: county commission, county executive, county auditor, county attorney, finance administrator.

"Other direct costs" include activities of those central offices that routinely perform services for all county agencies: personnel, accounting, financial management, data processing, and purchasing. Some portion of the activities of these offices would be directed toward the prison. The county physician worked part-time for the county, attending prisoners at the jail and the prison. Because the prison falls under the county's human services division, the services of the human services administrator and her secretary are "direct" rather than "indirect" costs.

"Other indirect costs" are those incurred by the activities of certain county officials at the executive level. These officials, and their staff, must spend some portion of their time dealing with matters pertaining to the prison. The matters requiring their attention may be occasional, periodic, regular, or seemingly constant, but they are distinct from the direct, routine services included in "other direct costs."

All these interagency costs, both direct and indirect, come from budgets other than those of the prison. For each one, the auditor used a prorating technique to calculate what proportion of those other budgets to attribute to the existence and operation of the prison. McGriff was very conservative in his choice of assumptions to use in these prorating techniques, thus consciously underestimating total costs under county management.

In contrast, total prison and related costs to the county under CCA management can be calculated much more clearly, simply, and thoroughly. The fee per prisoner day is fixed by contract and the number of prisoners, although not predictable in advance, is known precisely for any past or current period. To these per diem payments, however, three further sets of costs must be added:

1. The salary of the superintendent (who monitors the contract and makes all release and gain time decisions) and that of his secretary.

2. Certain other costs that the county continues to pay directly: interest and depreciation on construction prior to CCA, county hospital care for prisoners, and a clerk's salary in the office of workhouse records.

3. Some of the county's "other indirect" costs, a fraction of which the county will continue to incur despite the contract. Although the auditor underestimated these costs under county administration, he estimated generously the fraction to be added in under contracting.

Offsetting the "hidden costs" of contracting, which are incorporated in item No. 3, is what might be referred to as a "hidden rebate" from contracting. Every year, CCA pays about $64,000 back into the community in local sales, property, and business taxes that would not have existed without the contract.

The bottom line, or net effect, of all the cost components described here is shown in Table 3. This table compares the total costs to Hamilton County that occur when the prison is managed by CCA, with the total costs that would occur if the county resumed management itself.

Fiscal Year 1985–1986 was the first full fiscal year under the CCA contract. CCA's fee that year was $21 per diem. (The higher per diem in the table is based on total county costs under the contract, not just the payments to CCA.) In FY 1986–1987, the fee was raised to $22, where it remained the following year.

A clear pattern of savings is demonstrated. The savings were reduced at first when CCA raised its fee. However, they increased considerably the following year, when CCA held (or was held) to the same

TABLE 3. Hamilton County Penal Farm Costs, Under County Operation versus CCA Contract, Fiscal Years 1985–1986, 1986–1987, 1987–1988

	1985–1986	1986–1987	1987–1988
County operation	$2,853,513	$3,413,741	$3,642,464
(per diem)	($25.05)	($25.71)	($27.49)
CCA contract	$2,746,073	$3,312,428	$3,346,300
(per diem)	($24.10)	($24.95)	($25.25)
Savings	$107,440	$101,313	$296,164
(as %)	(3.8%)	(3.0%)	(8.1%)
Prisoner days	113,928	132,788	132,514
(average population)	(312)	(364)	(363)

fee whereas the county's own cost basis increased. The amounts saved, although large in dollar terms, are small as a percentage of total costs. It must be reiterated, however, that these figures are not exact, and most certainly underestimate the true savings. In discussions before the county commission, the auditor repeatedly emphasized the very conservative nature of his estimates of the costs of county operation. Where he could not get figures in which he had confidence, he either left costs out or used assumptions that he thought would err on the low side.

In addition, the commission took into consideration some costs and benefits that the auditor was not able to quantify at all. For example, CCA carries $5 million in liability insurance. In the event of a successful lawsuit, the indemnification clause in CCA's contract could save the county (and perhaps the commissioners personally) a considerable, but unpredictable, amount of money. Also, the commission believed that CCA was providing better management and more professional training than previously existed and was sparing county officials many of the daily hassles involved in running a prison. The additional staff training provided by CCA would have cost the county money to have achieved on its own. Grand jury reports were all positive after CCA took over, thus eliminating the time and expense required of the county to correct the sorts of problems criticized by earlier grand juries.

Two benefits in particular make the facility and its operation under CCA not truly comparable to the alternative county version. These are the physical improvements made by CCA and the added service gained by splitting the superintendent function from the warden function.

If the county took back the facility, it would gain the $1.6 million in new construction made by CCA. The auditor did factor in the cost of reimbursing CCA for the remaining unamortized cost of this construction if the county took back the prison. That, however, was based on CCA's construction costs. If the county had bid the construction itself (i.e., had there been no contract), it would have cost more.[7] Put differently, for the same price, the county would not have been able to add as much. In addition to the new construction, CCA invested capital and labor in repair and preventive maintenance of the physical plant, which it inherited from the county in a state of deterioration and neglect.

The contract added human as well as physical capital. Under the contract, the county has two full-time managers (each with a secretary) performing three functions: warden, superintendent, and monitor. Without the contract, the county would have only one person (with one

[7] Inmate housing constructed by the county in 1981 cost approximately $65 per square foot. CCA's cost to construct inmate housing in 1985 was $48.62 per square foot. (Figures supplied by CCA.)

secretary) to perform as both warden and superintendent, and it would have no monitor. It should be emphasized that monitoring is not just an added cost; it is an added benefit as well.[8]

The county has also added quality as well as quantity to its human capital. The warden under CCA is a man with much more experience than the county would have been able to attract on its own. Moreover, each CCA facility has behind it (and in Silverdale's case, nearby) the quite considerable experience and expertise of the top corporate officers in Nashville.

Thus the prison operation that the county has under the CCA contract is not the same as what it would have if it took the operation back, or if it had never contracted. It gets more, for less money, by contracting.

Meaningful comparison of public and private prison costs is very complicated. It requires not only accurate data but the ability to make difficult yet realistic assumptions and estimates about indirect, uncertain, or unknown cost components. In one case where this has been done to some extent, there appears so far to be definite savings under contracting. For this county, the estimated costs of public and private management are not very far apart in percentage terms, but even a small percentage difference can mean a lot of dollars in the costly business of imprisonment.

There is no detailed analysis and documentation yet available, at least in published literature, to support the much larger percentage savings frequently claimed for prison contracting. Such claims are often based on the simple comparison of a per diem fee charged by a contractor, with a per diem expression of costs shown in the public agency's operating budget. Because the contractor's fee is likely to be fairly inclusive, whereas the agency budget is apt to omit many indirect, interagency, or otherwise "hidden" costs, some of the larger claims of savings based on those simple comparisons may well be correct. However, they have not yet been rigorously demonstrated.

6. SUMMARY AND CONCLUSION

"Proprietary prisons" are secure confinement facilities that are managed by privately owned companies, under contract to government.

---

[8] Besides monitoring, the superintendent has at least one additional duty that he did not have before the contract. He supervises a new county program of electronic monitoring as an alternative to imprisonment for misdemeanants. Some of the time he would previously have spent as warden is now available for this sort of expansion of the county's total (including nonprison) correctional program. The superintendent spends two-thirds of his time at the prison and one-third downtown. However, all of his budget is added to the cost of the contract, which exaggerates the cost of imprisonment under contracting.

They are so recent that little can be said with confidence to be *known* about them. Hence, I have focused on a brief characterization of the early examples of these institutional contracts, on identifying the issues that are going to need study and debate, and on discussing the two issues that have led the public debate so far: propriety and cost.

The propriety of private prisons is an issue so deeply ideological that it may never be settled. However, the categorical declaration that, as a matter of principle, it is improper for anyone but the government to run a prison does not bear up under examination. The authority of the state to imprison is derived originally from the consent of the governed and may therefore, with similar consent, be delegated further. It is not owned by the state. Moreover, that authority is not absolute but is subject to the rule of law and the requirements of due process, whether it is exercised by salaried state employees or by contracted agents. Thus private contracting is not incompatible with either the legitimate exercise of authority or the protection of inmate rights.

On the issue of cost, there is not yet enough evidence to support any broad generalizations about the comparative costs of proprietary versus government prisons. One relatively complete set of figures was calculated by the auditor of a county whose prison was under private management. Using conservative assumptions thought to underestimate the costs of county management, the auditor nonetheless identified a small percentage (but significant dollar) difference in favor of private management for each of 3 years.

There have been many claims of large savings (ranging from 10% to 50%) due to contracting, and some counterclaims of higher costs. However, these generally have been based on simple comparisons of contractors' per diem fees with figures drawn from government agency budgets for "comparable" facilities. They have yet to be demonstrated by independent analysis.

Only time, and further research, will tell which side of the debate over private prisons has greater merit. We may never find out, however, if those prisons are not given a fair chance. That would leave us not only ignorant about proprietary prisons but with less information about government prisons. In penology as in any other branch of knowledge, we learn mainly from comparisons.

Private prisons will not, and should not, reduce the responsibility of government for imprisonment. Nor is it likely for the foreseeable future that they will significantly replace government in the total volume of prisoners held and facilities managed. Their most important contribution will be to provide a market test of costs and to serve as a comparative standard by which to measure government performance. Competition can be good for government agencies just as it is for private businesses. When government must compete with the private sector in the provision of a public service, that competition provides a powerful mechanism of evaluation, accountability, and control.

Whether proprietary prisons are less expensive than those run by the government or not, their greatest benefit will be the information they provide. They make more visible the true full cost of correctional facilities. As stated in a report to the National Institute of Justice (Mullen, Chabotar, and Carrow, 1985: 81):

> One of the advantages typically ascribed to contracting in other fields is its ability to reveal the true cost of public service. Corrections is no exception. Under a contract system, the costs of confining particular numbers of clients under specified conditions will be clearly visible and more difficult to avoid through crowding and substandard conditions. While corrections authorities might welcome the opportunity to demonstrate clearly that more prisoners require more resources, it remains unclear whether legislators and voters will be prepared to accept the real costs of confinement practices that meet professional standards.

Whether correctional authorities will welcome *all* the new information may depend on how it turns out. All of us, however, should welcome the chance to reveal the true costs as well as the best methods of providing uncrowded, properly run prisons and jails. Voters and legislators can then make more realistic choices. But to get this information, as well as to provide the maximum range of choices, there must be competition and information from the private market.

7. REFERENCES

American Correctional Association. *Private operation of a correctional institution.* Washington, DC: U.S. Department of Justice, National Institute of Corrections, 1985.

Camp, G., and Camp, C. *The real cost of corrections: A research report.* South Salem, NY: Criminal Justice Institute, 1985.

Lipset, S. M. Feeling better: Measuring the nation's confidence. *Public Opinion,* 1985, April/May, pp. 6–9, 56–58.

Lipset, S. M., and Schneider, W. *The confidence gap: Business, labor, and government in the public mind.* New York: The Free Press, 1983.

Logan, C. H. The propriety of proprietary prisons. *Federal Probation,* 1987, 51, 35–39.

Logan, C. H., and Rausch, S. P. Punish and profit: The emergence of private enterprise prisons. *Justice Quarterly,* 1985, 2, 303–318.

Mullen, J., Chabotar, K., and Carrow, D. *The privatization of corrections.* Washington, DC: Abt Associates, for the National Institute of Justice, 1985.

Roper, B. A. Market forces, privatization and prisons: A polar case for government policy. *International Journal of Social Economics,* 1986, 13, 77–92.

Savas, E. S. *Privatizing the public sector; How to shrink government.* Chatham, NJ: Chatham House Publishers, Inc., 1982.

Virginia, Commonwealth of. *Study of correctional privatization.* Richmond, VA: Secretary of Transportation and Public Safety, 1986.

Part II

LEGAL ISSUES IN CONTEMPORARY CORRECTIONS

Chapter 5

AMERICAN PRISONERS AND THE RIGHT OF ACCESS TO THE COURTS
A Vanishing Concept of Protection

KENNETH C. HAAS and GEOFFREY P. ALPERT

1. INTRODUCTION

In 1987, Americans celebrated the 200th anniversary of the United States Constitution. It is from this document that our basic rights and responsibilities have been developed. These rights, however, have never been distributed equally to all segments of the population. For example, the rights enumerated in the Constitution have never been fully extended to those who are incarcerated. Although the rights of free citizens have been generally preserved during this 200-year period, the history of prisoners' rights is a history of indifference and neglect.

Prisoners have always been the forgotten Americans in the United States Constitution. The original document of 1787 affirmed the fundamental right of habeas corpus (the right to challenge the legality of one's confinement) but did not specifically mention prisoners. Two years later, the Bill of Rights—the first 10 amendments to the Constitution— provided safeguards for those accused of crime. However, it would take nearly two centuries for the Bill of Rights to emerge as a major weapon in securing rights for those already convicted of crimes. And it would

KENNETH C. HAAS • Department of Criminal Justice, University of Delaware, Newark, Delaware 19716.   GEOFFREY P. ALPERT • College of Criminal Justice, University of South Carolina, Columbia, South Carolina 29208.

take the courts equally as long to recognize that "a right of access to the courts is one of the rights a prisoner clearly retains" (*Coleman v. Peyton*, 1966: 907).

The purposes of this chapter are to examine the prisoner's right of access to the courts and to comment on how changes in this area of law may affect research on prisons and on the role of the courts in spurring prison reform. The right of access is the most important of all prisoners' rights because it is the right upon which all other rights turn. Without it, prisoners would have no way to appeal their convictions or to vindicate their rights in such areas of law as the First Amendment's protections of speech, religion, and peaceable assembly; the Eighth Amendment's ban on cruel and unusual punishments; and the right to Fifth and Fourteenth Amendment due process in prison disciplinary proceedings.

We will explore the right of access by examining the two major types of cases that make up this body of law. First, we will focus on cases that involve the constitutionality of various *prison policies* that allegedly interfere with inmate efforts to seek judicial relief. Second, we will analyze recent trends in cases dealing with the *availability of judicial remedies* frequently sought by prisoners. These cases involve procedural and jurisdictional questions that can either make judicial remedies easier to obtain or place severe restrictions on the right of access.

2. PRISON POLICIES AND PRACTICES AFFECTING THE RIGHT OF ACCESS TO THE COURTS

2.1. U.S. Supreme Court Decisions

Until the past 20 years, federal and state courts followed a policy of declining jurisdiction in nearly all suits brought by prisoners. Generally known as the "hands-off" doctrine, this policy reflected the traditional view of the prisoner as a "slave of the state" (*Ruffin v. Commonwealth*, 1871: 796) without enforceable rights. As a practical matter, the judiciary's extreme reluctance to become involved in the internal operations of prisons made it virtually impossible for prisoners to seek judicial relief from alleged mistreatment and needlessly harsh conditions of confinement (Haas, 1977). Generally, the courts based their refusals to hear prisoner complaints on one or more of five rationales:

1. The separation of powers doctrine
2. The low level of judicial expertise in penology
3. The fear that judicial intervention would undermine prison discipline

4. The fear that opening the courthouse doors to prisoners would result in a deluge of inmate litigation
5. The view that considerations of federalism and comity should preclude consideration of the claims of state prisoners by federal courts (Haas, 1977).

A strict version of the hands-off doctrine prevailed among most courts until the late 1960s and early 1970s. Nevertheless, it was in 1941— a time when the hands-off doctrine remained strong—that the U.S. Supreme Court first recognized that the due process clauses of the Fifth and Fourteenth Amendments guarantee all Americans—even prisoners—the right of access to the courts. In the case of *Ex Parte Hull*, the Court struck down a Michigan prison regulation that required inmates to submit all their legal petitions to prison officials for approval. Whenever prison authorities felt that inmate petitions were frivolous, inaccurate, or poorly written, they would refuse to mail them to the courts. The Supreme Court held that this procedure amounted to an impermissible denial of the fundamental right of access to the courts. In no uncertain terms, the Justices told prison officials: "Whether a petition for a writ of habeas corpus addressed to a federal court is properly drawn and what allegations it must contain are questions for that court alone to determine" (*Hull* at 549).

Despite the *Hull* ruling, most courts remained extremely reluctant to interfere with prison policies restricting inmate access to the courts. In the 1950s and 1960s, many courts approved such prison practices as refusing to allow prisoners to purchase law books, prohibiting correspondence with law book publishers, allowing the confiscation of an inmate's legal documents found in another inmate's cell, refusing to permit a prisoner to type his or her own legal papers, and censoring or withholding legal correspondence between prisoners and attorneys (Edwards, 1968). Moreover, even when prison regulations were more accommodating to the right of access, ignorance, illiteracy, and poverty kept prisoners with arguably meritorious claims from filing their complaints.

Like their counterparts of yesteryear, today's prisoners often discover that legal barriers and personal handicaps can make court access very difficult. The right to a state-supplied attorney does not extend to inmate actions attacking prison conditions or to discretionary appeals of a criminal conviction (*Ross v. Moffitt*, 1974). Prisoners lack the money to hire attorneys, and they rarely possess the literacy needed to write and interest attorneys who might take a case without fee. As a result, the large majority of cases brought by prisoners originate from either the petitioning prisoner or from a "jailhouse lawyer" or "writ-writer"—

a prisoner who claims to have expertise in law and prepares legal documents for fellow inmates. Thus it is not surprising that the first major right of access case after *Hull* involved the limitations that prison officials could place on jailhouse lawyers.

In *Johnson v. Avery* (1969), the Supreme Court invalidated prison regulations that prohibited jailhouse lawyers from helping other prisoners with their legal problems. The Court conceded that jailhouse lawyers may burden the courts with frivolous complaints and undermine prison discipline by establishing their own power structure and taking unfair advantage of gullible prisoners (*Johnson* at 488). Nevertheless, the Justices declared that these concerns were outweighed by the importance of insuring that prisoners have reasonable access to the courts and "the fundamental importance of the writ of habeas corpus in our constitutional scheme" (*Johnson* at 485). Because most prisoners possess neither the necessary funds to hire their attorneys nor the necessary educational background to write their own appeals, their only recourse in most cases, reasoned the Justices, was to seek the help of a jailhouse lawyer (*Johnson* at 488–490). Consequently, the High Court concluded that prison officials could no longer enforce no-assistance rules unless the prison itself provided some type of legal services program that was reasonably effective in assisting prisoners with their petitions for post-conviction relief (*Johnson* at 490).

At first glance, the *Johnson* holding may seem to be rather narrow. However, the *Johnson* precedent, more than any other decision, paved the way for more effective efforts by prisoners seeking access to the courts. In the aftermath of *Johnson*, it became increasingly difficult to escape the logic that if inmates have the right to the assistance of another inmate in the preparation of legal documents, they cannot be absolutely restrained from acquiring the requisite legal materials and due process protection needed to assist in the preparation of petitions or to acquire an attorney or some other type of competent assistance to help them seek an appropriate and speedy judicial remedy (see Haas, 1982: 728).

However, the *Johnson* decision lacked precision. It provided prison officials with only the basic parameters of the right of access. Since 1969, the Supreme Court has resolved several important issues left unsettled by *Johnson*. In *Younger v. Gilmore* (1971), the Court affirmed a lower court ruling that required prison officials to provide inmates with a law library that contained a sufficient collection of books and materials to assure that prisoners were able to file petitions that demonstrate at least some legal proficiency. Three years later, the Court struck down a California prison policy that barred law students and legal paraprofessionals from working with prisoners (*Procunier v. Martinez*, 1974: 419–422). Also in 1974, the Justices invalidated a Nebraska regulation stating that prisoners could seek legal assistance only from a single "inmate legal adviser" who was appointed by the warden and who was permitted to provide assistance only in preparing habeas corpus petitions (*Wolff v. McDonnell*, 1974: 577–580). Finally, in *Bounds v. Smith* (1977), the Court held that even when prison policies allow jailhouse lawyers to operate, prison officials nevertheless must provide prisoners with either an adequate law library or adequate assistance from persons trained in the law.

Like the *Johnson* opinion, the *Bounds* opinion was far from specific in explaining what it would take to provide "adequate" legal services and materials for prisoners. The *Bounds* Court simply noted:

> While adequate law libraries are one constitutionally acceptable method to assure meaningful access to the courts, our decision here . . . does not foreclose alternative means to achieve that goal. . . . Among the alternatives are the training of inmates as paralegal assistants to work under lawyers' supervision, the use of paraprofessionals and law students, either as volunteers or in formal clinical programs, the organization of volunteer attorneys through bar associations or other groups, the hiring of lawyers on a part-time consultant basis, and the use of full-time staff attorneys, working either in new prison legal assistance organizations or as part of public defender or legal services offices. (*Bounds* at 828)

Thus there is still confusion after *Bounds* as to what prison officials must do to guarantee inmates meaningful access to the courts. Questions involving the adequacy of particular prison law libraries or legal services programs must be answered by the state and federal courts on a case-by-case basis. In states with small, homogenous prison populations, it may be sufficient to provide adequate law libraries and access to materials with some quasi-professional help. But in large, multilingual prison populations that are found in larger states, licensed attorneys may be necessary to guarantee access to the courts (Note, 1983; Alpert and Huff, 1981). A federal district court in Florida adopted that view in 1982 (*Hooks v. Wainwright*), holding that the state's plan to provide prisoners with law libraries staffed by inmate law clerks and librarians was insufficient to guarantee prisoners access to the courts. Accordingly, the court ordered the Florida Department of Corrections to provide some form of attorney assistance as part of its legal services plan.

However, on appeal, this decision was reversed by the Eleventh Circuit Court of Appeals (*Hooks v. Wainwright*, 1985). The court of appeals held that the lower court had interpreted *Bounds* too broadly and that attorneys were not required. In other words, a combination of law libraries and inmate law clerks will meet the *Bounds* mandate. The Ninth Circuit also approved the use of inmate law clerks rather than lawyers (*Lindquist v. Idaho Board of Corrections*, 1985) but indicated that the clerks must have received at least some sort of organized training.

Thus the issue of what must be done for illiterate inmates remains unsettled. But at a minimum, it appears that most courts will require both an adequate law library and assistance from persons who have some demonstrable understanding of the legal process. We now look at some of the available programs that provide legal services to inmates in state prisons, and we assess the impact of such programs.

2.2. Prison Legal Assistance Programs and Their Impact

Two frequently found types of prison legal aid programs are (1) institutionally supported networks of jailhouse lawyers, and (2) resident counsel programs staffed by actual attorneys. Among the states that have institutionalized the jailhouse lawyer as a source of legal assistance to other prisoners are Nebraska and Pennsylvania (Bluth, 1972; Rudovsky, Bronstein, and Koren, 1983). Although the participating jailhouse lawyers are not permitted to collect fees or special favors for their work, they are commonly awarded "good time" credits that earn them earlier release from prison. Under the Pennsylvania system, a group of writ-writers offers free legal services to other prisoners, with work credit, supplies, and office space provided by prison officials. There is no definite answer as to whether or not such writ-writer programs are truly successful in meeting the complex legal needs of prisoners. But many legal scholars believe that to be effective, jailhouse lawyers should be supervised by an attorney who can make sure that the writ-writers are capable of competent work and do not encourage frivolous or repetitious suits (Gobert and Cohen, 1981: 31).

The second type of legal assistance program, resident counsel, may be designed to include jailhouse lawyers and law students or paralegals under the supervision of lawyers at the prison (Alpert and Huff, 1981: 339). Early examples of such programs can be found in Washington, Texas, and Massachusetts. These programs, and others like them, provide legal assistance in non-fee-generating cases through the use of licensed attorneys and trained paralegals. It seems likely that resident counsel programs are generally superior to jailhouse lawyer-run programs in providing competent and comprehensive legal assistance to prisoners. Attorneys with some background in prison law are usually familiar with the technical aspects of drafting pleas and practical matters of legal strategy.

As to possible disadvantages, resident counsel programs can be very costly, depending upon the number of attorneys required. Moreover, problems may develop in the relationships among attorneys and correctional officials. On the other hand, the fact that these lawyers are state employees may cause inmates to stay away from the service—

seeing it as a "cop-out to the man" or as a token program designed merely to co-opt prisoners. If inmates fail to use state-funded attorneys for these or other reasons, access to the court has not been provided.

What affects the use of resident counsel programs by prisoners? In a study of such a program in the state of Washington, 120 out of 198 surveyed prisoners (61%) acknowledged that they had legal problems (Alpert, 1976). Ninety-one out of the 120 (76%) sought recourse to the legal aid project. Twenty-nine prisoners who had legal problems decided not to use the project. Out of these 29, five (17%) stated that they were retaining private counsel, 4 (14%) just "didn't give a damn," and 20 (69%) said that state funding discouraged their use of the Legal Services Project. Of those using the service, 63% felt that the project served the prisoners, whereas 37% felt it served the needs and goals of the state.

Research on resident counsel programs in Texas and Massachusetts also found that most of the inmate clients had positive attitudes toward the service (Alpert, 1980: 14–15). The research showed that for inmates in Texas

> participation in the legal aid project is a significant factor in producing positive changes in prisonization and in prisoners' attitudes toward police, lawyers, law and the judicial system. . . . A second significant finding which moves beyond attitudinal changes concerns the number of institutional infractions committed by members of our cohorts. The finding that users of legal aid experience fewer convictions for institutional infractions is significant in that it uses a behavioral measure as an independent variable. Providing legal services to prisoners is one step to reduce tension and anxiety, and reduce hostility among inmates. (Alpert, 1978: 44, 46–47)

The assertion that prison legal service programs can effectively reduce institutional tensions may seem surprising. However, this is a conclusion with which correctional administrators overwhelmingly concur. Two nationwide surveys of prison officials found that a large majority of the respondents believe that the inmate legal assistance programs mandated by court decisions have led to a decrease in disciplinary problems and have facilitated rehabilitation efforts. For example, Cardarelli and Finkelstein (1974) reported that over 80% of a large sample of state corrections commissioners, prison wardens, and treatment directors agreed that legal services provide a safety valve for inmate grievances, reduce inmate power structures and tensions from unresolved legal problems, and contribute to rehabilitation by showing the inmate that he or she is being treated fairly.

A second nationwide survey of prison officials (Haas and Champagne, 1976) disclosed that the prison systems that had hired attorneys to supervise legal aid programs had experienced a marked decline in problems with jailhouse lawyers and in friction between staff and inmates concerning alleged violations of rights. This study concluded that legal services programs supervised by attorneys help to maintain an atmosphere of discipline by undermining the power of the more unscrupulous jailhouse lawyers and by providing inmates with an outlet for their grievances and frustrations. Clearly, this is one area of correctional law that has contributed measurably to positive changes in American prisons.

3. PROCEDURAL AND JURISDICTIONAL OBSTACLES TO INMATE ACCESS

3.1. Section 1983 of the Civil Rights Act of 1871

We have just shown that over the past 20 years, the U.S. Supreme Court has broadened the prisoner's right of access to the courts by striking down prison regulations barring the activities of jailhouse lawyers and by requiring prison officials to establish reasonably adequate law libraries and/or legal assistance programs. However, it is important to understand that the right of access also encompasses questions involving judicial policies affecting the availability of the various judicial remedies sought by prisoners. Cases dealing with procedural and jurisdictional issues are of great importance because such cases can either limit or expand the availability of judicial relief for prisoners. And in this area of law, prisoners have not fared very well in recent years, for the Supreme Court has made it increasingly difficult for prisoners to secure full judicial review of their grievances.

Because over 90% of America's nearly 600,000 state and federal prisoners are housed in state prisons (Bureau of Justice Statistics, 1987), the large majority of lawsuits attacking allegedly unconstitutional prison practices are brought by state prisoners. Most of these suits are filed in federal court under Section 1983 of the Civil Rights Act of 1871 (hereinafter Section 1983). Although some state courts are more inclined to support civil rights and liberties than they were in the past (see generally Tarr and Porter, 1987), state prisoners generally believe that federal judges, as a group, are more sympathetic to their claims than are state judges. Indeed, research on comparative judicial behavior suggests that prisoners are correct in this regard. State courts that have been quite vigorous in protecting the rights of other minority groups generally have been less vigilant than the federal courts in safeguarding the rights of prisoners (Haas, 1981).

This state of affairs may change as an increasing number of President Reagan's appointees assume their duties on the federal bench. But there are important institutional and structural factors that militate against change. For example, whereas all federal judges enjoy lifetime appointments, the majority of the nation's state trial and appellate judges must stand in periodic elections and thus are more susceptible to public sentiments against prisoners. Moreover, federal court rules and procedures in such critical areas as pleading, fact finding, immunities, attorneys' fees, pretrial discovery, and class actions are more hospitable to prisoners' cases than the rules used by most state courts (Neuborne, 1981).

Section 1983 has been by far the most effective device for redressing the grievances of state prisoners (see generally Turner, 1979). Originally passed in an effort to combat the Ku Klux Klan in the aftermath of the Civil War, Section 1983 provides that any person acting under color of state or local law who violates the federal constitutional or statutory rights of another "shall be liable to the party injured in an action at law, suit in equity, or other proper proceeding for redress." Under Section 1983, state prisoners may challenge violations of their First Amendment freedoms of speech, religion, and association, or, for that matter, unconstitutional prison policies that deny or restrict their right of access to the courts. Most inmate Section 1983 cases, however, focus on allegedly unconstitutional conditions of confinement, covering such issues as privacy, unsanitary conditions, inadequate medical and dental care, overcrowding, nutritionally inadequate food, lack of exercise opportunities, inadequate heating, ventilation, and lighting, and unprovoked physical attacks by prison staff or other prisoners. Due process violations also are frequently litigated under Section 1983. Such cases may involve the rights of prisoners in disciplinary hearings, reclassification proceedings, interprison transfers, and parole eligibility hearings. Section 1983 actions also are commonly brought by probationers and parolees who claim that they were denied constitutionally mandated protections before or during revocation proceedings.

3.2. *Monroe v. Pape* (1961) and Its Progeny

Section 1983 was rarely invoked by prisoners or anyone else for nearly a century. But in a landmark 1961 case (*Monroe v. Pape*), the U.S. Supreme Court interpreted Section 1983 as giving federal courts original jurisdiction over any claims alleging violations of federal constitutional rights by state or local officials. This meant that petitioners suing state or local officials would not have to worry about the delays and expense involved in meeting the traditional requirement of exhausting all state judicial remedies before bringing suit in a federal court. They could instead bypass the state courts and go directly to the federal court with their Section 1983 claims. Three years later (*Cooper v. Pate*, 1964), the High Court made it clear that state prisoners could bring allegations of unconstitutional prison policies and conditions against state correctional employees under the provisions of Section 1983, thus creating a readily available and effective judicial remedy for prison abuses.

To be sure, there are other statutes, state and federal, under which prisoners can file legal claims. These include the federal Habeas Corpus Statute, the federal Tort Claims Act, state habeas corpus statutes, and state tort claims acts. However, for a variety of reasons, state prisoners and their attorneys prefer Section 1983 as the fastest and potentially most advantageous device for advancing claims against prison officials (see generally Manville, 1983: 163–220). Section 1983, for example, clearly is an appropriate vehicle for challenges to a prisoner's conditions of confinement. By contrast, many state habeas corpus statutes allow prisoners to challenge the legality of their conviction but not to challenge the conditions of confinement. Whereas Section 1983 is phrased in terms that permit the awarding of both compensatory and punitive damages to a victorious plaintiff, most state tort claims acts do not provide for punitive damages. The federal Habeas Corpus Act allows no monetary damages of any kind and strictly requires the exhaustion of all state remedies. The federal Tort Claims Act can be a useful remedy for some kinds of suits (especially those brought by federal prisoners who cannot use Section 1983), but the Tort Claims Act does not allow prisoners to sue governmental bodies for assault and battery claims or other intentional (as opposed to negligent) torts.

Because Section 1983 is the major device by which state prisoners seek to protect their rights to fair treatment and humane conditions, any new laws or court decisions that limit the usefulness of Section 1983 pose a major threat to prisoners. And, indeed, from the perspective of prisoners and the advocates of prison reform, there have been disturbing signs that Section 1983 may not survive into the twenty-first century. In a series of recent cases, the U.S. Supreme court has begun to diminish the effectiveness of Section 1983 as a means by which to combat violations of inmate rights.

Space limitations preclude a discussion of all of the Supreme Court decisions that have affected the use of Section 1983 by state prisoners (see generally Nahmod, 1986). Furthermore, it should be noted that a few of the Court's decisions have benefited inmate Section 1983 litigants. For example, inmates in city and county jails have profited from recent decisions establishing that local municipalities can be sued for compensatory damages under Section 1983 (*Monell v. Department of Social Services*, 1978) and that municipalities are unprotected by any kind of qualified immunity (*Owen v. City of Independence*, 1980).

The High Court also upheld the traditional scope of Section 1983 liability in a case involving a young inmate who suffered a night of rape and torture because a guard needlessly placed him in a cell with two prisoners known to have violent tendencies (*Smith v. Wade*, 1983). By a 5–4 vote, the Court affirmed that a prison employee may be held liable for punitive damages in a Section 1983 action alleging violations of the Eighth Amendment's cruel and unusual punishment clause. The *Wade* Court also determined that a Section 1983 plaintiff with Eighth Amendment claims is entitled to punitive damages if he or she can show that the defendant acted with reckless or callous disregard for the plaintiff's health or safety. The plaintiff, in other words, does not have to show that the defendant acted with malicious intent to injure the plaintiff, a more demanding standard.

Despite these victories for prisoners, most of the Supreme Court's jurisdictional pronouncements have sent a clear signal to the lower federal courts to cut back the availability of Section 1983 relief for state prisoners. For example, in 1973, the Court's decision in *Preiser v. Rodriguez* placed significant limitations on inmate use of Section 1983. *Preiser* established that whenever a state prisoner files a claim that, if successful, would result in a reduction in the length of his or her sentence (for example, a due process challenge to the fairness of a prison disciplinary committee's decision to take away an inmate's "good time" or early release credits), the prisoner can no longer sue under Section 1983. Instead, he or she will have to file the suit as a habeas corpus action, thus necessitating the time-consuming and often futile exhaustion of all state judicial and administrative remedies.

The *Preiser* majority conceded that the "broad language" of Section 1983 made it applicable to actions in which prisoners challenge prison practices that may unfairly lengthen their sentences (*Preiser* at 488–489). Nevertheless, the majority Justices held that the history of habeas corpus, the specific wording of the federal Habeas Corpus Statute, and the importance of allowing state courts the first opportunity to correct unfair state prison practices justified their decision to declare habeas corpus to be the *sole* remedy for state prisoners challenging the length of their confinement (*Preiser* at 477–490). In dissent, Justice Brennan asserted that the majority's effort to distinguish between prisoner challenges to prison practices affecting the conditions of confinement (where Section 1983 can be used) and prison practices affecting the duration of confinement (where habeas corpus, with its exhaustion requirement, must be used) was historically incorrect, analytically unsound, and certain to create unnecessary confusion that would inevitably thwart the fair and prompt resolution of legitimate inmate grievances (*Preiser* at 506–511).

More recent decisions have also narrowed the scope of liability under Section 1983. The Supreme Court has declared that states are not considered "persons" subject to suit under Section 1983 (*Quern v. Jordan,* 1979) and that local governments cannot be sued for punitive damages in Section 1983 cases (*City of Newport v. Fact Concerts,* 1981). State legislators have long enjoyed absolute immunity from Section 1983 liability (*Tenney v. Brandhove,* 1951), and the Court has made it clear that prison officials are protected by the affirmative defense of qualified or "good faith" immunity (*Procunier v. Navarette,* 1978).

In 1980, Congress passed legislation intended to curtail the use of Section 1983 by state prisoners. Section 1997e of the Civil Rights of Institutionalized Persons Act (hereinafter Section 1997e) requires state prisoners to exhaust state *administrative* remedies before they can file a section 1983 suit in a federal court. This requirement, however, applies only when either the attorney general of the United States or the federal court in which the suit is filed has certified that the state administrative remedy—some kind of inmate grievance system—meets minimally accepted standards of fairness. Section 1997e further states that a federal court must continue the case for no more than 90 days in order to require exhaustion of the administrative remedy.

In *Patsy v. Florida Board of Regents* (1982), the Supreme Court held that nonprisoner Section 1983 plaintiffs cannot be required to exhaust state administrative remedies. However, the Justices bestowed their approval on section 1997e's special filing requirements for prisoners, noting that it was reasonable to carve out an exception to the general no-exhaustion rule in order to relieve the burden of inmate complaints on the federal courts (*Patsy* at 509). It can be argued that a 90-day delay is not unreasonable and that Section 1997e may have the beneficial effect of motivating state prison administrators to improve their internal grievance systems (see McCoy, 1981). Nevertheless, prisoners can only find it unsettling to be singled out as the only class of Section 1983 litigants who cannot proceed directly to a federal court to seek relief from possible violations of their constitutionally protected rights.

3.3. From *Parratt* (1981) to *Daniels–Davidson* (1986)

In *Parratt v. Taylor* (1981), the Supreme Court announced the first of a series of decisions that have considerably weakened Section 1983 as a vehicle by which state prisoners can go to federal court to challenge prison policies. *Parratt* involved a Section 1983 suit brought by a Nebraska prisoner seeking $23.50 from prison employees for their alleged negligence in failing to follow the normal prison procedure for receiving mailed packages and thereby losing a mail-order hobby kit for which he had paid $23.50. The lower courts had determined that the loss of the prisoner's property was properly construed as a violation of the due process clause of the Fourteenth Amendment and thus was cognizable in a section 1983 suit.

The Supreme Court, however, disagreed, holding that when a plaintiff asserted the loss of *property* because of the *negligent* action of a state employee, the existence of a state postdeprivation remedy precludes a Section 1983 claim based on the due process clause. In this case, according to Justice Rehnquist's plurality opinion, the prisoner must bring his suit under the Nebraska Tort Claims Act—a state law that Justice Rehnquist conceded to be less efficacious than Section 1983 in that it contained no provisions for trial by jury or for punitive damages (*Parratt* at 543–544). Nevertheless, in Justice Rehnquist's view, a state remedy that may not be as advantageous as Section 1983 but that can potentially compensate a prospective Section 1983 plaintiff for his or her losses is "sufficient to satisfy the requirements of due process" (*Parratt* at 544). Therefore, the negligent conduct that had led to the loss of the prisoner's property had occurred with due process of law—the possibility of postdeprivation relief in the state courts—and was not actionable in the federal courts under section 1983 (*Parratt* at 543–544).

Legal commentators were quick to point out that the implications of *Parratt* were ominous for state prisoners (see, for example, Friedman, 1982; Blum, 1984), and they turned out to be absolutely correct. Three years later, the logic of *Parratt* was extended to *intentional* deprivations of property. In *Hudson v. Palmer* (1984), a state prisoner in Virginia brought a Section 1983 action against a prison guard who allegedly had conducted a "shakedown" search of the prisoner's cell and had intentionally destroyed his *noncontraband* personal property including legal papers, a letter from his wife, and a picture of his baby. The suit was based on two legal theories: (1) the assertion that prisoners retain some reasonable expectation of privacy in their cells and are thus constitutionally entitled to some minimal Fourth Amendment protections against unreasonable searches and seizures (i.e., the right to be present during cell searches); and (2) the contention that the guard's intentional destruction of the inmate's personal property should be actionable as a due process claim in federal court under Section 1983 regardless of whether an adequate state postdeprivation remedy was available.

In an opinion authored by Chief Justice Burger, the *Palmer* Court decided both of the previously mentioned issues in favor of the guard and against the prisoner. First, a 5:4 majority held that prisoners possess absolutely no recognizable expectations of privacy in their cells (*Palmer* at 529–530). Therefore, according to the majority, prisoners enjoy no Fourth Amendment protection against arbitrary searches or unjustified confiscation of their personal property, even if the sole purpose of the search and seizure is to harass the inmate (*Palmer* at 529–530).

Second, the Court voted unanimously to apply the reasoning behind *Parratt v. Taylor* to *intentional* deprivations of property by state employees. Pointing out that the destruction of the prisoner's property was a random, unauthorized act by a state employee rather than an established state procedure (in which case Section 1983 arguably could still be used), Chief Justice Burger argued that predeprivation due process was "impractical" because the state court "cannot predict when the loss will occur" (*Palmer* at 532). Therefore, according to the chief justice, the underlying rationale of *Parratt* must be applied to intentional deprivations of property because there is "no logical distinction between negligent and intentional deprivations of property insofar as the 'practicality' of affording predeprivation due process is concerned" (*Palmer* at 533).

Perhaps the weakest aspect of the chief justice's majority opinion is his failure to offer any explanation as to why prisoners who suffer unjustified, egregious, and humilitating property losses at the hands of state employees must use the arguably less efficacious state postdeprivation remedy rather than the federal postdeprivation remedy—Section 1983—that Congress has established as the means by which to redress wrongs committed by state employees. Nevertheless, the result of *Palmer* is that when the state provides an "adequate" postdeprivation remedy by which abused prisoners can seek compensation for their losses, they are barred from seeking compensation under Section 1983 in a federal court—even if they lose their state court lawsuit. Chief Justice Burger acknowledged that under the Virginia Tort Claims Act, a prisoner "might not be able to recover . . . the full amount he might receive in a section 1983 action" (*Palmer* at 535). However, the Chief Justice embraced Justice Rehnquist's *Parratt* argument that a state remedy need not be as efficacious as Section 1983 in order to satisfy the due process requirements of the Fourteenth Amendment (*Palmer* at 535).

In the aftermath of *Palmer*, one legal commentator accused the Supreme Court of "reviving the era of near total deference to prison administrators" (Leading Cases, 1984), whereas others speculated that the outlook for inmate litigants could become even worse if the rationale of *Parratt* and *Palmer* were to be applied to deprivations of *liberty* as well as to deprivations of *property* (Levinson, 1986). But this is precisely what the High Court did in two cases decided in January 1986—*Daniels v. Williams* and *Davidson v. Cannon*.

In *Daniels*, a county jail inmate had slipped on a pillow negligently left on the stairs by a guard. The inmate then brought a Section 1983 suit seeking compensation for his alleged back and ankle injuries on the grounds that the guard's negligence had deprived him of his *liberty* interest under the Fourteenth Amendment to be free from bodily injury caused by government employees. Writing for a unanimous Court, Justice Rehnquist (who would be confirmed as chief justice later in 1986), argued that the Fourteenth Amendment's guarantee that no state shall "deprive any person of life, liberty, or property, without due process of law" was originally intended to apply only to *intentional* deprivations of life, liberty, or property by government officials (*Daniels* at 331). Justice Rehnquist offered no evidence to support the contention that the 1868 Congress that enacted the Fourteenth Amendment held such a narrow view of the due process clause. However, he asserted that the history of the Supreme Court's handling of due process cases supported his argument:

> No decision of this Court before *Parratt* supported the view that negligent conduct by a state official, even though causing injury, constitutes a deprivation under the due process clause. (*Daniels* at 331)

The practical impact of Justice Rehnquist's extraordinarily brief examination of the history of the Fourteenth Amendment was devastating for state prisoners and local jail inmates. In one swift stroke, Justice Rehnquist overruled the one aspect of *Parratt* that had allowed prisoners any legal recourse when they had suffered losses at the hands of negligent state or local officials:

> Upon reflection, we . . . overrule *Parratt* to the extent that it states that mere lack of due care by a state official may 'deprive' an individual of life, liberty, or property under the Fourteenth Amendment. (*Daniels* at 330–331)

Thus state prisoners are not only barred from bringing negligence claims to federal courts under Section 1983; as a result of *Daniels*, they are not even constitutionally entitled to an adequate state postdeprivation remedy when they have suffered losses of life, liberty, or property at the hands of negligent state or local employees. In other words, under *Daniels*, negligent acts, however stupid or harmful, can never violate the Fourteenth Amendment. If the state has not enacted some kind of tort claim act under which the victim of negligent conduct can seek redress (and this was indeed the case for plaintiff Roy Daniels), he or she simply will have no right to go to any court—state or federal—to seek relief.

One of the nation's leading authorities on tort law described *Daniels* as "novel," "far-reaching," and as a "reinterpretation of the Fourteenth Amendment" (Mead, 1986: 27). But the damage done to the prisoner's right of access to the courts is perhaps best demonstrated by showing how the *Daniels* precedent was applied to the facts of *Davidson v. Cannon* (1986). Whereas *Daniels* was a simple slip-and-fall case that could arguably be called "insipid," *Davidson* involved egregious and inexcusable negligence on the part of state prison officials. After another prisoner had threatened him, Robert Davidson, the plaintiff, reported the threats both orally and in writing to the appropriate prison officials. His written request for protection found its way to the assistant superintendent of the prison who read it and sent it to the cellblock's corrections sergeant on December 19, 1980. But the sergeant, though informed of the note's contents and the identity of the threatening prisoner, forgot about the note and left it on his desk unread when he left the prison some 8 hours later. Because both the assistant superintendent and the sergeant did not work on December 20 or 21, the guards on duty knew nothing about the threat. On December 21, the inmate who had threatened Robert Davidson attacked him with a fork, breaking his nose and inflicting severe wounds to his face, neck, head, and body.

Without question, the facts of Robert Davidson's case are far more compelling than those of Roy Daniels' case. Surely Justice Rehnquist could not conclude that judicial willingness to consider Robert Davidson's claims "would trivialize the centuries-old principle of due process of law" (*Daniels* at 332). But in a four-page majority opinion, Justice Rehnquist, in effect, did just that. This was nothing more than a simple case of negligence, declared Justice Rehnquist, and therefore "the principles enunciated in *Daniels* [are] controlling here" (*Davidson* at 347–348).

It is notable that three justices dissented in *Davidson*. The three dissenters—Justices Blackmun, Marshall, and Brennan—expressed the belief that the conduct of the prison officials in *Davidson* arguably reached the level of *deliberate* or *reckless indifference* to the prisoner's safety (*Davidson* at 349–360). Thus they would have remanded the case to the lower courts to consider whether the actions of the prison officials should be treated as a "reckless indifference" claim under the Eighth Amendment's cruel and unusual punishment clause as in *Smith v. Wade* (1983). In Justice Blackmun's words:

> When the state incarcerated Daniels, it left intact his own faculties for avoiding a slip and a fall. But the state prevented Davidson from defending himself, and therefore assumed some responsibility to protect him from the dangers to which he was exposed. In these circumstances, I feel that Davidson was deprived of liberty by the negligence of prison officials. Moreover, the acts of the state officials in this case may well have risen to the level of recklessness. I therefore dissent. (*Davidson* at 350)

For prisoners and the supporters of prison reform, the implications of *Daniels* and *Davidson* are foreboding. The Supreme Court's next step could very well be to decide that *intentional* deprivations of *liberty* can no longer be litigated in federal courts when state remedies are available. For that matter, the Court may eventually go even further and apply the logic of *Daniels* to intentional deprivations of liberty, thus allowing the states to decide whether or not to provide remedies for such violations. Also in doubt is the continued vitality of *Smith v. Wade* (1983). Few legal scholars would be surprised if the Court were to hold that Eighth Amendment claims of reckless indifference to state prisoners' health or safety can no longer be brought under Section 1983 to the federal courts when adequate state remedies are available.

As a result of the Supreme Court's narrowing of Section 1983 jurisdiction, prisoners increasingly find themselves in a classic "Catch 22" situation. In *Johnson v. Avery* (1969), *Bounds v. Smith* (1977), and other cases, inmates won the right to challenge prison policies that violate their right of access to the courts and other substantive constitutional rights. But these hard-earned rights are rapidly becoming "rights without remedies" because of Supreme Court decisions that establish formidable and inflexible procedural and jurisdictional barriers to bringing suit in a federal or state court.

4. IMPLICATIONS FOR RESEARCH ON THE COURTS AND CORRECTIONS

Since *Monroe v. Pape* (1961), American prisoners have been transformed from "slaves of the state" to individuals with significant constitutional rights. The courts agreed to consider the complaints of prisoners only after years of neglect and the failure of prison administrators to manage their institutions appropriately. One consequence of the judiciary's willingness to review prison conditions was the raising of the iron curtain that had been drawn between the courts and prisoners. For a window in time, the pendulum was swinging toward the advantage of those who were incarcerated. As the previous analysis has demonstrated, the pendulum has reached its most advanced degree and is now moving rapidly in the opposite direction, toward the return of what can be termed a "modified hands-off" doctrine. In particular, the Supreme Court's recent decisions curtailing the availability of Section 1983 relief for state prisoners have, in effect, closed the federal (and, in some cases, the state) courthouse doors to prisoners who may have verifiable and meritorious claims.

The major justification for this trend is that inmate petitions—especially Section 1983 filings—are placing increasing burdens on the time and resources of judges and correctional officials. Several Supreme Court justices, notably Chief Justice Rehnquist and Justice O'Connor, have charged that inmate Section 1983 suits waste scarce judicial resources and create financial hardships for state and local governments (see *Monell v. Department of Social Services* (1978) at 724 (Rehnquist, J., dissenting; O'Connor, 1981: 808–815). Even judges who are generally more sympathetic to the need for federal protection of civil rights through Section 1983 have expressed concerns about the burdens that Section 1983 imposes on the federal courts (Coffin, 1971; Friendly, 1973: 87–107).

These concerns suggest that it is important to conduct a great deal more research on the financial and social costs of inmate Section 1983 claims and other types of lawsuits brought by prisoners. Is there really a deluge of prison litigation? Is the Section 1983 caseload a problem of crisis dimensions for court personnel and correctional employees? Or is it possible that the so-called flood of litigation is a largely illusory problem, created by the hyperbole of those who are simply hostile to prisoners as a class of litigants?

To answer the preceding questions will require increasingly sophisticated research on how the courts process prisoner petitions and how correctional personnel respond to inmate complaints. So far, the few empirical studies of how Section 1983 cases are handled by the federal courts tend to undermine the assertion that these cases are overburdening the federal docket (see, for example Bailey, 1975; Eisenberg, 1982; McCoy, 1981; Turner, 1979). It is especially interesting that most of these studies have indicated that the burden on the federal courts may be exaggerated by those who advocate limits on inmate Section 1983 cases. For example, Turner (1979: 637) discovered that "a large proportion of [Section 1983] cases are screened out and summarily dismissed before they get under way, . . . court appearances and trials are rare, and . . . prisoner cases are not particularly complex as compared to other types of federal litigation."

On the other hand, Roger Hanson (1987: 224) recently pointed out that the burdens of screening and disposing of Section 1983 cases—especially the typically inarticulate *pro se* complaints drafted by inmates without benefit of counsel—should not be underestimated. His study of four federal district courts revealed that the major workload of a majority of Section 1983 cases falls not on federal judges, but "on the shoulders of federal magistrates and *pro se* law clerks" (1987: 224). Moreover, Hanson stresses that we do not know—and thus need more research on—such important factors as:

(1) The cost to state attorneys general (or private counsel) in defending state officials.

(2) The cost to federal magistrates and their staff in the time spent handling cases through the pretrial stages.

(3) The time spent by federal district court judges and their staff in preparing for and conducting trials.

(4) The time spent by federal circuit court judges, and their staff in hearing appeals.
(5) The administrative costs to the federal district and circuit courts in the maintenance and processing of court documents.
(6) The costs in time and money to correctional officials in attending hearings, preparing answers, submitting to depositions, and transporting inmates to and from the courthouse. (1987: 225)

Even without additional research on the costs of prisoner litigation, it would not be premature to conclude that the costs are indeed significant. This is not to say that the costs necessarily outweigh the benefits. Some of the benefits are precious and priceless. For example, there is no way to put a dollar value on the importance of upholding the principle that all Americans—even those who have shown no respect for the law—are entitled to humane treatment, fundamental fairness, and due process of law. But if these values could be preserved while decreasing the social and economic costs of inmate litigation, everybody would benefit.

This intuitively appealing idea suggests the desirability of developing and refining inmate grievance systems that can resolve inmate complaints in a fair and prompt manner while reducing the caseloads of the federal and state courts. It was presumably with this intention that Congress passed the Civil Rights of Institutionalized Persons Act in May, 1980. This Act, discussed earlier, was designed specifically to reduce the Section 1983 caseload. It allows prison officials who have had their institutional grievance systems approved by either the United States Attorney General's Office or the federal court of jurisdiction to delay Section 1983 cases for up to 90 days in order to attempt to resolve inmate grievances internally. In other words, the Act provides for a period of negotiation in which a determination of the accuracy and importance of the allegations can be made, and a fair and just resolution can be negotiated.

Unfortunately, the states have shown an unwillingness to request certification for inmate grievance procedures and a reluctance to take advantage of the provisions of the Act. Only four states—Virginia, Wyoming, Iowa, and Louisiana—have certified grievance mechanisms in place, and only Virginia has had a certified procedure in place long enough to allow study of the effects of the Institutionalized Persons Act. Preliminary research by Hanson (1987: 227) indicates that "Virginia has experienced a substantial decrease in filing rates after gaining certification whereas adjoining states in the same federal circuit that have not been certified have experienced much smaller changes in litigation rates." This suggests that there is a compelling need for additional research on the effectiveness of certified grievance procedures and on how internal grievance systems generally affect the rights of both prisoners and correctional staff. Among the questions that need to be answered are:

1. What kinds of grievance systems are most effective in resolving inmate complaints?
2. Are certain kinds of grievance systems more effective than others in reducing Section 1983 litigation?
3. Is inmate participation (in a decisional capacity) in a grievance system helpful or counterproductive in settling disputes?
4. Can grievance systems offer fair compensation to prisoners who have suffered losses that are no longer compensable in the courts as a result of *Daniels, Davidson,* and other Supreme Court decisions?
5. Do grievance systems reduce—or merely postpone—frivolous and nonmeritorious Section 1983 suits?
6. How satisfied are prisoners and correctional staff with various kinds of grievance procedures?

Answers to these and other questions about the impact of internal grievance mechanisms on the courts and on the prisons may encourage the states to establish new and better dispute resolution procedures. However, it would be naive to be overly optimistic about this possibility. As Christopher Smith (1986: 149) warned, "[r]elying on the states for the development of remedies means [that the] implementation of protections for prisoners' rights is placed squarely in the hands of the elected legislatures and governors who fostered the unconstitutional prison conditions in the first place."

Thus it remains vitally important to continue earlier research on the realities of American prison conditions (see, e.g., Bowker, 1980; Toch, 1977) and to carry out new research on how these conditions affect the character, content, and number of suits filed by prisoners. In addition, it will be necessary to update earlier studies focusing on the impact of court decisions on prison policies and practices (Alpert, 1978; Haas and Champagne, 1976). Accordingly, our initial research agenda includes the following:

1. Comparative and longitudinal analyses of the conditions under which prisoners seek and are either provided or denied access to the courts.
2. Comparative and longitudinal analyses of how prisoners achieve access to the courts by type of prison and jurisdiction.
3. Studies on how the provision of legal assistance affects the attitudes and behavior of prisoners and staff.

4. Studies on how specific court decisions affect the attitudes and behavior of prisoners and staff.

The changing scope of the prisoner's right of access to the courts over the past century has reflected evolving judicial philosophies about the meaning of justice, the limits of punishment, and the proper role of the courts in a free society. It is our hope that a philosophy of humanitarianism, informed by carefully crafted and skillfully executed research, will shape correctional policies and provide guidance for the courts of the future.

5. REFERENCES

Alpert, G. P. Prisoners' right of access to courts: Planning for legal aid. *Washington Law Review*, 1976, 51, 653–675.

Alpert, G. P. *Legal rights of prisoners*. Lexington, MA: Lexington Books, 1978.

Alpert, G. P. Prisoners and their rights: An introduction. In G. P. Alpert (Ed.), *Legal rights of prisoners*. Beverly Hills, CA: Sage Publications, 1980.

Alpert, G. P., and Huff, C. R. Prisoners, the law and public policy: Planning for legal aid. *New England Journal on Prison Law*, 1981, 7, 307–340.

Bailey, W. S. The realities of prisoners' cases under U.S.C. Section 1983: A statistical survey in the northern district of Illinois. *Loyola University of Chicago Law Journal*, 1975, 6, 527–559.

Blum, K. M. The implications of *Parratt v. Taylor* for Section 1983 litigation. *The Urban Lawyer*, 1984, 16, 363–386.

Bluth, W. Legal services for inmates: Coopting the jailhouse lawyer. *Capital University Law Review*, 1972, 1, 59–81.

Bowker, L. H. *Prison victimization*. New York: Elsevier, 1980.

Bureau of Justice Statistics. *Prisoners in 1986*. Washington, DC: U.S. Government Printing Office, 1987.

Cardarelli, A., and Finkelstein, M. M. Correctional administrators assess the adequacy and impact of prison legal services programs in the United States. *Journal of Criminal Law and Criminology*, 1974, 65, 91–102.

Coffin, F. M. Justice and workability: Un essai. *Suffolk University Law Review*, 1971, 5, 567–587.

Edwards, J. A. The prisoner's right of access to the courts. *California Western Law Review*, 1968, 4, 99–114.

Eisenberg, J. Section 1983: Doctrinal foundations and an empirical study. *Cornell Law Review*, 1982, 67, 482–556.

Friedman, L. *Parratt v. Taylor*: Closing the door on Section 1983. *Hastings Constitutional Law Quarterly*, 1982, 9, 545–578.

Friendly, H. J. *Federal jurisdiction: A general view*, New York: Columbia University Press, 1973.

Gobert, J. L., and Cohen, N. P. *Rights of prisoners*. Colorado Springs: Shepard's/McGraw-Hill, 1981.

Haas, K. C. Judicial politics and correctional reform: An analysis of the decline of the "hands-off" doctrine. *Detroit College of Law Review*, 1977, 4, 796–831.

Haas, K. C. The "new federalism" and prisoners' rights: State supreme courts in comparative perspective. *Western Political Quarterly*, 1981, *34*, 552–571.

Haas, K. C. The comparative study of state and federal judicial behavior revisited. *Journal of Politics*, 1982, *44*, 721–746.

Haas, K. C., and Champagne, A. The impact of *Johnson v. Avery* on prison administration. *Tennessee Law Review*, 1976, *43*, 275–306.

Hanson, R. A. What should be done when prisoners want to take the state to court? *Judicature*, 1987, *70*, 223–227.

Leading cases of the 1983 term. *Harvard Law Review*, 1984, *98*, 151–165.

Levinson, R. B. Due process challenges to governmental actions: The meaning of *Parratt* and *Hudson*. *The Urban Lawyer*, 1986, *18*, 189–208.

Manville, D. E. *Prisoners self-help litigation manual*. New York: Oceana Publications, 1983.

McCoy, C. The impact of Section 1983 litigation on policymaking in corrections. *Federal Probation*, 1981, *45*, 17–23.

Mead, S. M. Evolution of the "species of tort liability" created by 42 U.S.C. Section 1983: Can constitutional tort be saved from extinction? *Fordham Law Review*, 1986, *55*, 1–62.

Nahmod, S. *Civil rights and civil liberties litigation*. Colorado Springs: Shepard's/McGraw-Hill, 1986.

Neuborne, B. Toward procedural parity in constitutional litigation. *William and Mary Law Review*, 1981, *22*, 725–787.

Note. A prisoner's constitutional right to attorney assistance. *Columbia Law Review*, 1983, *83*, 1279–1319.

O'Connor, S. D. Trends in the relationship between the federal and state courts from the perspective of a state court judge. *William and Mary Law Review*, 1981, *22*, 801–819.

Rudovsky, D., Bronstein, A. J., and Koren, E. I. *The rights of prisoners*. New York: Bantam, 1983.

Smith, C. E. Federal judges' role in prisoner litigation: What's necessary? What's proper? *Judicature*, 1986, *70*, 144–150.

Tarr, G. A., and Porter, M. C. State constitutionalism and state constitutional law. *Publius*, 1987, *17*, 1–12.

Toch, H. *Living in prison: The ecology of prison survival*. New York: The Free Press, 1977.

Turner, W. B. When prisoners sue: A study of prisoner section 1983 suits in the federal courts. *Harvard Law Review*, 1979, *92*, 610–663.

6. CASES

Bounds v. Smith, 430 U.S. 817 (1977).

City of Newport v. Fact Concerts, 453 U.S. 247 (1981).

Coleman v. Peyton, 302 F.2d 905 (4th Cir. 1966).

Cooper v. Pate, 378 U.S. 546 (1964).

Daniels v. Williams, 474 U.S. 327 (1986).

Davidson v. Cannon, 474 U.S. 344 (1986).

Ex parte Hull, 312 U.S. 546 (1941).

Hooks v. Wainwright, 536 F. Supp. 1330 (M.D. Fla. 1982), *rev'd*, 775 F.2d 1433 (11th Cir. 1985).

Hudson v. Palmer, 468 U.S. 517 (1984).

Johnson v. Avery, 393 U.S. 483 (1969).

Lindquist v. Idaho Board of Corrections, 776 F.2d 851 (9th Cir. 1985).

Monell v. Department of Social Services, 436 U.S. 658 (1978).

Monroe v. Pape, 365 U.S. 167 (1961).

Owen v. City of Independence, 445 U.S. 622 (1980).

Parratt v. Taylor, 451 U.S. 527 (1981).

Patsy v. Florida Board of Regents, 457 U.S. 496 (1982).

Preiser v. Rodriguez, 411 U.S. 475 (1973).

Procunier v. Martinez, 416 U.S. 396, 419–422 (1974).

Procunier v. Navarette, 434 U.S. 555 (1978).

Quern v. Jordan, 440 U.S. 332 (1979).

Ross v. Moffitt, 417 U.S. 600 (1974).

Ruffin v. Commonwealth, 62 Va. (21 Gratt.) 790 (1871).

Smith v. Wade, 461 U.S. 30 (1983).

Tenney v. Brandhove, 341 U.S. 367 (1951).

Wolff v. McDonnell, 418 U.S. 539, 577–580 (1974).

Younger v. Gilmore, 404 U.S. 15 (1971).

Chapter 6

GENDER AND JUSTICE
The Equal Protection Issue

NICOLE HAHN RAFTER

1. OVERVIEW

In meting out punishments for crimes, our society defines justice in terms of both proportionality—the fit between offense and consequence—and equal treatment, the imposition of penalties without regard for such personal characteristics as gender, race, or social class. This chapter is concerned with justice in the second sense. It focuses on the gap between the ideal of equal treatment and the reality that prisons punish inmates differently on the basis of gender.

Over the past 20 years, various observers have compared conditions under which men and women are confined (Advisory Commission on Intergovernmental Relations, 1984; Alpert and Wiorkowski, 1979; Connolly, 1983; Fabian, 1979; Glick and Neto, 1977; Note, 1973; Rafter, 1985; U.S. Comptroller General, 1980; U.S. General Accounting Office, 1979). Without exception, they have concluded that women's prisons provide different and generally inferior care. Women have fewer educational and vocational programs; less opportunity for work release, recreation, and visitation; and fewer medical and legal resources. Their institutional job assignments are often more limited in number and type, and they may be classified according to criteria established for men (American Correctional Association, 1984). Despite the popular belief that female

NICOLE HAHN RAFTER • College of Criminal Justice, Northeastern University, Boston, Massachusetts 02115.

prisoners live under less rigid conditions, in acutality they frequently are subjected to higher levels of security and stricter discipline (U.S. Comptroller General, 1980). Differential and usually less adequate care for women, it is now clear, has been the rule since the prison system began (Rafter, 1985). What is new, today, is that incarcerated women are challenging this tradition in the courts.

In recent years, women have brought a series of suits charging jail and prison officials with discrimination on the basis of sex—failure to meet the ideal of justice as equal treatment. Although such cases are still few in number, there are indications that they will be brought with increasing frequency in the years ahead. They have been litigated, moreover, throughout the United States and in the context of diverse institutional arrangements ("coed" jails and coed state prisons, separate women's jails and separate women's prisons). The cases have developed out of varying circumstances: One addresses gender disparities in access to recreational facilities, for example, another differences in the sizes of cells to which men and women, respectively, are assigned. However, their underlying approach is much the same: All contrast the conditions of male and female prisoners; conclude that women's conditions are poorer; and argue that the differences constitute sex discrimination in violation of the Fourteenth Amendment's Equal Protection Clause. Courts have started to agree with this argument, holding that inequities that have characterized the U.S. prison system for 200 years are unconstitutionally discriminatory and no longer permissible. These decisions require changes that may radically restructure ways in which penal systems allocate funds, plan programs, and make institutional assignments.

In what follows, I examine the issue of gender and justice by analyzing, first, the historical roots of unequal treatment. Next I identify two structural problems that perpetuate the problem today. A third section describing the new equal protection litigation is followed by one that explores possible responses—steps penal systems can take to alleviate the problem. I conclude by suggesting that we fight fire with fire: Given the long history of inequitable care and the intractability of the structural problems involved, judges should consider differential prison conditions at sentencing and "discriminate" by making special efforts to use nonincarcerative sanctions with women.

2. ORIGINS OF THE PROBLEM

2.1. Women in Custodial Prisons

In analyzing the incarceration of women from a historical perspective, it is useful to begin by distinguishing two models or types of treatment, custodial and reformatory. The *custodial model*—the only one in existence until the late nineteenth century—was punitive in nature: Uninterested in rehabilitation, its aim was to confine inmates at the lowest cost (a profit, if possible) until their sentences expired. Custodialism was basically a masculine model in that it treated women like men, holding them under conditions of high security, demanding hard labor, and ignoring female-specific needs. Women's units of the custodial type were usually attached—at least initially—to a men's prison. They became associated with the problem of *neglect*; their inmates received less attention than their male counterparts. Moreover, even when the circumstances of the two sexes were outwardly similar, women in custodial units suffered more just because those circumstances were designed by and for men.[1]

The very earliest prisons did not separate the sexes. In the late eighteenth and early nineteenth centuries, a state's few female felons were confined in the midst of hundreds of men at the central penitentiary and guarded by all-male staffs. As time went on and more women accumulated, they were gathered in small units of their own—the end of a cell block, a space over the guard room, sometimes a little building in a corner of the prison yard. The men who ran prisons viewed female convicts as an annoyance; in their eyes, it was the women, not men, who had to be kept separate to prevent sexual mischief and scandals. Thus women were increasingly isolated. *Their* windows were nailed shut, *they* were kept from exercising in the yard, *their* quarters were located as far as possible from the main activities of the prison. In time, women were moved outside the walls, to a building across the street from the penitentiary, perhaps, or one several miles away on the prison farm.

The more women were isolated, the more they experienced the neglect that came to characterize women's units of the custodial type. Removed from the mainstream of prison life, they had less access than men to the mess hall and yard, the chaplain and physician. Separated, they might now have a matron—and thus be less vulnerable to sexual coercion by guards and other convicts; but the matron, always subordinate to the principal keeper of the adjacent men's prison, also experienced neglect. She and her charges lived in small quarters that could not be expanded as easily as those of male prisoners; thus these units became overcrowded more rapidly. When the women's building needed repairs, it was less likely than the men's cell blocks to receive attention.

---

[1] The rest of Section 2 is based on Rafter, 1985; to avoid frequent citations in the text, I refer readers generally to this work for substantiation and exemplification of points made here.

Even when male and female inmates of custodial institutions were treated with apparent evenhandedness, the latter suffered more hardship. Consider, for example, the circumstances of a woman held alone, or with but a few others, in a predominantly male penitentiary. She had less privacy from the opposite sex and less company of her own kind. Male guards held the keys to her cell. If pregnant, she had at best access to a physician accustomed to dealing with men. If nursing, she had to find ways to care for the child in her cell—a nearly impossible task, as high rates of infant mortality in early custodial prisons attest. Moreover, the female was regarded as far worse than the male criminal and thus treated with more derision. Francis Lieber voiced a common opinion in his preface to Beaumont and Tocqueville's *On the Penitentiary System in the United States* when he maintained that "a woman, when she commits a crime, acts more in contradiction to her whole moral organization, i.e., must be more depraved, must have sunk already deeper than a man" (1964 [1833]: 11). Because they violated role prescriptions as well as the law, female criminals were doubly scorned. Penitentiary conditions that appeared similar for men and women, then, usually spelled more misery for the latter.

The custodial model, although eventually supplemented by women's institutions of the reformatory type, did not disappear. Most states that established a separate reformatory for women continued to operate a custodial unit, in or nearby their central prison, for female offenders convicted of the most serious crimes and those transferred out of reformatories for misbehavior. Other states—particularly those in the South and West—never created a women's reformatory. In them, the women's unit sometimes became an independent prison in the early twentieth century, but it maintained the tradition of neglect and subjection to masculine standards that had become typical of custodial institutions.

2.2. Women in Reformatory Prisons

The *reformatory model* began to evolve after the Civil War in the Northeast and Midwest. Based on the concept of rehabilitation and on a view of women as innately different from men in both needs and abilities, the reformatory model feminized punishment. The first independent prisons for adult females, reformatories were founded through efforts of organized women's groups and run entirely by women. Many were designed along the lines of reform schools for children: Unwalled, covering large rural tracts, they consisted of a series of cottages in which small groups lived family-style, supervised by a motherly matron. Methods of rehabilitation were dictated by the ideal of domesticity (Welter, 1966); taught to sew, cook, and wait on tables, inmates learned how to comport themselves as "good" women. Often they were paroled to live-in positions as domestic servants; if they failed to satisfy the mistress, they could be returned to prison.

The reformatory model became associated with its own constellation of problems, drawbacks best characterized, from today's perspective, as those of *protectionism*. Institutions of the reformatory type were based on a view of women as more childlike than men: They adopted the cottage system used to reform wayward children, and they punished refractory inmates by denying them supper and sending them to their "rooms."[2] To prevent fallen women from falling again, reformatories attempted to instill the values of home and hearth. But by the same token, they discouraged inmates from acting as independent adults—from competing with men in the industrial job market and participating in the activities (meeting men in dance halls, smoking cigarettes, traveling alone) of other working-class women.

The disadvantages of protectionism become clearest when we look at its consequences for sentencing and time served. Although women's reformatories were state prisons, they could—and often did—receive misdemeanants as well as felons. Reformatories for young men were also established in the late nineteenth and early twentieth centuries, but these, like traditional state prisons, limited intake to felons; men convicted of misdemeanors were punished in jails, not state institutions. Many of the misdemeanants sent to women's reformatories, moreover, were convicted of minor sex offenses: lewdness, prostitution, being pregnant out of wedlock, "delinquency." Adult men were rarely prosecuted, much less incarcerated, for such transgressions. Through their very existence, women's reformatories, with their loose commitment restrictions and assurances of rehabilitative care, encouraged judges to apply the double standard at sentencing. Some reformatory inmates were released after a few months, but many were held on indefinite sentences for periods of years. Justified by the belief that women deserved special consideration, differential treatment in fact resulted in harsher punishment.

2.3. Convergence of the Two Models

About 1930, the custodial and reformatory models merged, pooling their respective disadvantages to create the women's prison system as we know it today. The merger occurred mainly in the Northeast and

---

[2] Discipline in reformatories occasionally devolved into brutality; but such harshness was antithetical to the reformatory ideal.

Midwest, regions where the two models had long coexisted, and was precipitated by the Great Depression. States that had been operating reformatories found they could no longer afford expensive programs to rehabilitate petty offenders. At the same time, they came under increasing pressure from wardens of predominantly male prisons who proposed to relieve overcrowding by getting rid of women in adjoining custodial units. The solution, adopted in the 1930s by states from Connecticut to California, Nebraska to Virginia, was to turn women's reformatories into institutions for felons only. Misdemeanants were sent to local jails, as they had been before the reformatory movement began. Women's custodial units at mainly male prisons were closed and their inmates transferred to reformatory grounds. At these locations, reformatory traditions persisted, most importantly that of infantilization. (As we shall see, one of the arguments in today's equal protection litigation is that women's prisons treat inmates like children, placing on them more restrictions than are required of males.) But the reformatory legacy now mixed with elements of the custodial style, especially its tradition of neglect. (The resulting impoverishment of programs in women's prisons is another complaint in current litigation.)

States that never established a reformatory continued to adhere to the custodial model. As noted earlier, some, when faced with large populations of female convicts, turned custodial units into independent women's prisons. Even with their own superintendents, however, these institutions still received less attention and lower levels of funding than men's prisons. Thus today they, too, provide targets for suits based on the Fourteenth Amendment.

3. NUMBERS AND "NATURE": SOURCES OF SEX DISCRIMINATION TODAY

Two structural factors combine with these historical traditions to produce gender discrimination within penal systems today. One is a "numbers" problems—the simple fact that there are many fewer women than men in correctional institutions. In 1987, only 5% of state and federal prisoners, and 8% of jail inmates, were female. In and of themselves, the numbers were considerable—almost 29,000 women in state and federal prisons, another 24,000 in local jails. But compared to male prisoners, females constitute only small proportions of total inmate populations. The results, as Fabian has put it (1979: 17), are "remoteness and heterogeneity."

Remoteness results because most states have just one prison for women, who are thus likely to be incarcerated at a greater distance than men from family, friends, legal contacts, and community resources. Some states have no women's prison at all, sending females to neighboring jurisdictions. Similarly, many counties send women to other jurisdictions to avoid maintaining quarters for just a few in the local jail (Connolly, 1983; Kerle and Ford, 1982). These prisoners, too, are thus further removed than men from community, legal, and personal resources. At the federal level, women are also more likely than men to be incarcerated far from their home base.

Due to their relatively small numbers, women's units perforce hold *heterogeneous populations*. Men's prisons, being numerous, can specialize in youthful offenders, the mentally ill, low or high security, and so on. But most women's institutions must try to provide the full range of security and services. In sum, as an American Correctional Association report has observed (1984: 30), the "fewer programs and treatment options available to [female] than male inmates . . . [are] a direct result of a small number of offenders and the limited number of institutions which house women prisoners."

The second source of inferior care is a "nature" problem—the fact that treatment is shaped by the structure of relationships between the sexes, including stereotypes of women's "true nature" and the realities of gender roles. For example, assumptions about gender influence the content of vocational programs. In women's institutions, training frequently is limited to courses in grooming ("cosmetology"), sewing, and typing (Glick and Neto, 1977; Note, 1973; Ryan, 1984; Weisheit, 1985). Poorly paid within prisons, such work also reduces women's ability to compete for jobs after release. Furthermore, beliefs about women's nature may encourage prison officials—nearly all of whom are male—to perpetuate the reformatory tradition by dealing with women in a protective, even infantilizing manner. As a U.S. district court put it in one of the leading sex discrimination cases, *Canterino v. Wilson*, "restrictions are imposed solely because of gender with the objective of controlling the lives of women in a way deemed unnecessary for male prisoners" (1982: 207).

Women's lower level of violence—another aspect of the nature problem—also fosters second-class treatment (Mecoy, 1987). Women are less likely than men to riot or assault one another within the walls (Fabian, 1979; McBride, 1987). Ironically, their pacific nature can work against them: Because women do not create trouble, they are often taken less seriously than male prisoners.

Finally, "nature" puts women at a disadvantage because they have more to lose when separated from children (Bird, 1979). When men go to prison, child care is less likely to be an issue. Either they are not living with their children at the time of arrest, or they can leave children with

a female relative. But women who go to prison often have several children dependent solely on them. Anxiety about children is a major source
of psychological pain for incarcerated women (Baunach, 1985; Potter,
1978).

Neither the numbers dilemma nor that of "nature" is susceptible
to quick fixes. Combined with the historical factors described in the last
section, they make sex discrimination within the prison system a problem highly resistant to solution. Yet some inroads have been made
through litigation.   .

4. LEGAL CHALLENGES

The current interest of women prisoners in equal protection issues
is part of a broader shift toward legal activism. Historically, female inmates have been far less litigious than males (Alpert, 1981; Smith College
School of Social Work, 1982). The explanation, as the cases discussed
later suggest, probably lies with the fact that women have had less access
to legal resources and thus lacked opportunities to develop a tradition
of jailhouse lawyering (cf. Alpert, 1978). Some observers continue to
find incarcerated women "quiescent" on legal matters (Aylward and
Thomas, 1984), but others have detected signs of change. For example,
Leonard (1983) has drawn attention to three issues around which female
inmates are becoming legally active—sex discrimination, medical care,
and parental rights (also see Fabian, 1979). Other writers have noted a
growth of suits around rights of pregnant inmates (McHugh, 1980; Note,
1981–1982). One indication of the new activism emerged from a 1983
survey by the American Correctional Association, which found (1984:
31) 23 states facing court decrees and/or pending litigation concerning
female prisoners. Similarly, a National Institute of Corrections survey
of state prisons for women identified 27 states involved in litigation of
this type (Ryan, 1984: 23).

Equal protection suits of the past 15 years have used a comparative
approach that has enabled women to raise questions about a wide range
of conditions[3] they could not have successfully challenged by focusing
on women's units alone—a point that may be illustrated with an example concerning prison labor. Inmates have no right to a specific job
within an institution or to payment for their work. Thus it would be
fruitless for Inmate A to sue on the ground that she was assigned to

---

[3] An earlier series of sex discrimination suits centered around not conditions but *sentencing*
inequities; see Fabian, 1979; "Sex Discrimination—Prison Inmates," 1982; and Temin,
1980.

kitchen duties while Inmate B was assigned to maintenance, or that she was paid less than Inmate B, so long as the differences were not based on a suspect classification such as race. But if female inmates as a group can show that, compared to male equivalents, they have a more limited range of job assignments, or are consistently paid less, they may be able to persuade a court that their equal protection rights are being violated.

In what follows, I discuss five cases of this type, dealing first with three jail suits, next with two that pertain to state institutions.[4]

4.1. Jail Cases

In *Mitchell v. Untreiner*, decided by a U.S. District Court in 1976, equal protection issues remained peripheral. This was a class action by inmates (male and female) of the Escambia County Jail at Pensacola, Florida. The central issue was living conditions, which the court found "punitive and inhumane" (p. 893). The court identified two conditions that made incarceration especially onerous for the jail's female inmates. First, only convicted males were designated as trustees and allowed to eat in a dining room. Second, only convicted males were held at the jail's satellite road camp, where in "marked contrast to living conditions at the Jail," inmates received clothing and newspapers, were allowed contact visits, and had opportunites for education and exercise. The court concluded that "[f]emale inmates are doubly denied equal protection of the laws by not being permitted to be trustees . . . [or] to serve their sentences in a less severe facility as is available to male prisoners at the . . . Road Prison" (p. 895).

Cooper v. Morin, decided by the Supreme Court of Monroe County, New York, in 1977, was a class action by female inmates held in a section of the county jail. Although the inmates' main concerns lay elsewhere, their suit included two equal protection claims to which the court added a third. It was on two of these three equal protection issues—not on the matters that comprised the bulk of the complaint—that the plaintiffs won the most territory.

---

[4] As of this writing (1987) there is no up-to-date inventory of sex discrimination cases brought by female jail and prison inmates, although the ACLU's National Prison Project plans to compile one in the near future. I am grateful to Miriam Berkman of the Yale Law School's Legal Services Organization for sending me a copy of a recent memorandum by Kate Silverman that lists reported and pending litigation. Other cases are mentioned in Fabian, 1979; Leonard, 1983; "Sex Discrimination—Prison Inmates," 1982; and U.S. Comptroller General, 1980. The three jail cases discussed here were selected for their ability to illustrate the range of issues around which jailed women are litigating. The two state examples are the leading cases of their type.

The first of the inmates' equal protection charges concerned the gymnasium, to which the jail's male inmates had more access. Noting that "[m]ale prisoners outnumber females on the order of ten to one," the court concluded that "[t]hat factor alone justifies greater male access time to the gymnasium facilities" (p. 68). It was more sympathetic to the plaintiffs' second equal protection claim, concerning a paucity of paying jobs for women. Although both male and female sentenced inmates were assigned to trusty positions for which they apparently were paid at the same rate, the court found that the women were assigned to a smaller *range* of jobs. Their assignments were limited to the women's quarters and the tailor shop, whereas men could work in six areas. County officials attempted to justify these differences on the ground that "every female inmate outside her immediate housing area must be accompanied by a matron" (p. 68)—a very old excuse for limiting the movements of women (but not men) in mixed-sex institutions. The court held, however, that neither "administrative convenience" nor the "expense of having an additional matron" constituted "an acceptable justification for sex discrimination" (p. 69).

The third equal protection issue in *Cooper*, raised by the court itself, involved differences in cell dimensions and locations. The men's cells were 11 square feet larger and faced windows; the women's fronted on other cells, making it more difficult to use the toilet with privacy. The court declared it "a clear violation of plaintiffs' equal protection rights . . . to be housed under conditions substantially inferior to those under which the majority of male prisoners are confined," adding that "if men's cells face windows, women's cells must likewise" (pp. 70–71).

In *Molar v. Gates* (1979), officials of Orange County, California, unsuccessfully appealed a lower court decision in favor of the county's female prisoners. Here equal protection was the sole issue. The trial court had ruled that the practice "of providing minimum security jail facilities with their attendant privileges, including outside work assignments, for male prisoners while denying such facilities to female inmates . . . was violative of the equal protection clause of the state as well as the federal Constitutions" (p. 242). Inmates of the women's jail were subjected to high security, had little opportunity for outdoor recreation, and were denied contact visits; moreover, at any one time, only two or three went outside the jail on work furlough. Sixty-five percent of the county's male inmates also served their sentences at a high-security main jail; the rest, however, were assigned to two branch jails with lower security, many opportunities for outdoor recreation and work furlough, and the privilege of contact visits.

County officials appealed on several grounds. With a logic that echoed the philosophy of the women's reformatory movement, they argued, first, that the only way to protect the women was to keep them completely separated from men at all times. The court responded that this "'protection' argument is . . . nothing more than a defense based on the 'administrative costs' of providing equal facilities and programs for women. . . . [B]udgetary considerations do not justify governmental violation of the right to equal protection of the laws" (p. 250). Defendants also argued that given the relatively small number of female inmates, it would be too expensive to run a minimum security jail for them. Again the court declared that administrative cost and convenience could not justify denial of constitutional rights.

With varying degrees of focus on equal protection issues but nearly complete success, these three cases addressed disparities that can be found in many jails holding both men and women: allocation of the best jobs to men; greater restrictions on the movements of women; the availability to men, but not women, of placements at subsidiary jails with lower security and more programs; and differences in cell sizes and opportunities for recreation and contact visits. Similar disparities can be found between single-sex jails for men and women. Moreover, the three cases did not consider other common jail practices such as assignment of men to guard women (Kerle and Ford, 1982; Sims, 1976) and the transfer of women out of jurisdiction (Fabian, 1979; *Park v. Thompson*, 1973; "Sex Discrimination—Prison Inmates," 1982). These may well form the basis for other jail cases in the years ahead (Rafter, 1987).

4.2. State Prison Cases

Less than a week before the *Molar* decision, plaintiffs in a Michigan class action won a major equal protection suit against state prison officials. Decided by a federal district court, *Glover v. Johnson* (1979) is significant for not only its specific holdings but also the judge's preliminary decisions about scope and procedure.

The *Glover* court began by rejecting officials' contention that it should compare Huron Valley, Michigan's women's prison, only to men's institutions of a similar size—and hence with a similar level of programming. According to the court, in making this argument "the State avoids the fact that *all* State female felons are sent to Huron Valley while *all* male felons are *not* confined in a facility of comparable limitations" (p. 1078; emphases in original). By deciding that the critical comparison involved gender, not similarly sized institutions, the court was able to address the "numbers" issue head on. It concluded (p. 1078) that in the context of an entire state prison system, "'institutional size' is, frankly, not a justification but an excuse for the kind of treatment afforded to women prisoners" (also see *Bukhari v. Hutto*, 1980).

Turning to procedural matters, the court referred extensively to *Barefield v. Leach* (1974), in which female inmates of the New Mexico Penitentiary had successfully raised a wide range of equal protection issues. *Barefield* had concluded that *"'what the Equal Protection Clause requires in a prison setting is parity of treatment, as contrasted with identity of treatment, between male and female inmates with respect to the conditions of their confinement and access to rehabilitation opportunities'"* (*Barefield*, slip op. at 37–38, cited and with emphases added in *Glover* at 1079). The *Glover* court adopted this standard.

Preliminaries over, the court turned to specific issues raised by the plaintiffs.

The first concerned rehabilitation opportunities, which the court found "substantially inferior to those available to the State's male prisoners in terms of both the quality and variety of programming offered" (p. 1101). For instance, Huron Valley provided vocational education in only 5 areas, compared to 20 at the men's institutions; and whereas the women's programs taught noncommercial skills such as how to make personal calendars, the men's prepared inmates for the job market. Differences in wages and in opportunities to earn good-time credits were among many others that emerged at trial. But whereas the court decided that "the Constitution requires a greater degree of parity in rehabilitation programming," it did not order the state to provide women with *identical* opportunities. Rather, with the *Barefield* standard in mind, it required counseling, followed by a survey, to determine the women's "actual educational and vocational interests" (p. 1101).

The most innovative aspect of *Glover* was its response to the claim that the Huron Valley law library was less adequate than that available to male prisoners. The court found that, although the library did meet constitutional standards, women lacked the access to the courts guaranteed by the Fourteenth Amendment's Due Process Clause. Male prisoners, with their tradition of jailhouse lawyering, had developed the expertise to use legal resources. But "the women do not have a history of self-help in the legal field; the evidence tends to show that until recently they have had little access to adequate legal resources" (p. 1097). Thus the court ordered that women be given a special legal education course to bring their level of skills up to that of men—not on equal protection grounds "but because skilled women inmates are needed to provide meaningful access to the courts" (p. 1097).

Canterino v. Wilson (1982), the other major suit won against a state system, closely resembled *Glover*. The U.S. Department of Justice joined inmates of the Kentucky Correctional Institution for Women (KCIW) in this class action against prison officials. A federal district court found that KCIW inmates "were denied access to many vocational education and training programs . . . available to male prisoners" and that "[o]f the programs which are available to the females at KCIW, many are inferior in quality to the corresponding programs at [Kentucky's] male institutions" (p. 188). Whereas women had only 2 part-time domestic training courses, men had 14 full-time courses that could lead, after release, to well-paid jobs. Women were excluded from community study, work release[5] the farm centers, and on-the-job training; and because they were denied comparable institutional jobs, they received lower wages. The men's institutions ran industries, partly through a federal grant that prohibited sex discrimination in expenditure of funds; yet "not a single prison industry is operated at KCIW" (p. 191). The court decided that these and other disparities violated both federal statutes and the equal protection clause. Drawing extensively on *Glover*, it rejected defendants' attempts to justify inferior treatment on grounds of the smaller size of the women's prison, security considerations, and the women's alleged lack of interest in nondomestic employment (pp. 209–212).

The *Canterino* court also responded positively to a host of complaints about general conditions of confinement. It ordered KCIW to reduce overcrowding until it met the standards established for the state's men's prisons. Finding that "men at the most restrictive male institution have more access to the outdoors in one day, than women at KCIW have in a normal week" (p. 202), it instructed officials to provide more opportunities for outdoor activity. (Women were kept in their cells "for all but a few minutes during each day" [p. 202] to isolate them from the male maintenance crew; the court pointed out that women could be assigned to maintenance.) The court further ordered KCIW to provide more due process in disciplinary and grievance proceedings, improve the women's law library, and give them more legal assistance.

The major difference between *Glover* and *Canterino* lay in the attention the latter paid to KCIW's Levels System, a behavior modification program that "rigidly" governed "such elementary decisions as to when to go to bed and even the ability of a mother to display a picture of her child" (p. 183). Observing that none of the state's men's prisons imposed such restrictions, the court condemned the Levels System as infantilizing. "[T]he Levels System teaches the women to be docile and childlike" (p. 184), "tends to . . . [produce] depression and childlike responses" (p. 186), and "has been imposed at KCIW because defendants have implicitly, if not consciously, decided that women are less capable

---

[5] Along the same lines, in 1983 a Massachusetts prisoner brought suit after being denied assignment to a work-release program at a forestry camp near her home; the law establishing the camp restricted its use to male inmates (Marantz, 1983).

than men of exercising basic privileges" (p. 207). The court concluded that such "restrictions, based on gender and unrelated to any important government objective, violate . . . the equal protection clause" (p. 207).

4.3. The Limits and Potential of Litigation

Significant though these cases are for both the principles they enunciate and the changes they require, litigation is no more a panacea for sex discrimination than any other prison problem. Suits are a slow and costly means of redress. Often they do little more than raise false hopes (Mays and Taggart, 1985), and they can precipitate staff retaliation (Smith College School of Social Work, 1982; Thomas, 1984). Even when courts decide in inmates' favor, corrections officials resist compliance (e.g., *Canterino v. Barber*, 1983). "Prison conditions decrees," observes Alvin Bronstein, executive director of the National Prison Project,

> whether consented to or court-imposed, are not self-executing. Change is resisted, either actively or passively. In each and every case the implementation stage requires a greater commitment of time and resources than was required to achieve the decree in the first instance. (1987: 6)

Yet the benefits of litigation outweigh its drawbacks. Bronstein points out that, despite the difficulties, litigation has achieved "profound and permanent changes" in prison conditions and policies (1987: 6–7; also see Jacobs, 1980, and Advisory Commission on Intergovernmental Relations, 1984). In a study designed to measure the effects of legal assistance to female prisoners in particular, Noblit and Alpert (1979) conclude that legal efforts decrease inmate alienation and promote rehabilitation. Not only does legal engagement ameliorate "at least some of the worst abuses of the prison system," it also may help women overcome institutionally induced apathy by giving them some measure of control over their lives (Thomas 1984: 152, 161). Research for this chapter has indicated that equal protection litigation is in fact most effective as a *threat*: The majority of cases that have come to my attention have either had no legal outcome whatsoever or resulted in a consent decree; yet they have prodded officials into action. As a result of a suit brought by 23 New Hampshire women sent to out-of-state prisons, for example, New Hampshire is now being forced by court decree to build a women's prison of its own (n.a., 1987). And in 1982, when California women challenged the protectionist rationale that barred them from low-security firefighting camps, the state caved in and created the country's first firefighting camp for women (Mecoy, 1987). Changes instituted in response to the threat or actuality of litigation cannot solve all of female inmates' problems—not even all of their equal protection problems; but they do increase parity with male counterparts.

5. AVOIDING THE INEVITABLE: WAYS TO ALLEVIATE
THE PROBLEM

Jails and prisons faced with court orders, and others interested in avoiding litigation entirely, have begun devising ways to reduce gender disparities. To my knowledge, no one has taken an overview of these proposals. What follows, then, is a compendium of measures put forth as means of (in the words of Wright and Magid [1983]) "avoiding the inevitable." No one of these steps, alone, can overcome the obstacles of history, numbers, and "nature"; used simultaneously, they might be equal to the task.

In addition to the constructive measures described next, there is another possibility: moving toward equal treatment by downgrading the care of men. Mentioned (though not endorsed) as an alternative to improving the care of women in *Molar v. Gates* (1979: 251), this route would risk riots by worsening the already abysmal conditions under which most men serve their terms. It would, moreover, probably fail to achieve even low-grade equity: historically, as we have seen, poor but outwardly evenhanded treatment has masked disregard for women's special legal, medical, and family needs.

5.1. Pooling Resources

The most obvious step to minimize disparities is "co-corrections"— holding all women in coed institutions and thus providing them with facilities and programs identical to those of (some) men (Herbert, 1985). Sexual integration has been tried in a number of jurisdictions since the early 1970s, with some good results, but it has failed to achieve equality due to the numbers and "nature" problems. When states "go coed," they end up incarcerating all their women—but just some men—in a mixed-sex institution, providing more options for the latter. In other ways, too, co-corrections does not address the problem identified in *Glover*: Determinations of equity must look beyond care within individual institutions to the resources available to men and women, respectively, in the entire system. In co-correctional states, most women, perforce, are still assigned to an institution farther than men from their home base. Coed programs sometimes are instituted merely to improve conditions for or control over men—to relieve overcrowding at men's prisons, for example, or to reduce homosexual attacks among men (Heffernan, 1978; Ross, Heffernan, Sevick, and Johnson, 1978). The level of security may rise when men are introduced into a formerly female institution; women (but not men) may be barred from work details when there is insufficient supervision; and, as in the outside world, the burden of avoiding pregnancy tends to fall on women (Ross *et al.*, 1978; SchWeber, 1984). Moreover, in some co-correctional prisons, men have forced women out of programs and assumed a right to the highest status positions (Campbell, 1982; Ross *et al.*, 1978; SchWeber, 1984). Finally, transformation of a women's prison into a co-correctional facility can result in replacement of the female superintendent by a male.

But the co-correctional model, though problematic, has considerable potential. In the early 1980s, Alaska worked out a promising "coordinate" variation by building a women's and men's prison in close proximity and giving each its own superintendent to insure equal authority (Campbell, 1982; Heffernan, 1979). The women were free to use the resources of the larger men's institution; those who elected against participation or were deemed irresponsible could remain in the women's unit, which had its own library, classroom, and areas for visitation and recreation. This equal-but-separate coordinate model can be adopted by states that already have a women's prison close to one for men (Wright and Magid, 1983): Women can be bussed to the nearby men's institution for classes and job training.

An entirely different method of sharing resources, recommended by the U.S. Comptroller General's office (1980), is for federal, state, and local systems to pool resources for handling female prisoners. By increasing the number of placements available, this would make it easier to locate women near their homes. It would also enable women's institutions to become more specialized, in the manner of men's, thereby increasing the number of programs and encouraging diversification in security level. This approach requires a good deal of cooperation across jurisdictions. That such cooperation is possible is demonstrated by recent mergers of some state and county systems (Advisory Commission on Intergovernmental Relations, 1984). The next step is to turn merger into a tool for advancing equal protection.

5.2. Utilizing Community Resources

Attempts to provide a greater range of programs in women's prisons are frequently thwarted by the institutions' relatively small size. This obstacle can be overcome, at least in part, through more reliance on community and private resources. There is no reason why women's prisons should continue trying to provide all services through programs run within the walls by departments of correction. Through work release and study release, institutions located near towns and cities can make much use of community-based programs (Rafter, 1987; Wright and Magid, 1983). In addition, rural and urban institutions alike can follow the lead of men's prisons and contract out more extensively to the private sector (see, generally, Sexton, Farrow, and Auerbach, 1985).

A recent survey of administrators of state prisons for women found that, although they make little use of private sector services, they are open to more collaborations of this sort (Weisheit, 1985). The growing interest of both inmates and officials in nontraditional training for women (auto mechanics and plumbing, for instance), and in programs for victims of physical abuse, makes contracting out an attractive possibility. Indeed, at a time when officials are mapping plans for entire prisons to be privately run (Immarigeon, 1985; Wray, 1986), it is astonishing that women's institutions turn so seldom to private agencies.

5.3. Architectural Innovations

Inequitable treatment by gender is often cast in concrete, if not stone: Architectural arrangements isolate women prisoners in rural areas or in corners of mixed-sex institutions from which access to the gym and other facilities is difficult. In this era of prison building, however, new institutions can be designed to promote equity. Vermont's Chittenden County Correctional Center, an institution for state and county prisoners, demonstrates the potential of imaginative architecture. It confines men and women separately in areas subdivided by security level, each with its own yard; thus men and women assigned to each grade of security have recreational facilities, and no group has to be locked up to allow another access. The cafeteria, library, and classrooms are centrally located so both sexes can reach them without passing through the others' quarters. Although observers report that women are not permitted as many *hours* in some of the common rooms, the institution's architecture makes equal treatment a real possibility.

5.4. Greater Use of Nonincarcerative Sanctions

None of the correctives mentioned so far questions the use of incarceration *per se*, and all are expensive. As Marilyn Haft pointed out near the start of the movement to combat sex discrimination within penal institutions:

> Theoretically the routes are open for courts and legislatures to force the . . . states . . . to expend untold sums of money to build "equal" prisons for women. This would be a calamity. Society does not need more fortress-like schools for crime and human degradation. Instead, this set of circumstances should be viewed as an unusual opportunity for states . . . to spend money on alternatives to prison. (1980 [orig. 1973]: 329–330)

To be sure, alternatives are not suitable for all female offenders: Some women are dangerous, and others have been convicted of offenses so heinous as to warrant, in the public's view, a punitive response. But many incarcerated women have been convicted of nonviolent property crimes and drug offenses, others of violence in response to abuse by a spouse or lover (American Correctional Association, 1984; California Bureau of Criminal Statistics, 1987; McBride, 1987; McDermott, 1985; Potter, 1978; Ryan, 1984; U.S. General Accounting Office, 1979). These women can be sentenced to community-based alternatives—restitution programs, high-intensity probation, halfway houses, special treatment centers. In the community, such women can support themselves, care for their children, and receive better services (Immarigion, 1987). More extensive use of nonincarcerative sanctions would, moreover, free funds to improve conditions for those left behind the walls.

Goaded by the current crisis in overcrowding, policymakers are again undertaking the search for alternatives to imprisonment that began in the early 1970s. They might well concentrate their efforts on women—less dangerous as a group than male prisoners and, importantly, perceived as such by the public. I would go so far as to urge that judges develop an explicit policy of considering gender at sentencing and making special efforts to use nonincarcerative sanctions with women. Just as judges currently consider prison overcrowding before making the in-or-out decision, so, too, should they consider prison conditions related to gender. The policy would be based on recognition of the pervasiveness of sex discrimination within penal systems and the enormous difficulty of eradicating it. It would acknowledge that apparently equal treatment—giving the same sentence to a man and a woman with identical records—usually results in unequal treatment at the next stage in the criminal justice process.

Discrimination at sentencing may be thoroughly legitimate, as Parisi has observed:

> Although the term *discrimination* has developed negative connotations, it merely means "differentiation." If justifiable on legally relevant criteria, differentiation is permissible in sentencing and parole decisions. . . . [D]*isparity* refers to unwarranted differences in dispositions among groups with similar characteristics. If the differences are linked to such factors as race, religion, or class, then *disparity* is the appropriate term to describe the unjustifiable variation. (1982: 205–206)

Parisi goes on to hold that discrimination on the basis of sex is justifiable at sentencing when a woman has a dependent child who would be harmed by her incarceration:

> From a child's infancy, the child-raising duties are primarily allocated to the mother. Although both mother and father are equally capable, society is not yet prepared to recognize and accomodate this. Why should the judiciary

blindly impose equal treatment on parents, when the rest of society does
not? (1982: 216)

I am arguing that sentencing judges should take *prison conditions*, not
the presence or absence of dependent children, into consideration; but
my point is the same: Such discrimination would not be disparity. Taking
conditions at women's prisons, among other factors, into consideration
at sentencing would be a legitimate means to balance inequities, an
interim measure to achieve gender justice. If prisons and jails eventually
eliminate differential treatment on the basis of sex, then judges could
abandon the gender criterion, confident that equal sentences would in
fact result in equal punishment.

6. REFERENCES

Advisory Commission on Intergovernmental Relations. *Jails: Intergovernmental dimensions
    of a local problem*. Washington, DC: Advisory Commission on Intergovernmental Re-
    lations, 1984.
Alpert, G. P. The determinants of prisoners' decisions to seek legal aid. *New England Journal
    on Prison Law*, 1978, 4, 309–325.
Alpert, G. P. Women prisoners and the law: Which way will the pendulum swing? *Journal
    of Criminal Justice*, 1981, 10, 37–44.
Alpert, G. P., and Wiorkowski, J. J. Female prisoners and legal services. *Quarterly Journal
    of Corrections*, 1979, 1, 28–33.
Aylward, A., and Thomas, J. Quiescence in women's prisons litigation: Some exploratory
    issues. *Justice Quarterly*, 1984, 1, 253–276.
American Correctional Association. *Female classification: An examination of the issues*. College
    Park, MD: ACA, 1984.
Baunach, P. J. *Mothers in prison*. New Brunswick, NJ: Transaction Books, 1985.
Bird, M. The women in prison: No escape from stereotyping. *New York Times*, 23 June
    1979.
Bronstein, A. J. Fifteen years of prison litigation: What has it accomplished? *Journal of the
    National Prison Project*, 1987, 11, 6–9.
California Bureau of Criminal Statistics. Women in crime: The female arrestee. *Outlook*
    1987, 4 (pam.).
Campbell, C. F. *Shared resources: The implementation of co-corrections at the Hiland Mountain
    and Meadow Creek Correctional Centers, Eagle River, Alaska*. Report to Division of Cor-
    rections, State of Alaska, July 1982.
Connolly, J. E. Women in county jails: an invisible gender in an ill-defined institution.
    The Prison Journal, 1983, 63, 99–115.
Fabian, S. L. Toward the best interests of women prisoners: Is the system working? *New
    England Journal on Prison Law*, 1979, 6, 1–60.
Glick, R. M., and Neto, V. V. *National Study of Women's Correctional Programs*. Washington,
    DC: National Institute of Law Enforcement and Criminal Justice, LEAA, U.S. De-
    partment of Justice, 1977.
Haft, M. G. Women in prison: Discriminatory practices and some legal solutions. Reprinted
    in S. K. Datesman and F. R. Scarpitti, *Women, Crime, and Justice*. New York: Oxford,
    1980 [orig. 1973].

Heffernan, E. Female corrections—History and analysis. Opening Address: Conference on the Confinement of Female Offenders, U.S. Bureau of Prisons, Lexington, Kentucky, March 28–30, 1978 (unpublished).

Heffernan, E. *Women offenders in the Alaska criminal justice system.* Report to Division of Corrections, State of Alaska, Department of Health and Social Services, July 15, 1979.

Herbert, R. Women's prisons—An equal protection evaluation. *Yale Law Journal*, 1985, *94*, 1182–1206.

Immarigeon, R. The trend to privatization. *Jericho*, 1985, *40*, 1, 6, 10.

Immarigeon, R. Women in prison: Is locking them up the only answer? *Journal of the National Prison Project*, 1987, *11*, 1–5.

Jacobs, J. B. The prisoners' rights movement and its impacts, 1960–1980. In N. Morris and M. Tonry (Eds.), *Crime and Justice.* Vol 2. Chicago: University of Chicago Press, 1980.

Kerle, K. E., and Ford, F. R. *The state of our nation's jails, 1982.* Washington, DC: National Sheriffs' Association, 1982.

Leonard, E. B. Judicial decisions and prison reform: The impact of litigation on women prisoners. *Social Problems*, 1983, *31*, 45–58.

Lieber, F. Translator's preface. In G. de Beaumont and A. de Tocqueville, *On the penitentiary system in the United States and its application in France.* Carbondale: Southern Illinois University Press, 1964. (Originally published 1833)

Marantz, S. A question of female inmates' options: Framingham prisoner's suit alleges bias in favor of men. *Boston Globe*, June 10, 1983.

Mays, G. L., and Taggart, W. A. The impact of litigation on changing New Mexico prison conditions. *The Prison Journal*, 1985, *LXV*, 38–53.

McBride, N. C. U.S. putting more women in prison, victimizing many children. *Christian Science Monitor*, June 16, 1987.

McDermott, M. J. *Female offenders in New York State.* Albany: New York State Division of Criminal Justice Services—Office of Policy Analysis, Research and Statistical Services, 1985.

Mecoy, L. Plight of women inmates. *Sacramento Bee*, March 15, 1987.

McHugh, G. A. Protection of the rights of pregnant women in prisons and detention facilities. *New England Journal on Prison Law*, 1980, *6*, 231–263.

N. A. New Hampshire women's prison ordered. *Boston Globe*, January 18, 1987.

Noblit, G. W., and Alpert, G. P. Advocacy and rehabilitation in women's prisons. *Law & Policy Quarterly*, 1979, *1*, 207–222.

Note. The sexual segregation of American prisons. *Yale Law Journal*, 1973, *82*, 1229–1273.

Note. Nine months to life—The law and the pregnant inmate. *Journal of Family Law*, 1981–1982, *20*, 523–543.

Parisi, N. Are females treated differently? A review of the theories and evidence on sentencing and parole decisions. In N. H. Rafter and E. A. Stanko (Eds.). *Judge, lawyer, victim, thief: Women, gender roles, and criminal justice.* Boston: Northeastern University Press, 1982.

Potter, J. In prison, women are different. *Corrections Magazine*, 1978, December, 14–24.

Rafter, N. H. *Partial justice: Women in state prisons, 1800–1935.* Boston: Northeastern University Press, 1985.

Rafter, N. H. Even in prison, women are second-class citizens. *Human Rights*, 1987, *14*, 28–31, 51.

Ross, J. G., Heffernan, E., Sevick, J. R., and Johnson, F. T. *National Evaluation Program, Phase 1 Report: Assessment of coeducational corrections.* Washington, DC: National Institute of Law Enforcement and Criminal Justice, LEAA, U.S. Department of Justice, June 1978.

Ryan, T. A. *Adult female offenders and institutional programs.* Washington, DC: National Institute of Correcctions, 1984.

SchWeber, C. Beauty marks and blemishes: The coed prison as a microcosm of integrated society. *The Prison Journal*, 1984, *1*, 3–14.

Sex discrimination—Prison inmates. In *American Law Reports ALR4th: Cases and Annotations*. Vol. 12. Rochester, NY: Lawyers Co-operative Publishing Co., 1982.

Sexton, G. E., Farrow, F. C., and Auerbach, B. J. *The private sector and prison industries*. Washington, DC: National Institute of Justice, August 1985.

Sims, P. Women in jail, the plight of the forgotten. *Poverty Law Report*, 1976, *4*, 3–4.

Smith College School for Social Work. *Legal issues of female inmates*. Report prepared for National Institute of Corrections, 1982.

Temin, C. E. Discriminatory sentencing of women offenders: The argument for ERA in a nutshell. In S. K. Datesman and F. R. Scarpitti (Eds.), *Women, crime, & justice*. New York: Oxford, 1980.

Thomas, J. Law and social praxis: prisoner civil rights litigation and structural mediations. In S. Spitzer and A. T. Scull (Eds.), *Research in law, deviance and social control*. Vol. 6. Greenwich, CT: JAI Press, 1984.

U.S. Comptroller General. *Women in prison: Inequitable treatment requires action*. Washington, DC: General Accounting Office, 1980.

U.S. General Accounting Office. *Female offenders: Who are they and what are the problems confronting them?* Washington, DC: General Accounting Office, 1979.

Weisheit, R. A. Trends in programs for female offenders: The use of private agencies as service providers. *International Journal of Offender Therapy and Comparative Criminology*, 1985, *29*, 35–42.

Welter, B. The cult of true womanhood: 1820–1860. *American Quarterly*, 1966, *18*, 151–174.

Wray, H. Cells for sale. *Southern Changes*, 1986, *8*, 3–6.

Wright, C., and Magid, J. Litigation in women's prisons: Avoiding the inevitable. American Correctional Association, *Proceedings 1983*, 53–56.

7. CASES CITED

Barefield v. Leach, Civ. No. 10282 (D.N. Mex., 1974)

Bukhari v. Hutto, 487 F. Supp. 1162 (E.D. Va., 1980)

Canterino v. Barber, 564 F. Supp. 711 (W.D. Ky., 1983)

Canterino v. Wilson, 546 F. Supp. 174 (W.D. Ky., 1982)

Cooper v. Morin, 398 N.Y.S.2d 36 (1977)

Glover v. Johnson, 478 F. Supp. 1075 (E.D. Mich., 1979)

Mitchell v. Untreiner, 421 F. Supp. 886 (N.D. Fla., 1976)

Molar v. Gates, App., 159 Cal. Rptr. 239 (1979)

Park v. Thompson, 356 F. Supp. 783 (D. Hawaii, 1973)

Chapter 7

CRIMINAL SENTENCING REFORM
Legacy for the Correctional System

KAY A. KNAPP

1. EARLY SENTENCING REFORMS

Determinate sentencing laws enacted in the 1970s and presumptive sentencing guidelines implemented in the 1980s wrought major changes in criminal justice. For most of the twentieth century, an indeterminate system of sentencing held sway in the United States (Rothman, 1980). The key elements of indeterminate systems include (1) wide sentencing ranges with high statutory maximum sentences, such as 10, 20, or 30 years established by the legislature; (2) judicial determination of whether prison or probationary sentence will be imposed in a given case; (3) judicial pronouncement of a largely symbolic sentence duration for prison cases, usually consisting of the high statutory maximum sentence; and (4) administrative control over the actual prison term exercised by a parole board. The structure encouraged the judge and parole board to fashion a sentence to achieve whatever purpose of sentencing (deterrence, incapacitation, rehabilitation, or punishment) deemed appropriate (von Hirsch, 1976).

Critics of indeterminate sentencing proliferated beginning in the early 1970s (American Friends Service Committee, 1971). Sentencing disparity, which resulted from the wide discretion of individual decision makers, was chief among the concerns (Dershowitz, 1976). Sentencing

KAY A. KNAPP • Institute for Rational Public Policy, Inc., 40 Philadelphia Avenue, Takoma Park, Maryland 20912.

disparity was viewed as unfair, especially insofar as the exercise of broad discretion appeared to favor more affluent, white offenders and disfavor poor, minority offenders. A practical result of disparity was inmate anger and frustration that caused unrest within the prisons (Shane-Dubow, Brown, and Olsen, 1985).

A related concern was the uncertainty of prison release dates that resulted from the broad discretion exercised by parole boards in releasing offenders. Uncertainty was deemed unfair to inmates who were unable to adequately plan for their return to the community and unfair to the public who deserved "truth" in sentencing (Fogel, 1975). Critics also charged that the indeterminate sentencing system was "lawless" in that broad sentencing ranges coupled with broad sentencing discretion provided inadequate standards for sentencing, effectively eliminating the possibility of meaningful appellate review of sentences (Frankel, 1972). Finally, critics argued that selection of sentencing purpose should not be left to the discretion of individual decision makers but rather should be specified within a broader public policy statement (von Hirsch, 1976).

Early reform efforts grappled with those concerns and attempted to address them. Legislative determinate sentencing systems, such as those enacted in California (1976), Indiana (1977), and Illinois (1978), significantly changed the distribution of sentencing discretion. The California Determinate Sentencing Law specified punishment as the sole purpose of sentencing (Penal Code of California, Sec. 1170 [a] [1]). Generally, the sentencing reforms deemphasized the sentencing purpose of rehabilitation and emphasized punishment and deterrence (von Hirsch and Hanrahan, 1981). Judges retained discretion to determine whether to imprison an offender or place the offender on probation. Legislatures, however, reduced the statutory sentence duration ranges available to judges. Aggravating and mitigating features were generally specified in the law to guide the judge in choosing a specific sentence within the range or to specify the exact amount to be added or subtracted with respect to the presumptive sentence (Shane-Dubow et al., 1985).

Parole boards were abolished along with the "back-door" release authority they had exercised. The back-door discretion under indeterminate sentencing was transferred to the front door under determinate sentencing. Judges pronounced sentences that were actually to be served, reduced only by statutorily defined good time that was generally limited to one-third to one-half of the pronounced sentence (Jacobs, 1982). Through this redistribution of sentencing discretion, legislative determinate sentencing attempted to move toward certainty and truth in sentencing. The narrower sentencing ranges provided standards for sentencing that were somewhat more specific than provided by indeterminate sentencing systems. As a result, appellate review of sentences became somewhat more meaningful and "lawful" than it had been under indeterminate sentencing.

2. Sentencing Reform in the 1980s

Legislatively authorized sentencing guidelines followed closely on the heels of legislative determinate sentencing systems. The first legislatively mandated sentencing guidelines were implemented in Minnesota in 1980 (Minnesota Sentencing Guidelines Commission, 1980). The state of Washington followed with similarly structured guidelines adopted in 1983 and implemented in 1984 (Washington Sentencing Guidelines: Revised Code of Washington, 1983). Pennsylvania implemented statewide sentencing guidelines in 1982 but retained the discretionary release authority of parole (Pennsylvania Administrative Code, 1982). Florida, Maryland, and Michigan developed guidelines within the jurisdiction of the courts, with Florida's judicial guidelines eventually receiving legislative authorization (Tonry, 1988).

Sentencing guidelines as enacted in Minnesota and Washington share one key feature with legislative determinate sentencing. Parole and its discretionary back-door release authority were eliminated; the sentences that judges pronounced were to be served reduced only by statutorily limited good time. The guidelines, however, differ from legislative determinate sentencing in a number of respects. First, the statutory sentencing ranges were not reduced by the legislature. Rather, legislatively established commissions devised very narrow sentencing ranges for specific combinations of offenses, ranked by seriousness, and criminal history records. The narrow sentencing ranges were "presumptive" sentences to be imposed by the judge in a usual or typical case. The statutory range was available for judges to use when unique case circumstances suggested a departure up or down from the presumptive sentence. A second difference between guidelines, as enacted in Minnesota and Washington, and legislative determinate sentencing is the level of detail contained in the sentencing policy. Guidelines policy tends to be much more specific in several respects. More offense differentiations are generally made in guidelines systems. Burglary, for example, might be classified in four or five different categories (e.g., unoccupied building, residence, occupied building or residence, occupied building or residence with a weapon or assault) for sentencing purposes under guidelines; burglary might fall into two categories (building and residence) under legislative determinate sentencing. Guidelines policy is also generally more specific with respect to sentencing on multiple counts, that is, concurrent and consecutive sentences. Guidelines provide specific guidance with respect to whether prison or probation should be imposed in a particular case. Guidelines in Minnesota and Washington clearly specified sentencing purposes of proportionality and uniformity (essentially just deserts or punishment) as the primary purposes of sentencing.

Both legislative determinate sentencing in the 1970s and sentencing guidelines reforms in the early 1980s were motivated by substantive concerns such as sentence disparity, proportionality, and truth in sentencing. To the extent that attention focused on corrections, discussions involved (1) the certainty provided to inmates (and the public) with determinate sentences, and (2) the desirability of sentence uniformity so that inmates confined together would not perceive their sentences to be inequitable and unfair. Little attention was paid in the 1970s to the level and distribution of correctional resources and correctional management issues. However, any significant alteration in sentences will have automatic repercussions in the correctional system. The legacy for corrections of these early reforms is still unfolding.

Interest in sentencing reform continues among the states. By 1987, Oregon, Tennessee, and Louisiana were developing legislatively mandated sentencing guidelines (Knapp, 1988). In 1988, New Mexico enacted legislation (New Mexico HB 136) establishing a sentencing guidelines commission. Although interest has not diminished, the motivation driving sentencing reform has changed significantly since the 1970s. Current efforts appear to be motivated by a desire to better manage corrections systems and in particular to control prison populations. Both Louisiana and Tennessee are operating under a federal court order with respect to corrections (National Prison Project, 1987). The sentencing reform enabling legislation in both Oregon and Tennessee specifies correction resource constraints within which the guidelines must be developed. Architects of these sentencing reforms appear to place less emphasis on the substantive issues of sentence disparity, uniformity, certainty, proportionality, and crime control than did the creators of the earlier efforts.

In this chapter I will argue that an exclusive focus on either substantive issues or population management is unlikely to yield a comfortable legacy for corrections systems. Neither focus, by itself, is likely to achieve its primary objective—substantive reform on the one hand and population management on the other. The evidence derived from reform efforts to date suggest that effective sentencing reform requires close attention to both substantive issues and resource issues.

3. THE CORRECTIONAL LEGACY OF SENTENCING REFORM

As noted before, legislative determinate sentencing and sentencing guidelines share common substantive goals of truth and certainty in sentencing; they redistribute discretion in similar ways among criminal justice actors; and they tend to emphasize just deserts and deterrence purposes of sentencing. The two forms of sentencing reform differ significantly, however, in structure, operation and, most importantly, correctional legacy. They are structurally different in that the legislature develops sentencing policy in determinate systems and the sentencing commission develops sentencing policy, subject to legislative review, in a guidelines system. Legislative determinate systems and guidelines systems operate differently in that guidelines sentences tend to be closely monitored, with policy modifications informed by the monitoring. Legislative determinate systems tend not to be monitored as closely, and policy modifications appear to occur in reaction to sensational cases.

Finally, determinate sentencing and sentencing guidelines differ significantly in correctional legacy. Prison population control and correctional management issues were not primary in the development of either determinate sentencing or sentencing guidelines. The two forms of sentencing reform, however, differ importantly in their ability to effect the legacy for corrections.

3.1. Legislative Determinate Sentencing Systems

The indeterminate sentencing systems that were replaced by legislative determinate systems controlled prison populations primarily through the parole function, using back-door release if space were needed for new inmates. That safety valve was lost with the determinate sentencing system. The authority that parole boards had to set the actual time served was transferred to other parts of the system, and the judges lost some of their "in/out" discretion where mandatory minimum sentences were included.

The substantive reforms embodied in legislative determinate sentencing, that is, reducing sentence disparity and increasing the uniformity, proportionality, and certainty of sentences, thus translated into a substantial redistribution of sentencing discretion. Under determinate sentencing, the legislature retained significantly more sentencing authority by defining relatively narrow sentencing ranges for offenses such as robbery or murder compared to those under indeterminate sentencing. Judges generally had considerable discretion to determine sentence disposition and had some authority to determine whether aggravating or mitigating factors were present in a case. This authority allowed judges to directly influence sentence length, which was often beyond their control under indeterminate sentencing (Rothman, 1980). Prosecutors also obtained more sentencing discretion. The offense of conviction became more important in determining the sentence than previously, and consequently the prosecutor's charging and negotiating decisions directly affected sentences. "Real" or "total" offense behavior (the behavior the criminal actually engaged in, not merely what they were charged with) generally did not disappear from the sentencing decision under the determinate structure, but the prosecutor would generally determine whether to present evidence regarding an aggravating factor or whether to argue for or against a mitigating factor. The existing parole authority was eliminated under determinate sentencing. If the legislature was to set the period of imprisonment within a narrow range, there was no need for an early release authority. Indeed, such an authority would have undercut the whole concept.

This distribution of sentencing discretion clearly invested a greater share of authority in more politically sensitive, vulnerable, and accountable actors (i.e., legislatures, judges, and prosecutors) rather than politically isolated parties such as parole boards.

In addition to redistributing discretion in sentencing, legislative determinate sentencing also changed the focus of sentencing purposes from rehabilitation toward just deserts and deterrence. In an indeterminate system, the actual length of incarceration was not determined until some period after the person had been incarcerated. The parole board theoretically evaluated the person's progress toward rehabilitation and set a release date based on that progress. In a determinate system, the legislature made a judgment as to how long a person should stay in for committing a particular type of offense. Such a system necessarily concentrates on the offense because the offender is obviously unknown to the legislature. In concentrating on the offense conduct, the legislature would only be able to weigh the consequences of the act, the moral culpability of a person who would commit such an act, and the general "deterrability" of persons likely to commit such an act.

3.1.1. Legislative Reform and Sentencing Purposes

The structure created by the legislative type of substantive reform furthered the movement toward desert and deterrence as primary purposes of sentencing (Fogel, 1975). Not only did legislation suggest a larger role for punishment as a purpose of sentencing, but the distribution of discretion under determinate sentencing reinforced that tendency. Discretion is exercised by judges and prosecutors who are closer to the offense that was committed and more directly aware of the consequences of the offense. They see the victims of an offense and observe for themselves the consequences of the offender's conduct. As a result, they give more weight to culpability and consequence factors. Additionally, judges and prosecutors are trained in substantive criminal law rather than social work. This "legal" orientation interacts with the establishment of evidentiary standards for sentencing and appellate review to create a relatively hospitable environment for a desert-based sentencing system.

3.1.2. Correctional Aspects of Legislative Reform

As noted, the primary focus of legislative substantive reform with respect to corrections was on inmate perceptions of sentence fairness and certainty. Certainty and truth in sentencing were deemed important both to deter the commission of offenses and to allow inmates to better plan their time in prison and their transition out of prison. It was hoped that the relationship between inmates and corrections officials would improve with release discretion removed from inmates' "keepers." Equity in punishment, it was believed, would lead to inmate perceptions that sentences were fairer than under indeterminate sentencing (American Friends Service Committee, 1971).

Although substantive reform, not system management, was the primary focus of the early determinate sentencing systems, implementation and resource concerns were not entirely ignored. Statutory determinate sentences were considerably shorter than the largely symbolic statutory maximums they replaced. There was an effort, particularly in California but also in Illinois, to incorporate something akin to past "real time" sentences, with some adjustments to account for a more proportional sentencing system and to rectify specific areas thought to have been treated too leniently in the past (Shane-Dubow et al., 1985).

Critics of determinate sentencing systems were concerned that the new structure would politicize sentencing and the result would be longer periods of imprisonment and less rational decision making. Many corrections and parole officials argued that parole boards could better determine sentence duration away from the glare of publicity that sometimes accompanies adjudication. Corrections officials expressed fear that without strong incentives such as early release for program participation in prison, inmates would refuse to participate in rehabilitation programs that might serve to better their chances of a successful transition to society upon release.

The actual legacy for correctional systems appears to have been both less positive than proponents had hoped and less negative than critics feared. Certainty and truth in sentencing did not result in better behaved inmates, as had been hoped. Disciplinary infractions were as frequent among offenders with determinate sentences as indeterminate sentences. Notably, infractions were no more frequent among determinate sentenced offenders. Although inmate behavior did not improve with determinacy, determinate-sentenced inmates reported significantly less stress than indeterminate-sentenced inmates (Goodstein, 1982, 1984).

Program participation decreased very little among determinately sentenced inmates. By and large, determinately sentenced inmates were as socially active as indeterminately sentenced offenders. It was also learned that corrections departments found various "coercive" incentives to substitute for early release. Some departments awarded "meritorious good time" for program participation; others could impose special release conditions (e.g., residential treatment) if an inmate failed to participate in prison treatment programs. All departments used information regarding program participation for decisions on classification and jobs (Goodstein, 1983, 1984; Hepburn and Goodstein, 1986).

The impact of the early determinate sentencing systems on prison populations is difficult to determine (Blumstein, Cohen, Martin, and Tonry, 1983; Cohen and Tonry, 1983). There is no question that prison populations increased substantially in states that adopted determinate sentencing. By the same token, prison populations increased substantially in states with indeterminate sentencing systems. It is difficult to disentangle the causes of the prison population increases during the 1970s and 1980s. In addition to changes in sentencing laws, the crime rate for serious offenses increased significantly in the 1970s. Public attitudes regarding crime, sentences, and corrections became more punitive. Law Enforcement Assistance Administration (LEAA) money funneled into state and local law enforcement for more than a decade produced more efficient and effective law enforcement. These confounding events make it impossible to clearly define the causes of prison population increases.

Whether or not legislatively established determinate sentencing caused prison overcrowding, it clearly did nothing effective to avoid or alleviate prison crowding problems. It is easy to understand why the rudimentary efforts to coordinate early sentencing reform efforts with correctional policies were ineffective. Effective substitution of legislative "real-time" sentences for long symbolic sentences was improbable for a number of reasons. First, the judicial disposition decision was discretionary and largely unguided. Once judges started imposing relatively short real-time sentences instead of long symbolic sentences, it was likely that they might be willing to send more offenders to prison (Lipson and Peterson, 1980). After all, the danger of a midlevel serious offender being imprisoned for an excessive period was eliminated with judicially imposed real-time sentences. These judges had, at best, only an anecdotal knowledge of the effect of their sentencing on prison crowding. Moreover, prisons were not their responsibility. It was not their function to control prison populations. In addition, sentence length was significantly affected by aggravating and mitigating circumstances that relied upon prosecutorial fact finding and plea negotiation. No one knew how many offenders committed a certain type of offense or how often certain aggravating or mitigating factors would be associated with that offense. Because those factors were the primary determinates of sentence length and thus of prison populations, no one knew what effect the determinate sentencing system would have on the correctional system. All in all, determinate sentencing systems continued to be far too discretionary to allow for the coordination of sentencing and correctional policies, even if that had been a major focus of the reform.

Subsequent modifications of determinate sentencing laws were similarly disengaged from implementation issues and resource allocation questions. Penalties were frequently enhanced, especially in California, but seldom were correctional resources enhanced to correspond with changes in sentencing policy. The same legislature that may have felt that sentences were too lenient might not have been willing to pay the vast sums of money needed to expand the prison system. In short, the political decision to establish a determinate sentencing system was often not followed by another decision to fund the consequences of such a system.

The legacy of prison crowding, whatever its origin, undermined sentencing reform's substantive objectives. Redistribution of sentencing discretion, just deserts and deterrence, and certainty and truth in sentencing were impossible to achieve in an overcrowded setting. Invariably, overcrowding resulted in the establishment of back-door mechanisms (e.g., good time, meritorious credits, program credits, administrative leave, emergency release) that effectively transferred sentencing discretion from the "front door" (judges and prosecutors) to the "back door" (corrections and parole administrators) (Jacobs, 1982; Shane-Dubow et al., 1985). Such mechanisms are invariably used in the manner for which they are intended, that is, to regulate prison populations. Thus certainty and truth in sentencing, deterrence, and desert are sacrificed for the more immediate goal of population control.

3.2. Sentencing Guidelines Reforms

Legislatively authorized sentencing guidelines followed closely on the heels of legislative determinate sentencing systems. The first legislatively mandated sentencing guidelines were implemented in

Minnesota in 1980. The state of Washington followed with similarly structured guidelines in 1984. Pennsylvania implemented statewide sentencing guidelines in 1982 but retained parole (discretionary release authority). Florida, Maryland, and Michigan developed guidelines within the jurisdiction of the courts, with Florida's judicial guidelines eventually receiving legislative authorization.

3.2.1. Advantages of Sentencing Guidelines Reforms

Although guidelines and legislative determinate sentencing have the same general substantive objectives, legislatively mandated guidelines have proven to be the more promising vehicle to effect those objectives for a number of reasons (Tonry, 1987, 1988; von Hirsch, Knapp, and Tonry, 1987). First, guidelines policy tends to be more specific and refined than legislatively defined sentences. It contains greater detail as to aggravating and mitigating factors and provides more specific weights to be applied to those factors. Guideline policy is thus more subtle and rich and consequently less likely to be circumvented to achieve a specific result. As noted earlier, legislative determinate policy tends to be tied to gross statutory categories that do not finely differentiate among offenses for sentencing purposes (Clarke, 1987; Schuwerk, 1984, 1985). Such policy inevitably allows greater discretion and thus greater uncertainty and disparity.

Another reason legislatively established guidelines tend to be more effective is that a monitoring system that measures policy compliance generally accompanies guideline implementation. The specific policy encourages responsibility among sentencing participants, and the monitoring system ensures that those participants will be held accountable for their sentencing decisions. The monitoring system also acts as a feedback mechanism for modifying sentencing policy. Experience indicates that *ad hoc* policy modifications are less likely to be made by a commission than by a legislative body. Legislatures may respond to a particular, well-publicized case. Commissions, with a broader range of data available to them, respond to broader trends. For instance, a legislature may respond to a report that a stock broker has used the phone to perpetrate a billion dollar scandal by raising the determinate sentence for phone fraud. A commission would know that most such frauds involve long-distance calls by college students and relatively small amounts of money.

The way discretion is distributed under sentencing guidelines is similar to that of legislative determinate sentencing except that, under the guidelines model, the legislature exercises its authority by establishing a sentencing commission. The discretion that had been exercised by the parole board is redistributed to judges, prosecutors, the commission, and legislature. Appellate review of sentences adds another source of sentencing control in the judicial branch. Generally, the exercise of appellate review in sentencing has been more authoritative in guidelines systems than in legislative-determinate sentencing systems (Knapp, 1985).

As in legislative determinate sentencing systems, substantive issues were the principal focus in developing the Minnesota and Washington state sentencing guidelines. Unlike legislative determinate sentencing systems, the guidelines efforts also dealt seriously (albeit secondarily) with correctional resource issues. The architects of these guidelines understood that coordinating sentencing and correctional policies was necessary in order to achieve substantive sentencing reform (Minnesota Sentencing Guidelines Commission, 1982, 1984). Moreover, the specific sentencing policy inherent in a guidelines structure also made it feasible to coordinate the policies.

Sentencing guidelines in Minnesota and Washington guided disposition decisions (i.e., prison "in"/"out" decisions) as well as durational decisions. Additional guidelines for consecutive sentencing, probation revocation, and departure reasons resulted in a sentencing structure detailed enough to develop reasonably grounded simulations showing the impact of various sentencing scenarios on correctional resources. Without guidelines in these areas, major decisions having significant impact on correctional resources would have been unstructured and incapable of even generalized prediction (Knapp, 1986).

Prison overcrowding was avoided in Minnesota and Washington, which enabled the implementation and maintenance of the substantive reforms (Minnesota Sentencing Guidelines Commission, 1982, 1984; Miethe and Moore, 1987; Washington Sentencing Guidelines Commission, 1987). Both systems monitor sentencing practices under guidelines and recommend substantive modifications. The commissions provide their respective legislatures with information on sentencing practices and projected resource needs. The legislatures thus have the necessary information for coordinating sentencing and correctional policies.

Even well-structured guidelines may be undercut if a significant, discretionary "back-door" mechanism remains. Thus, if significant amounts of time can be subtracted from (or added to) a sentence by a parole commission or correctional authorities in an unstructured way, the certainty of punishment and the control on resources are both diminished.

Executive branch early release procedures have not been utilized in Minnesota or Washington. There has, however, been retroactive resentencing of indeterminate prison cases. The redistribution of sentencing authority instituted by sentencing reform has remained intact. Truth and certainty in sentencing continue.

Not all guidelines efforts have resulted in such a comfortable corrections legacy. Pennsylvania, as noted, maintains discretionary parole releasing authority. In addition, the Pennsylvania guidelines contain relatively wide sentencing ranges. Those guidelines do not provide a comprehensive enough structure or specific enough policy by which to coordinate sentencing and corrections policies. Florida's guidelines operate in an environment of substantial prison overcrowding. As with legislative determinate sentencing, the substantive guidelines' policy cannot be implemented in that environment. Executive branch early release procedures overrule judicially imposed guideline sentences.

The demonstrated ability of two states to coordinate sentencing and corrections systems by means of presumptive sentencing guidelines has inspired some other states such as Oregon, Louisiana, New Mexico, and Tennessee to pursue similar sentencing reform. The driving force in the most recent efforts, however, appears to have switched from substantive reform of criminal sentencing to prison population control.

4. CURRENT SENTENCING REFORM EFFORTS

4.1. Current Concerns for Sentencing Reform

Current interest in state sentencing reform comes from several sources. Judges want more discretion over sentence duration and want more certainty in time served. Judges often want more sentencing options such as a short incarceration period followed by significant non-incarcerative controls available for use with offenders whose offenses that are midrange in seriousness.

Executive branch administrators are also unhappy with the pattern of sentencing and correctional practices, especially in this period of prison overcrowding. Despite the fact that corrections budgets have increased much more dramatically than other state spending areas, it has been difficult for correctional administrators to maintain institutions and systems that meet constitutional standards (National Conference of State Legislatures, 1987).

Legislative bodies are particularly frustrated with current systems. Ultimate responsibility for sentencing policies lies with legislators, yet they are provided with little relevant information for making the difficult policy and allocation decisions for sentencing and corrections. The position of legislators is especially difficult given their responsibility to allocate resources across a diverse range of issue areas, including education, social services, and transportation, as well as government operations (courts) and corrections. Even with substantial increased allocations for corrections in recent years, correctional institutions or systems are under federal court order or consent decrees in a majority of states (National Prison Project, 1987). It is clear that further spending increases will be necessary absent significant changes in sentencing policies and practices.

4.2. Characteristics of Current Reforms

Legislators appear to be looking for such changes as evidenced in the nature of current sentencing reform legislation. Three states—Tennessee, Louisiana, and Oregon—enacted sentencing guidelines legislation in the late 1980s. In the case of at least two of these, the impetus for sentencing reform clearly came from concerns for population control. The corrections systems in both Louisiana and Tennessee currently operate under federal court consent decrees. Oregon has less serious crowding, but executive branch early release procedures are frequently used to regulate prison populations.

The inclusion of legislative language for structuring the coordination of sentencing policy with correctional resources indicates that implementation issues are being taken seriously by these states. The Tennessee sentencing commission is mandated "to the extent possible" to develop guidelines consistent with "a prison capacity figure arrived at by taking ninety-five percent (95%) of the present constitutional capacity of the prison system and adding any new prison beds constructed in accordance with American Correction Association (ACA) standards" (Tennessee Statutes 40-37-203). The Oregon Criminal Justice Council is required by statute to take effective capacity of state and local correctional facilities and other sentencing options available into consideration in developing guidelines (Oregon HB 2715, 1987). If the council finds that correctional resources are insufficient and therefore inappropriately limit the guidelines, the council shall recommend needed changes in correctional resources. The Louisiana legislature is required to report on the fiscal impact of the proposed guidelines. If the impact exceeds $1 million, the proposal is subject to the review of appropriations committees.

Prior guidelines projects in Minnesota and Washington included similar legislative direction. Enabling legislation in Minnesota mandated that the commission take into substantial consideration correctional resources including but not limited to the capacities of local and state correctional facilities. The Washington commission was instructed to develop a second set of guidelines that could be implemented with current correctional resources if the first set exceeded existing correctional resources. Options for coordinating sentencing and corrections policies were thereby ensured for the legislatures of these two states as implementation of substantive reform progressed.

Although the language specifying the coordination of sentencing and correctional policies is similar in current and prior guidelines efforts, the situations facing current jurisdictions are quite different. It is clear that a major impetus for current sentencing reform efforts is the perceived crisis in corrections. States are pressed to deal with the problem because, internally, they need to better manage correctional systems and, externally, the federal courts are requiring them to run constitutional systems.

There is a real danger that the corrections crisis will cause a shift in guideline focus, with substantive issues neglected in favor of correctional management issues. Up to this point, no guidelines have been implemented in which the dominant goal or main purpose is prison population control. Such a switch in focus is understandably attractive because a system of presumptive guidelines is one of the few mechanisms that can give policymakers control of sentencing practices and impacts. However, unless guideline development seriously addresses substantive issues of sentencing purpose, disparity, rationality and enforcement, the system will be unable to effectively guide sentences and unable to control prison populations.

4.2.1. First and Foremost—Sentencing Purposes

It is well to note that the sentence imposed in a case is primarily dependent upon the sentencing purpose that is being pursued. One commonly identified purpose of sentencing is just deserts (or, with subtle differences, punishment or retribution), in which the sentence is an end in itself. Utilitarian sentencing purposes include deterrence, incapacitation, and rehabilitation under which sentences are designed to reduce crime through incapacitation, specific or general deterrence, or reformation.

It is a common observation at sentencing institutes and workshops that the major source of sentence differences among judges is selection of different sentencing purposes. For example, sentences pronounced for hypothetical embezzlement cases at a sentencing institute will vary from long periods of imprisonment, to short periods of imprisonment, to probation. The reasons for sentencing differences revealed in debriefing sessions invariably relate to sentencing purposes. A relatively long prison sentence is justified on the basis of just deserts (e.g., culpability due to a position of responsibility or breach of trust) or general deterrence (sending a message to others in positions of responsibility or trust). Short periods of incarceration for embezzlement are more often justified on the basis of specific deterrence (giving this offender a message). Probation for this type of offense is generally justified on the basis of incapacitation (this offender is not a threat to the public and is unlikely to recidivate) or rehabilitation if a condition of monetary or community service restitution is attached to the probation.

Occasionally, a similar sentence is suggested by each of the four purposes. For example, there are crimes so heinous and offenders so dangerous that a very long prison sentence is required for desert, deterrence, incapacitation, and rehabilitation purposes. Or a minor crime committed by a nondangerous offender may result in minimal social control with each sentencing purpose. Frequently, however, the various purposes lead to inconsistent sentences. Purposes must be addressed in order to control sentencing discretion and disparity.

It is notable that sentence differences do not result primarily from different perceptions of sentence severity. When judges are in agreement as to the primary purpose(s) to be served by a sentence, it seldom happens that one judge in a jurisdiction argues that 10 years in prison is the appropriate duration and another judge argues that 2 years is the appropriate duration. Nor is it frequently argued that "10 years is a long time" versus "10 years is a short time." "Fiddling with the numbers" in terms of sentence duration is not as central to substantive sentencing reform as a determination and prioritization of sentencing purposes and rationales.

The tendency of those whose primary concern is the management of prison populations is to neglect or to avoid the difficult, controversial, and sometimes subtle substantive discussions of sentencing purpose and rationale. In the context of pressing correctional management problems, philosophical issues related to sentencing purposes are often perceived to be esoteric, academic, and nonessential. Indeed, it is not uncommon for corrections administrators to observe that they "cannot afford" to think about such philosophical issues because they have "real problems" to deal with.

Thus substantive issues are often slighted by those whose primary concerns involve correctional management issues. The idea of achieving the end product can dominate over the structure and policies needed to attain the goal. The focus becomes one of "fiddling with the numbers" rather than exploring and resolving key issues of sentencing purposes and rationale. This approach not only yields unsatisfactory substantive sentencing policy, it also fails in its objective to effectively manage corrections systems. The failure to address and resolve criticial substantive sentencing issues manifests itself in two structural features that undermine coordination of sentencing and correctional policies. One feature relates to the maintenance and distribution of sentencing discretion. A second feature involves the enforcement mechanism of appellate review.

4.2.2. Discretion in Sentencing

The planned coordination of sentencing and corrections policies requires the development of sentencing policy that is articulated, specific, embodying limited discretion, and accompanied by an enforcement mechanism. *Ad hoc* control of prison populations generally relies upon general procedures (e.g., parole, good time, early release, emergency release), the specific application policies of which are not formally articulated. Generally, wide decision-making discretion rather than narrow discretion is desired for *ad hoc* prison population control, and there is generally no effective mechanism for reviewing release decisions.

The structure needed for planned sentencing and corrections coordination is therefore just the opposite of the structure needed for *ad hoc* control. Those wanting to better manage correctional systems often recognize how effective a substantively based guidelines system can be in coordinating sentencing and correctional policies. But they are generally unwilling to relinquish the *ad hoc* control mechanisms they have in case the sentencing policy is implemented differently than anticipated or in case the legislature does not provide correctional resources needed for implementation. Therefore, policies that provide substantial discretion tend to be favored. For example, correctional managers often favor making it relatively easy for a judge to depart from the presumptive sentence so that judges can easily mitigate sentences, and favor wide sentencing ranges so that symbolically harsh sentences can be mitigated in practice. The broad discretion afforded individual decision makers makes planned policy coordination impossible.

In addition to relatively broad discretion, the location of discretion is affected. The locus of decision making under a substantively based, specific sentencing policy is usually the judge. Both the sentencing policy and information relevant to all sentencing purposes, save rehabilitation, are available at the time of judicial sentencing. There is little need for substantive purpose to delay the sentencing decision. Also for planning purposes, it is useful to focus decision making, rather than distributing it over many points and useful to have the decision made relatively early in the process, rather than 2, 5, or 10 years after imprisonment. If decision making is unfocused, there will be an increasing disparity in results. If decision making is delayed until well after a term of imprisonment has begun, it will be difficult to make useful projections.

The locus of decision making for *ad hoc* control of prison populations is executive branch corrections or parole administrators. Administrators concerned with correctional management are loath to relinquish releasing authority in case the coordinated effort is ineffective. *Ad hoc* releasing authority not only undermines the ability to coordinate sentencing and correctional policies, but it also affects judicial behavior in that it relieves judges of responsibility for sentencing and also relieves them of accountability. Judges often adjust their sentences to account for the anticipated behavior of corrections and parole administrators that in turn undermines the ability of *ad hoc* measures to effectively control prison populations. Rather than encouraging responsible behavior by judges, *ad hoc* release structures deprive judges of responsibility.

Removing responsibility for prison population control from articulated sentencing policy and from judges and placing it in an *ad hoc* releasing authority reduces the range of options available by which to control populations. Essentially, reducing the duration of prison sentences is the only method open to corrections and parole administrators. A more systemic approach, such as guidelines, opens a wider range of sentencing options, such as intermediate sanctions like fines, short terms in local jails, community service, or home detention as well as prison sentences of various durations, to be used to allocate offenders and thereby control correctional populations. But to be effective, such sanctions must be incorporated in systemic sentencing policy and not used as part of an unsystematic, *ad hoc* approach.

4.2.3. Enforcement Mechanisms

The tendency to view sentencing purpose and rationale as esoteric and academic in the face of prison overcrowding is problematic in the context of appellate review as the primary enforcement mechanism. Guidelines that focus on the numbers rather than on the purpose and rationale result in departures from the guideline number based on any commonly identified purpose of sentencing—desert, deterrence, incapacitation, or rehabilitation. If sentencing purposes are neglected in the guidelines policy, that discretion will be exercised by judges, and disparity will result. One judge might depart from a 24-month prison sentence for a property crime and impose a longer sentence because there has been a rash of similar crimes and a deterrent effect for this and other offenders is deemed necessary. Another judge might mitigate the sentence for the same case because the offender is not a particular danger to persons in the community and probation is deemed to be a better alternative. Still another judge might conclude that the offender suffers from chemical dependency and mitigate the sentence in favor of sending him or her to a residential treatment center; or alternatively aggravate the prison sentence so a longer time in prison is available for dealing with the serious chemical dependency problem. Discretion to select the sentencing purpose is discretion to select the sentence.

Focusing on numbers or neglecting purpose altogether undermines the ability of appellate review to act as an effective enforcement mechanism. If a credible case for a departure can be made (and credible cases can easily be made if the sentencing purpose is discretionary), the appellate courts can do little in reviewing or overturning sentences.

Unless purposes and reasons for departure are dealt with, sentencing discretion will not have been structured, and prison populations will not have been controlled or coordinated.

5. FUTURE SENTENCING STRUCTURES

The tension between structures that can support planned coordination of sentencing and correctional policies and structures that support *ad hoc* prison population control has parallels in other correctional areas. Prison classification systems waver between serving the psychological and treatment needs of offenders and serving the management needs of correctional administrators (MacKenzie, Chapter 9 this volume). Certainly justice and utilitarian sentencing purposes conflict in many ways. The choices given these tensions are difficult, and values supporting the various perspectives are dearly held.

There may be instances when an optimal solution can emerge without explicitly addressing and resolving the issues underlying the tension. That is a happy, if rare, circumstance. The circumstance is not likely to emerge with respect to sentencing and corrections coordination. There is much empirical evidence to suggest that substantive sentencing reforms cannot be achieved absent adequate correctional resources (Tonry, 1988). There is much logic and some evidence to suggest that prison populations cannot be controlled by or coordinated with sentencing policy unless that policy is clearly articulated (Knapp, 1986).

The sentencing structure for planned, coordinated policies, then, involves dispensing with discretionary *ad hoc* releasing authority and investing judges with real rather than symbolic sentencing authority within a framework of specific sentencing policy and appellate review of sentences. This creates a tension for corrections administrators. On the one hand, they are strong supporters of sentencing guidelines. On the other hand, they are strong detractors of reform in terms of distribution of discretion and substantive issues. By straddling the structures in this fashion, they serve to undermine the effectiveness of both a planned and an *ad hoc* approach to prison population control.

Concern with prison crowding has not done much to improve sentencing structure or to develop an effective systemic approach as yet. It could spur the development of a new generation of guidelines, however, if philosophical issues are addressed instead of ignored. A new generation of guidelines is needed that will encompass a whole range of punishments rather than limiting the notion of punishment to prison, as the *ad hoc* approach is wont to do. There has been significant innovation in the development of intermediate sanctions in recent years (Peterselia, 1987). In addition to the traditional use of short jail terms, other options like community service, residential treatment, nonresidential treatment, fines, restitution, home detention, electronic monitoring and drug testing schedules, and various levels and forms of probation supervision are commonly used as sentencing options by judges or as administrative tools by a corrections agency.

These options have yet to be structured into a comprehensive sentencing system. Their unstructured use has raised concerns about their efficiency and effectiveness in a number of respects. One area of concern is disparity and lack of proportionality in the use of sentencing options. Another area of concern involves the effectiveness of sentencing options in achieving utilitarian purposes of rehabilitation and specific deterrence, to the extent that they are goals of the programs. Additionally, it is difficult to determine the resource needs and the efficiency of sentencing options and prison, absent detailed policy prescribing their use.

A general approach for structuring more systemic guidelines and broadening the concept of punishment might be to establish sanctioning levels measured in some generic scale of units (e.g., 10 sanctioning units, 16 sanctioning units) for categories of offenders. Exchange or equivalency rates among sanctions would be established by policy in terms of sanction units (e.g., 6 months in jail is 12 sanctioning units; 120 community service hours is 8 units; a year of probation is 15 units). Essentially, the court would be provided with a menu of sanctions from which to fashion a sentence to meet the sanctioning level contained in the sentencing policy. This approach establishes general policy regarding sanctioning levels and defines the level of resource use for the intermediate range of offenses and offenders.

Such a system has the advantage of coordinating a richer array of sentencing options with a broader array of correctional resources. It can provide for the complexities of sanctioning given the array of sentencing purposes while avoiding the disadvantages of a highly indeterminate or discretionary system. For this type of system to work, corrections administrators must still relinquish *ad hoc* controls and work with the rest of the system to fashion substantive sentencing policy. A comfortable legacy for corrections must await a sentencing system that combines a substantive sentencing policy that is coordinated with correctional resources with which to implement the reforms.

6. REFERENCES

American Friends Service Committee. *Struggle for justice.* New York: Hill and Wang, 1971.

Blumstein, A., Cohen J., Martin S. E., and Tonry M. H. (Eds.). *Research on sentencing: The search for reform.* Washington, DC: National Academy Press, 1983.

Clarke, S. H. *Felony sentencing in North Carolina 1976–1986: Effects of presumptive sentencing legislation.* Chapel Hill: Institute of Government, University of North Carolina at Chapel Hill, 1987.

Cohen, J., and Tonry, M. H. Sentencing reforms and their impacts. In *Research on sentencing: The search for reform.* Washington, DC: National Academy Press, 1983.

Dershowitz, A. *Fair and certain punishment.* New York: McGraw-Hill, 1976.

Fogel, D. *We are the living proof.* Cincinnati: W. A. Anderson, 1975.

Frankel, M. E. *Criminal sentences: Law without order.* New York: Hill and Wang, 1972.

Goodstein, L. A quasi-experimental test of prisoner reactions to determinate and indeterminate sentencing. In N. Parisi (Ed.), *Coping with imprisonment.* Beverly Hills: Sage, 1982.

Goodstein, L. Sentencing reform and the correctional system: A case study of the implementation of Minnesota's Determinate Sentencing Law. *Law and Policy Quarterly,* 1983, 5, 478–501.

Goodstein, L. *Determinate sentencing and the correctional process: A study of the implementation and impact of sentencing reform in three states.* Washington, DC: U.S. Government Printing Office, 1984.

Hepburn, J. R., and Goodstein, L. Organizational imperatives and sentencing reform implementation: The impact of prison practices and priorities on the attainment of the objective of determinate sentencing. *Crime and Delinquency,* 1986, 32, 3339–365.

Jacobs, J. Sentencing reform by prison personnel: Good time. *UCLA Law Review,* 1982, 30, 217–270.

Knapp, K. A. Next step: Non-imprisonment guidelines, *Perspectives,* 1988, 12, 8–10.

Knapp, K. A. Proactive policy analysis of Minnesota's prison populations. *Criminal Justice Policy Review,* 1986, 1, 37–57.

Knapp, K. A. *Minnesota sentencing guidelines and commentory annotated.* St. Paul: Minnesota Continuing Legal Education Press, 1985.

Lipson, A. J., and Peterson, M. A. *California justice under determinate sentencing: A review and agenda for research.* Prepared for the State of California, Board of Prison Terms, The Rand Corporation, 1980.

Meithe, T. D., and Moore, C. A. Evaluation of Minnesota's felony sentencing guidelines. Washington, DC: National Institute of Justice, U.S. Department of Justice, 1987.

Minnesota Sentencing Guidelines and Commentary. St. Paul: Minnesota Sentencing Guidelines Commission, 1980.

Minnesota Sentencing Guidelines Commission. *Preliminary report on the development and impact of the Minnesota sentencing guidelines.* St. Paul: Minnesota Sentencing Guidelines Commission, 1982.

Minnesota Sentencing Guidelines Commission. *The impact of the Minnesota sentencing guide-*

lines: *Three-year evaluation.* St. Paul: Minnesota Sentencing Guidelines Commission, 1984.

National Conference of State Legislatures. *State Budget Actions in 1987.* Denver: National Conference of State Legislatures, 1987.

National Prison Project. *Status report—The courts and prisons.* Washington, DC: American Civil Liberties Union Foundation, 1987.

New Mexico House of Representatives. HB 136, 1988.

Oregon Legislative Assembly. House Bill 2715, 1987.

Penal Code of California, Sec. 1170 (a) (1).

Petersilia, J. *Expanding options for criminal sentencing. R-3544-EMC.* Santa Monica: Rand, 1987.

Rothman, D. J. *Conscience and convenience: The asylum and its alternative in progressive America.* Boston: Little, Brown and Co., 1980.

Schuwerk, R. P. Illinois experience with determinate sentencing: A critical reappraisal Part 1: Efforts to structure the exercise of discretion in bargaining for, imposing, and serving criminal sentences. *DePaul Law Review,* 1984, *33,* 631–739.

Schuwerk, R. P. Illinois experience with determinate sentencing: A critical reappraisal Part 2: Efforts to impose substantive limitations on the exercises of judicial sentencing discretion. *DePaul Law Review,* 1985, *34,* 241–407.

Shane-DuBow, S., Brown, A. P., and Olsen, E. *Sentencing reform in the United States: History, content, and effect.* Washington, DC: Government Printing Office, 1985.

Tonry, M. *Sentencing reform impacts.* Washington, DC: U.S. Government Printing Office, 1987.

Tonry, M. Structuring sentencing. In *Crime and justice.* Chicago: University of Chicago Press, 1988.

von Hirsch, A. *Doing justice: The choice of punishments.* New York: Hill and Wang, 1976. Reprint: Boston: Northeastern University Press, 1986.

von Hirsch, A., Knapp, K. A., and Tonry, M. *The sentencing commission and its guidelines.* Boston: Northeastern University Press, 1987.

Washington sentencing guidelines. In *Revised code of Washington,* secs. 9.94A.340 through 9.94A.420.

Washington Sentencing Guidelines Commission. *Report to the legislature: January 1, 1987.* Olympia: Washington Sentencing Commission, 1987.

Part III

MANAGING THE PRISON

Chapter 8

PRISON LABOR AND INDUSTRY

TIMOTHY J. FLANAGAN

The most desirable system for employing convicts is one which provides primarily for the punishment and reformation of the prisoners and the least competition with free labor, and, secondarily, for the revenue of the state.
U.S. House of Representatives
Industrial Commission, 1900

The modern concept of prisons as institutions for treatment does not contemplate the "busy prison factory" or the self-supporting prison as a goal. Nevertheless, in any well-rounded program directed toward the needs of those confined, some employment projects have their place.
F. Flynn, 1950

We can continue to have largely human "warehouses," with little or no education and training, or we can have prisons that are factories with fences around them . . . [to] accomplish the dual objective of training inmates in gainful occupations and lightening the enormous load of maintaining the prison system of this country.
Chief Justice Warren E. Burger, 1982

TIMOTHY J. FLANAGAN • School of Criminal Justice, State University of New York at Albany, Albany, New York 12222.

1. INTRODUCTION

Work has been one of the defining characteristics of incarceration throughout the history of American prisons. "Work was in fact the core of the penal experience both at the Eastern Penitentiary, the first such institution in the United States, and at Auburn in New York" (Schaller, 1982: 3). The celebrated debate between the designers of the Pennsylvania "solitary" system and the Auburn "congregate" system of prison organization was largely a controversy about the most efficient way to organize production within the confines of maximum security.

Today, strong support exists among correctional experts, policymakers, and the general public for the principle that inmates should perform constructive and useful labor. In a 1982 Gallup poll, 94% of the American public felt that it was a "good idea" to "require prisoners to have a skill or learn a trade, to fit them for a job before they are released from prison". Eighty-three percent felt that "keeping prisoners busy constructing buildings, making products and performing services that the state would have to hire other people to do" was a good idea, and 81% favored paying prisoners for their work but requiring inmates to return two-thirds of their wages to their victims or to the state for the cost of maintaining the prison (Gallup, 1982). Cullen and Travis concluded that "Americans are convinced of the beneficial, if not curative, nature of putting inmates to work" (1984: 53). It is not surprising, then, that former Chief Justice Burger's call for reshaping American prisons into "factories with fences" has been received with enthusiasm.

It is tempting to read too much into these supportive statistics, for as Hawkins observes, "Opposition to productive labor by prisoners is as old as the penitentiary system itself" (1983: 90). Americans have heartily supported the *concept* of work for prisoners, but the historical record reveals deep-seated ambivalence about the application of the principle (Funke, Wayson, and Miller, 1982). In an observation that is as pertinent today as three decades ago, Barnes and Teeters wrote that "the public believes, in theory at least, that prisoners should work—and work hard. It is actually ambivalent about the matter; when jobs are plentiful, prisoners should work but during periods of recession, criminals should not 'take jobs from law-abiding citizens'" (1959: 522). Implementing the principle of prison labor also produces dissensus about the types of work that prisoners should perform, incentive and reward structures, the distribution of rewards among the inmate, the inmate's family, victims of crime, and the state, the place of work within the goals of the correctional organization, and many other issues.

TABLE 1. Contemporary Goals of Prison Labor[a]

Offender based	Institution oriented	Societal
Good work habits	Reducing idleness	Repayment to society
Real work experience	Structuring daily activities	Dependent support
Vocational training	Reducing the net cost of	Victim restitution
Life management experience	corrections	
Gate money		

[a] Randall Guynes and Robert C. Greiser, "Contemporary Prison Industry Goals." Chapter 2 in *A study of prison industry: History, components, goals*. College Park, MD: American Correctional Association, 1986, p. 21.

2. THE MANY FACES OF PRISON WORK: THREE CONCEPTUAL MODELS

Support for the principle of inmate labor is due to the fact that such labor serves many goals. As a result, people of diverse correctional ideologies support work programs for very different reasons. In fact, prison work programs have always sought multiple goals, but the primacy of specific objectives has waxed and waned over time. Guynes and Greiser (1986) constructed a typology of contemporary goals of prison labor that classifies the objectives in terms of the various constituencies served by inmate work. This typology is presented in Table 1.

Utilizing inmates for institutional maintenance tasks reduces operating costs and therefore has economic appeal. Employment of prisoners also reduces idleness, long thought to be an undesirable and counterproductive feature of prison life, and provides a routine or structure for organizing the daily activities of the prison (Guynes and Greiser, 1986). Work programs also expose offenders to the norms and practices of the "world of work," including responsibility for time accounting, the linkage between individual effort, productivity and economic reward, self-discipline, and others. Because many offenders enter prison with sketchy work records, teaching inmates the elements of the "work ethic" is thought to be an important function of prison work programs.

Many prison jobs provide the inmate with specific work skills, but the marketability of these skills after release is a problem that has plagued prison labor systems for some time. Observers note that many prison jobs are in fields with no counterpart or labor surpluses in the free economy, utilize outmoded equipment and production techniques, or require licenses that are difficult for ex-offenders to obtain. Despite these problems, providing prisoners with job skills, regular work experience, and "gate money" is thought to be a mechanism to increase the likelihood of inmates' gainful (and legitimate) employment upon release. Recidivism research highlights the link between postrelease employment and crime, so providing work skills and experience are thought to improve the postrelease adjustment of offenders as well.

In addition to these offender-focused goals and institution-oriented objectives, inmate labor has also been promoted in terms of benefits to the larger society. An objective of some models of inmate labor is the payment of restitution to victims; other systems require that inmates reimburse the state for a portion of the costs of confinement through wages earned in prison or that these wages help support dependents, thereby reducing the demand on other government sponsored support programs.

2.1. Implications of Multiple Goals

The many objectives assigned to prison work programs create several problems, and trying to determine if *any* of these goals are being met is a difficult empirical question. Guynes and Greiser have commented, "It takes little reflection to note that achieving a variety of objectives can result in apparently unresolvable conflicts. All the goals assigned to prison industry cannot be attained simultaneously" (1986: 25). For example, the objective of reducing idleness among inmates may lead to overassignment to prison jobs, a practice that is counterproductive if the goals of providing "real-world" work experience, teaching job skills, or making work programs profitable are taken seriously. Similarly, job training efforts may lower productivity and deflate employment opportunities as a result of declining output. These examples illustrate conflicts between inmate-focused objectives and institution-oriented goals, but competition between institutional and societal goals also arises. "Both victim restitution and dependent assistance increase [prison] industry's expenses—they require adequate inmate compensation. These increase costs, reducing the likelihood that goods and services can be provided to the state and the community at a less costly level than production by the private sector" (Guynes and Greiser, 1986: 25).

Goal ambiguity and tension between multiple objectives characterizes many other dimensions of correctional organization and other complex service delivery organizations such as universities, hospitals, and police departments. Goal conflict creates problems for these organizations, but benefits also accrue through the widening of policy domains, diffusion of accountability among different criteria, and the ability to promote the program on a number of different grounds. However, the absence of a "mission statement" for prison labor programs is regarded by many as the fundamental policy issue facing contemporary prison industry.

3. HISTORICAL DEVELOPMENT OF INMATE LABOR SYSTEMS

As mentioned earlier, work has been a feature of American corrections ever since *institutions* have been used as a mechanism for *correcting* offenders. As David Rothman (1975) observed in *The Discovery of the Asylum*, colonial Americans relied on a variety of punishments and protective measures to deter crime and punish criminals, but these measures did not include confinement in institutions for "correctional purposes." Rather, physical and psychological punishments (the stock, whipping, hanging, and others), fines, and banishment comprised the armament of crime control during this period. Some workhouses for the poor were developed during this period, but these institutions were last-resort measures for those who fell through the safety net of family or neighborhood aid, assistance from religious congregations, and other forms of noninstitutional aid. Local jails housed persons awaiting trial. Rothman noted that "the jails facilitated the process of criminal punishment but were not themselves instruments of discipline" (1971: 53). Organized along the same "household model" as the almshouses of the period:

> The keeper and his family resided in the jail, occupying one of its rooms; the prisoners lived several together in the others, with little to differentiate the keeper's quarters from their own. They wore a special clothing or uniforms and usually neither cuffs nor chains restrained their movements. They walked—not marched—about the jail. . . . Nowhere were they required to perform the slightest labor. (1971: 55)

Americans experimented with different approaches to crime control and order maintenance in the late eighteenth and early nineteenth centuries, as the society responded to fundamental challenges presented by immigration, urbanization, expansion, and growing industrialization. Communal prisons were developed during the late eighteenth century but were quickly assailed as "schools of crime" that operated "with alarming efficacy to increase, diffuse and extend the love of vice, and a knowledge of the arts and practices of criminality" (Rothman, 1971: 94). The American penitentiary system, born in the 1820s, first wedded the concepts of institutional confinement as a method of correction and work as the mechanism to promote self-discipline necessary for the reformation.

The Pennsylvania "solitary system" and the New York "congregate system" of prison organization were premised on the reformative effects of order, disassociation from the temptations of the larger society, and the benefits of regular work. In the Pennsylvania system implemented at penitentiaries in Pittsburgh (1826) and Philadelphia (1829), work was a reward to be earned after a period of isolation and self-reflection. Rothman described the Pennsylvania plan:

> After a period of total isolation, without companions, books, or tools, officials would allow the inmate to work in his cell. Introduced at this moment, labor would become not an oppressive task for punishment, but a welcome diversion, a delight rather than a burden. The convict would sit in his cell and work with his tools daily, so that over the course of his sentence regularity and discipline would become habitual. He would return to the community cured of vice and idleness, to take his place as a responsible citizen. (1971: 86)

In contrast, the New York system implemented at Auburn (1823) and Ossining (1825) kept prisoners isolated at night but organized production within congregate workshops during the day. The debate between proponents of the models is among the most colorful vignettes in American penology, but the efficiency of the New York labor system won the day. McKelvey wrote that within 20 years of the establishment of the penitentiaries in New York and Pennsylvania, "new prisons . . . copied the Auburn pattern, . . . largely because of the relative economy of construction and the promise of profits from congregate labor" and observed that "the development of prosperous prison industries was the most earnest concern of wardens, and indeed the rivalry between the officers of different prisons over their financial records gradually pushed aside the argument (of the relative merit) between the two systems, leaving it to the cranks and the historians to settle if they could" (1972: 29–30).

4. MODELS OF PRISON LABOR ORGANIZATION

The concept of inmate labor conjures an image of a factory where inmates produce goods for consumption by the prison system itself or other state agencies. The license plate, road sign, or shoe factory comes immediately to mind. In fact, prison labor has been organized in diverse ways in different times and places, and some forms include direct involvement of private sector entrepreneurs and firms. Six organizational models have been used, and three models inure benefits to private interests.

As early as 1790, the labor of inmates of the Walnut Street Jail in Philadelphia was *contracted* to private parties. The contractor supplied equipment, raw materials, and supervision of the laborers; the prison supplied inmate labor for a stipulated fee. The contractor was left to his own devices to enforce productivity standards and quality control. A variation of the contracting scheme, called the *piece-price* system, incorporated supervision by prison personnel, and the contractor paid for the finished goods on a per-unit basis for each acceptable product. In both cases, formulae were devised to establish the fee for the inmates' labor and the distribution of the income between the inmate and the prison. These early systems of prison labor organization included many features of Chief Justice Burger's model of "factories with fences." One observer described the system at the Walnut Street Jail as follows:

> Each convict has a book in which he enters his bargain with the outside employer, and in which his earnings are also set down in order. The convict's outgoings, whether an account of his prosecution, his fine, the price of the instruments which he breaks, or injures, of his clothing, and of his board, are likewise set down in his book which is audited every three months in the presence of the inspectors. (LaRochefoucald, in Barnes and Teeters, 1959: 524)

In 1803, the New York legislature turned over the operation of its industrial program at Newgate prison to a private contractor, a decision that prompted the resignation of the prison's superintendent, Thomas Eddy (McKelvey, 1972: 7).

Another form of "private benefit" prison labor organization was the *lease system*, first implemented in Kentucky in 1825 and widely used in Southern states during the post-Civil War period. A private entrepreneur purchased inmate labor for an annual fee and was responsible for all care and custody of inmate workers. Both the fee and the maintenance of inmates had to be recovered before the lease became profitable, creating a system in which profit was based on reaping the maximum work from each inmate for the minimum investment. Leased inmates were used on farms, in mines, in road construction, and many other industries, including the construction of new prisons. The abuses that characterized this model of prison work and claims of unfair advantage from competing firms and early labor organizations resulted in the virtual abolition of this form of prison labor by the mid-1930s.

Prisoner labor has also been organized in ways that produce no direct benefits to private parties; these systems have characterized inmate labor during most of the twentieth century in America. Prison work has focused on a *public works* objective, in which inmate labor is used in road and bridge construction, construction of public facilities such as parks (and even prisons themselves), and many others. The image of Southern prison "road gangs" in the film *Cool Hand Luke* comes immediately to mind, but correctional agencies throughout the country have employed inmates in these activities.

The two final models of public benefit prison labor organization involve little direct involvement of the private sector in the *production* of goods and services but vary in the *market structure* for prison-made products. The *state account* system, introduced in Minnesota in the late nineteenth century, involved the state takeover of an industry (the production of binder twine, a commodity that was essential for farming—a major economic activity of the state). When this system was organized, there was no in-state producer of this product, so private sector resistance was minimal. Under these favorable conditions, McKelvey wrote, "Producing and selling cheap in an almost unlimited market to the benefit of the chief portion of its electorate, and at the same time paying its prison expenses, Minnesota had an unassailable system" (1972: 104). Other states have organized prison production along similar lines, dealing with opposition from private interests by limiting the employment of prisoners within certain industries. The advantages of this system are minimal opposition from private sector producers and the wide market that enables near full employment of prisoners. Critics pointed out a key deficiency, however—because no comparable manufacturing facilities existed in the state, the possibility of prisoners finding employment in an industry for which they were trained and experienced was all but precluded (Barnes and Teeters, 1959).

The final method of organizing prisoner labor is most common today. In the *state-use* system, the correctional agency develops and operates prison industries. Private-sector involvement is limited to the sale of raw materials to prison industry and is subject to competitive bidding, procedures that govern marketing to all governmental agencies. The prison system also markets its products—but the market is restricted to state and local government agencies and some nonprofit organizations. To buttress this system, legislation in many states *requires* governmental agencies to purchase prison-made products when the correctional system provides the products and *forbids* the sale of prison-made goods on the open market.

In theory, the state-use model creates an enormous market for prison-made goods and services and provides protection for private sector manufacturers against competition from prison industries with artificially deflated wage structures. Several deficiencies in the state-use model have given rise to complaints by all concerned, however, and proposals to modify or eliminate the state-use system emerge directly from these complaints.

5. THE DECLINE AND RESURGENCE OF PRISON WORK

The placid descriptions of nineteenth century prisons as beehives of industriousness evaporated as the concept of prisoner-as-worker ran into conflict with private interests and a changing penological philosophy. Throughout the late nineteenth and most of the twentieth century, the importance of prison labor, measured by economic impact or by the centrality of work within the confinement experience, dramatically declined. Only within the last 5 to 10 years has interest renewed in the promise and problems of prison labor.

Corruption of prison officials and abuse of prisoners were the seeds of destruction of the early contract and lease systems of prison labor. Social reformers and penologists decried the ascendancy of the profit motive as the raison d'être for prisoner labor and criticized the concomitant reduction in emphasis on the reformative, educational aspects of prison work. At the same time, the fatal blow for full employment of prison inmates was struck by the dual forces of the nascent organized labor movement in the United States and the rise of the industrial society.

Manufacturing interests criticized the employment of prisoners to produce goods for the open market as unfair competition. Because the prison was supported by taxes, the intrusion of the prison into the marketplace was assailed as a form of double taxation. At the same time, the organized labor movement exerted tremendous political pressure against the employment of prisoners in jobs that might be held by persons who had not been convicted of crimes. The prevailing ideology has been the "principle of least eligibility," a view that convicted offenders should be least eligible for sharing the benefits of society, including benefits that accrue from participation in the economic life of society. The adoption of state-use systems that restricted sale of prison-made goods to the governmental sector was a direct result of these challenges. A series of increasingly restrictive federal laws circumscribed the sale of prison-made goods in the 1930s and effectively eliminated the interstate market. State legislatures also responded to pressure from the external environment by limiting the product areas in which prisons would participate.

The impact of these forces on prison employment was direct and dramatic. Barnes and Teeters reported that in 1885, 75% of state prison inmates were "employed at productive labor." Of these working prisoners, two-thirds were in contract or lease labor systems. By 1940, the employment rate in state prisons had fallen to 44% and 88% of employed prisoners were in state-use or public works labor systems. The value of commodities produced by state prisoners fell by more than 33% between 1923 and 1940 (1959: 535, 537).

Hawkins (1983) reminds us that the decline of prison labor, especially during the twentieth century in America, was not wholly attributable to the efforts of organized business and labor to thwart prison production. At this time, a "new penology" began to develop in America. The emergent ideology of American corrections focused on the "medical model" of correctional intervention and placed rehabilitative treatment methods at the core of the prison experience. Counseling and education programs of unlimited variety replaced work experience as the principal reformative mechanism of American corrections. As an example of the new order, Hawkins cited the observation of sociologist Walter Reckless that "work must be relegated to secondary importance, to be done when not interfering with the schedule of attitude and habit retraining. . . . There must be no interference with the main business of the prison or reformatory—namely social re-education" (Reckless, 1950, in Hawkins, 1983:89). Similarly, Sutherland and Cressey wrote in 1960 that although it "cannot be argued that prison labor has no rehabilitative effects. . .it is doubtful that labor is the most important activity which is, or could be, provided for the reformation of prisoners" (in Hawkins, 1983: 89). Clearly, the status of work within the prison experience had fallen precipitously from the lofty position of the penitentiary designers of the early nineteenth century, and rates of idleness among prisoners or overassignment to institutional maintenance tasks to create the illusion of industriousness bore witness to the implications of this ideological shift.

During the last decade, there has been a revival of interest in prison labor. There are several reasons for this resurgence of interest in productive labor for prisoners. First, the treatment ideology in American corrections has undergone fundamental questioning by researchers, policymakers, and the public. Without belaboring the point, since the publication of Lipton, Martinson, and Wilks's compendium, *The Effectiveness of Correctional Treatment* in 1975, proponents of the view that effective treatment programs that succeed in altering the criminal behavior of offenders can be developed and implemented in prisons have been on the defensive. As a result, the primacy of these programs within the correctional organization has greatly diminished.

Second, American correctional systems have experienced tremendous increases in the prisoner population during the 1980s. The *rate* of new commitments to state prisons has increased, and the average *length* of prison sentences has risen simultaneously. Population pressures force correctional administrators to focus on activities that reduce the level of idleness among their changes *and* hold promise for containing geometrically increasing correctional budgets. Hawkins captures these twin objectives in writing that "at a time when the *real* cost of incarceration has been estimated at $50,000 per year over a ten-year sentence and $80,000 per year over a twenty year sentence . . . the failure to provide productive activity for prisoners which could reduce correctional operating costs not only confers no benefit on the prisoners, it imposes a substantial burden on the public" (1983:121). These comments must be read in context: The recent American political agenda has been headed by a concern for reducing the cost of government at all levels, while simultaneously demanding protection from crime through the greater use of incarceration.

A third reason for renewed interest in prison labor has been the reentry of the private sector. After achieving a near complete demarcation between prison labor and the free market in the 1930s and 1940s, American business has again shown interest in the prison as a production center, in part because many of the arguments advanced to curtail prison labor 50 years ago are no longer relevant today. The scope of the postwar American economy has broadened so widely that prison labor is not regarded as the threatening force of the past. Schaller argues that:

> In today's market the private manufacturer, the "mom and pop" type operation that served as the principal competition for prisons in the last century, has been largely replaced by the giant corporation and the industrial conglomerate. Those large manufacturers have no reason to fear competition from the small production outlets that typically operate in a prison setting. Nationwide marketing strategies, along with vastly improved transportation systems available to today's manufacturer, have so broadened a producer's sales potential that limited competition within the confines of a state poses no threat to business at all. (1981:61)

In an ironic development, Schaller notes that labor-intensive production tasks for which prisons are best suited are those that American business has directed to foreign countries in recent years. This conclusion does not suggest that real and angry opposition to expansion of prison labor has diminished. The passion with which these objections are voiced is reflected in legislative hearings and debates concerning the relaxation of state-use laws and expansion of prison industry operations (New York State Assembly, 1985). Nevertheless, recent changes in correctional philosophy, crime control ideology, the scale of prisoner populations, and the free economy have focused new attention on prison labor.

6. A CONTEMPORARY PORTRAIT

In American prisons today, work is grouped in three principal activities: prison industry, institutional maintenance/service tasks, and agriculture. The relative size and importance of these operations varies from state to state, particularly in the role of farming. Recent proposals to improve and expand work activities in prisons focus primarily on the industrial and institutional maintenance areas.

6.1. Institutional Maintenance/Service Tasks

A variety of service-oriented and maintenance tasks must be completed in prisons on a regular basis. Lawns must be mowed, laundry cleaned, meals prepared and served, cell blocks cleaned and painted, plumbing and electrical systems maintained, and so forth. In most prisons, these tasks are performed by inmates under the supervision of custodial staff and civilian supervisors. Because of the scope and immediacy of these activities, the largest proportion of inmate jobs are within this maintenance/service sector.

An assessment of work programs in federal prisons found that because these maintenance functions are "generally the foremost concern of institution officials, they often assign institutional work a higher priority than other [industrial] work programs" (U.S. General Accounting Office, 1982: 3). The study found that 60% of employed prisoners in the federal correctional system were assigned to institutional maintenance tasks. Comparable data for state prisons are not available on a uniform basis, but because the federal prison system administers the most extensive prison *industry* operation in the United States, it is reasonable to conclude that the share of employed inmates assigned to service tasks in state systems is higher than the federal system.

"Institutional work is important for the day-to-day operations of prisons, but the typical institutional job does little to enhance inmate work skills" (U.S. General Accounting Office, 1982). All too often, these assignments are used to reduce idleness rather than further the administration of the prison. There are many more prisoners available than are required to accomplish the tasks. As a result, the goals of reducing idleness and providing legitimate and meaningful work experience come into conflict. The GAO study found that Bureau of Prisons' policy mandated employment for all able-bodied prisoners, but the bureau had "no consistent criteria or methodology for determining the number of inmates that institutional work programs need," with the result that "there has not been sufficient work to provide all inmates meaningful, productive and full-time employment" (1982: 7).

Charges of overassignment or "featherbedding" institutional assignments have plagued prison work programs for many years. The recurring (and frequently accurate) image is of three inmates assigned to a broom, and responsible for sweeping a single corridor during an 8-hour shift. John Conrad provides an illustration of the problem that reveals the custodial interests that are served. He wrote of

> my observations of the mess hall at the Indiana State Prison at Michigan City, where, a few years ago, I had a depressing but significant dialogue with the chief steward. He told me that overassignment to the mess hall was so serious

that he had several times as many men as he could keep occupied. His solution was to assign one four-man table to each man and require him to clean it up after each meal—a task that might occupy him for five whole minutes out of the day. Yet the Captain's assignment board would show that all these men were on full-time assignments. Was such a job meaningful, I asked? (1986: 75)

Conrad's respondent argued that many of his charges had *no* previous job experience, that the "quality" of the work was more important than the number of hours, and that learning to take pride in one's work was important and beneficial to the inmate after release.

The problems of institutional service work are exacerbated by at least three related factors. First, many inmates do not *want* to work (for a variety of reasons), and the ability of the prison to provide incentives for productive and legitimate work is restricted. Second, unlike the larger society, where for many, time is a precious commodity to be apportioned among work, family, and other interests and commitments, prisoners live in a setting where time is abundant and useful activities to structure time are scarce (Calkins, 1970). Third, the opportunities for work that approximate "real-world" employment are especially limited. For this reason, efforts to enhance the economic and rehabilitative potential of inmate work have focused on the prison industry sector.

6.2. Prison Industry

An mentioned earlier, the scope and importance of contemporary prison industry bears little resemblance to that of the nineteenth century. Funke, Wayson, and Miller (1982) found that between 1885 and 1979, the percentage of state prison inmates employed in correctional industries decreased from 90% to 10%. A survey of state correctional departments conducted in 1983 found the employment rate was less than 10% (Freiser, Miller, and Funke, 1984). According to Funke, Wayson, and Miller, "these facts describe what is undoubtedly the longest economic depression of any U.S. industry" (1982: 27).

The employment rate of federal correctional institutions is somewhat higher. As of September, 1987, Federal Prison industries, Inc. employed 33% of the total federal prison inmate population and 47% of those inmates actually available to work (U.S. Department of Justice, Federal Prison System, 1987).

The state-of-the-art survey by Greiser, Miller, and Funke in 1983 investigated several other indicators of the health of prison industry programs. "Prison industries directors were asked to estimate the percent of production capacity at which they were currently operating. There was wide variation in the responses which ranged from a low of

40 percent to full capacity. The mean production capacity of prison industry operations in the states was 68 percent" (1984: 15).

An indicator of the *efficiency* of contemporary prison industry was a question concerning the probable impact on employment levels if industries were to operate "under conditions analogous to the private sector and assuming production levels remained constant." The researchers reported that under these assumptions, "36 states said they would be employing fewer inmates than they are at present" (Greiser et al., 1984: 15).

Nationwide, the average wage for inmate workers in 1983 was $3.00 per day, but of 41 states that were able to provide profit/loss information for Fiscal Year 1983, 15 states reported a loss from manufacturing/service industries; of 18 states that were able to report separate profit/loss information for agricultural activities, 11 states reported a loss. The researchers attempted to identify specific shops or types of industrial operations that were most profitable or nonprofitable but concluded that "with one consistent exception, i.e., farming, the results demonstrate no clear pattern of profit-making or loss industries. Agricultural operations were quite often losing money and being subsidized by profits from manufacturing operations" (1984: 16). These general figures must be regarded cautiously, as the states vary in the calculation of overhead charges and the accounting of inventories and accounts receivable (see, for example, Association of the Bar of the City of New York, 1985). As Greiser, Miller, and Funke reported, "The definition of all those factors assigned as industries costs, e.g., reimbursement to DOC for security staff, is likely to play a significant role in any bottom line profit or loss reported" (Greiser et al., 1984: 15).

Finally, the *scope* of prison industry operations in 1983 ranged from a single shop in Hawaii to 37 different industrial operations in Florida, and the products and services produced in state prisons ranged from foundries to flag making and from concrete products to chewing tobacco (American Correctional Association, 1986b). However, *problems* facing industry managers were common in many states. Industry directors reported in 1983 that

> at the top of the list of concerns were overcrowding and the resulting problems that emerge such as lack of space and high inmate turnover. An almost equal number . . . responded that organizational issues and/or the lack of clear goal definition were among the most immediate problems which industries must address. . . . The third most pressing issue expressed was the lack of resources necessary to develop new programs. (Greiser, Miller, and Funke, 1984: 23)

7. TOWARD MORE EFFECTIVE PRISON LABOR: EMPIRICAL AND POLICY ISSUES

In this decade, the most pressing policy issue facing American corrections has been providing space for the ever-growing prisoner population. The crowding problem has created immediate and serious dilemmas for correctional administrators, state policymakers, and others concerned with prison management. Crowding has also made judicial intervention in correctional administration a regular occurrence, as overcrowded facilities give rise to complaints regarding the conditions of confinement. John Conrad observed that the "torch of correctional innovation and reform" has been borne largely by the judiciary during this period.

In contrast, the development of more effective prison labor programs requires attention and action from a broad range of actors, including correctional administrators, the legislatures, and private sector interests. Conrad notes that when pressure to develop an adequate supply of prison space begins to ease (either because of demographic changes in the population, wider use of alternatives to confinement, or the completion of capacity expansion efforts), attention must shift to the question: "What will these people *do* during their period of confinement?" Moreover, because much of the increase in prison populations is due to longer sentences, these periods of confinement will be even longer than in the past. Given widespread disillusionment with the effectiveness of prison-based treatment programs, the cycle of prison reform has come full circle to an interest in prisoner labor, both as a means of accomplishing reformative goals and as a mechanism for reducing the costs of confinement.

Many approaches and policy directions are being implemented already, to rejuvenate the prison labor programs that became moribund during most of this century. Current policy activity can be summarized in two generic directions. First, a number of efforts focus on making prison work more "realistic," in the sense that prison labor more closely emulates the "businesslike" practices of labor in the free economy. Second, renewed interest in involving the private sector in prison labor programs is often seen as the most promising way to accomplish the aims of more productive, relevant, and useful inmate work.

Examples of the first policy direction—making prison labor more "businesslike"—have proliferated for at least a decade. The "free venture" model of prison industry, developed during the mid-1970s, incorporates many standard features of "real-world" business practices, such as an 8-hour workday, shop-level hiring/firing authority, meaningful productivity standards and accounting methods, and others (U.S. Department of Justice, 1978). These features represent a dramatic change in the goals and organization of prison work from that which has characterized prison labor during most of this century. On a less grand scale, many correctional agencies have adopted modern management practices in an effort to approximate "businesslike" administration.

The second general policy direction—greater involvement of the private sector in prison labor—has taken different forms from state to state. In some jurisdictions, the creation of "business advisory councils" to work with correctional administrators in developing more relevant and profitable prison labor programs is a recent development. In others, these councils also advise policymakers concerning relaxation of restrictive state-use statutes to widen the market for prison-made products or serve as liaisons with organized labor groups to foster a less acrimonious atmosphere toward expanding inmate labor programs.

The most dramatic examples of this policy shift are the new laws, promulgated in 20 states as of 1982, that expand the market for prison-made products beyond the limits of state-use legislation or that authorize private-sector-controlled business operations within prisons (Auerbach, 1982). As of year-end 1984, there were at least 26 such prison-based businesses operating in 17 U.S. prisons in 9 states, in conjunction with 19 private firms, and employing almost 1,000 inmates. Legislation in 21 states authorized private sector employment or contracting of prisoner labor (U.S. Department of Justice, 1985). A recent assessment of these developments found widespread interest in private sector involvement among state corrections directors, legislators and governors, and concluded that the reinvolvement of the private sector in prison labor "seems to be a lasting trend rather than a passing fad." The study cautioned that many issues must still be resolved, however, and the resolution of these issues by local decision makers "will largely determine the success or failure of this promising innovation on a nationwide scale" (U.S. Department of Justice, 1985: 9–10).

These policy directions have produced promising results, but it is clear that rejuvenating of the concept of productive and meaningful labor by prisoners involves the resolution of many interdependent and nettlesome issues. Responsibility for resolving these issues cannot be avoided; some of the unresolved issues are political in nature and can only be resolved by legislatures that are willing to make decisions regarding goals and policies to further these goals. Other issues are empirical in nature; they involve examination and questioning of assumptions about the presumed benefits of inmate labor and the presumption that prison work *can* become profitable and productive. A brief discussion of several of these issues follows.

7.1. What Is the Goal of Prison Labor?

Articulating and ranking the goals of prisoner labor may seem an academic exercise, but there is great practical significance in having policymakers specify and order the many (and often competing) objectives of inmate work. A recent study of prison industry programs by the American Correctional Association concluded that "legislative and executive orders often offer unclear directives and goals for correctional industry programs," thus "a major issue facing prison industry is a determination of its mission" (1986a: 74, 78).

Developing a "mission statement" for prison labor programs is critical for several reasons. Most important, goal specification provides the benchmarks for evaluating of efforts to improve prison labor programs. Second, goal definition provides an opportunity for the correctional organization to clarify the role of work within the hierarchy of objectives and variety of programs available within the prison. For example, because prisoners bring low educational and skill levels to prison, strengthening the mission of inmate labor programs will require the rational integration of work, training, and education programs (Coffey, 1986). Many inmates are simply not equipped for productive work careers within the prison unless this experience is preceded by remedial education programs and vocational training. (Federal Prison Industries, Inc., the industrial arm of the federal prison system, has recognized this interdependence between work, training, and education for some time; since 1964 the profits from FPI sales have been reinvested in the Bureau of Prisons' vocational and basic education programs.)

Third, a mission statement for prison labor programs would provide managers with direction for resolving conflicts among objectives. For example, if the development of marketable postrelease job skills is a primary objective of prison work, this will influence decisions about staffing levels, the selection of production activities to complement employment opportunities in the free economy, and many others. The relevance of goal clarification for program managers was underscored in a recent survey, in which industry directors from state correctional agencies listed "the lack of clear goal definition" as one of the "most immediate problems which industries must address" (Greiser, Miller, and Funke, 1984: 23).

Implementation of the goals of prison labor requires investment of public funds, so responsibility for developing these mission statements rests with the state legislatures. However, it is clear that the definition of goals cannot take place in a vacuum; the goals must be reconciled with the external environment of corrections. Therefore, not just correctional experts, but business leaders, organized labor, and the public at large must take part in defining the mission of prison labor programs, because all these parties have substantial interests at stake.

7.2. Can Prison Business Run Like a Business?

A second general issue to be considered in the development of effective prison labor programs is whether institutional work programs *can* emulate the "businesslike" practices of the free economy. The adoption of businesslike management practices and procedures is a worthy goal, but there may be inherent limits to the productivity of prison labor. At least three different aspects of the problem are worth considering.

7.2.1. The Inmate Labor Force

As a group, inmates of American state prisons lack many of the basic educational and experiential prerequisites of a productive labor force. Compared to the labor pool in the free economy, prisoners are educationally disadvantaged and lack regular work experience and training that an employer in the larger economy would consider essential for even entry-level employment. Even if one assumes that inmates are motivated to productive labor, substantial remedial education and training will be needed for many to reach reasonable competency levels.

Many prisoners also lack motivation to work while confined, viewing such labor as involuntary servitude or preferring to live off the profits of their criminal careers or from careers in "hustling" while confined. Legge (1978) observed that work does not enjoy the same *status* in prison as in the larger society, in part because of the restricted range of *rewards* available to workers in the prison environment and the virtual absence of effective *sanctions* for poor work performance.

7.2.2. The Correctional Environment

The issue of effective rewards and sanctions for productive work by prisoners illustrates one constraint imposed by the correctional environment. Economic rewards are the most common incentive to productive labor in the free economy, where workers are free to sell their labor to competing firms. However, payment of even minimum wages to inmates raises thorny political issues. Hawkins observed that this manifestation of the "principle of least eligiblity" is the most significant obstacle to the development of productive labor programs in prisons. A number of proposals exist that link the payment of "real-world" wages to chargebacks against room and board, restitution to victims, enforced savings, and family support payments, but even these features do little to assuage opposition to paying prisoners real wages.

Nonwage incentives are also available to promote productive labor among inmates, such as granting "good time" credits, providing preferential housing within the prison, and others. Even these incentives anger critics, as some view these rewards as an unwarranted linkage between productivity and diminution of deserved punishment. Differential treatment of productive and nonproductive inmates also violates a traditional maxim of correctional administration that all prisoners be treated the same, without regard to their economic or social status. The creation of economic "classes" of inmates, based on productivity in work programs, raises concerns about the treatment of prisoners who are physically unable to work, who would benefit from training or basic educational programs prior to employment, or who are assigned to institutional maintenance programs because these tasks must be completed or because a sufficient supply of industrial opportunities is not available.

In addition, Legge (1978) observed that decision making in prisons is dictated by the inmate's status *as a prisoner* rather than *as a worker*, so the range of available employment opportunities may be artificially circumscribed. For example, if an inmate classified as maximum security would benefit from placement in an industrial setting that exists only in a medium security prison, the mismatch will be resolved in favor of the security consideration rather than the employment issue.

Many other features of the prison environment limit the productive capacity of inmate labor. The prison workday is punctuated by numerous intrusions that serve the superordinate goal of security; these include regular counts, callouts for visitation or medical, legal, or counseling sessions, and lockdowns for security purposes. Inmate turnover rates that far exceed those of private industry are another problem. The dilemma of attracting and keeping civilian supervisors is another serious problem limiting expansion of prison industry (U.S. General Accounting Office, 1982).

Finally, one of the most deeply rooted problems is the perspective of correctional administrators toward expanded prison labor. The goals of private enterprise and of running an efficient and safe prison are by no means complementary. Modern prison superintendents are unaccustomed to having their professional competence judged by profit and loss statements, and traditional practices of private business (variable wage scales, promotion to supervisory positions, collective bargaining, and others) run counter to deeply rooted correctional management traditions. Inmate movement within the facility, access to tools and raw materials that can be fashioned into weapons, the presence of large groups of inmates in industrial shops, and many other requirements of manufacturing processes represent security nightmares to institutional managers.

7.2.3. The External Environment

The social, legal, political, and economic environment in which prisons exist also presents obstacles to productive prison labor. As mentioned earlier, legislation in many states restricts the markets and industries in which prison labor can participate. For example developing public/private sector joint ventures involving prison labor in New York state would require revision of the state's constitution because an amendment provides that no inmate "shall be required or allowed to work . . . at any trade, industry or occupation, wherein or whereby his work, or the product or profit of his work, shall be farmed out, contracted, given or sold to any person, firm, association or corporation" (New York State Constitution, Art. 3, Sect. 24). Constitutional revisions involve a complicated process of legislative and voter approval that takes several years. The political struggle involved to open markets and permit public/private cooperation for the benefit of prison inmates is uninviting, especially because powerful business and labor constituencies are likely to oppose these measures on many grounds. The fears of private business and organized labor about unfair competition from prisoner labor and the principle of least eligibility that continues to dominate public attitudes toward correctional reform are tremendous political and social obstacles to legal change.

Expansion of prison labor programs will also require major capital investment. Correctional budgets in many states have undergone unprecedented increases in recent years as a result of new prison construction, hiring of additional staff, and increased operating expenses, so garnering funds to develop new industries from governmental sources may be difficult. If investment capital is available from the private sector, correctional agencies will be forced to compete for this capital against more traditional and less risky ventures. In addition to demonstrating the availability of a reliable labor pool at competitive wages, financial incentive packages to attract private investors in prison-based business may involve tax credits, improvements to existing production facilities, favorable utility rates, and many other incentives that breed political and economic controversy. Finally, because many states have long pursued a policy of building prisons away from population centers, existing facilities are often located in remote areas. This situation will create problems in transportation of raw materials and finished goods, relocation of private business managers, and creation of programs to employ prisoners on work release or provide continuity of employment after release.

In summary, there are many obstacles to the goal of full and productive prison labor. The correctional administrator who seeks to achieve the goal of productive work for every inmate will have to be politically adept, a proficient organizational manager, well versed in the needs and requirements of private business operations, and very patient.

7.3. Does It Make a Difference?

Prison labor programs have always assumed that work is beneficial in reforming offenders. Whether these benefits exist is an empirical question on which there is surprisingly little evidence.

The Corrections Committee of the Association of the Bar of the City of New York reviewed the literature on this question in 1984 and concluded:

> Real work, it is argued, not only alleviates idleness and tensions within the prison but also makes it more likely that inmates will be employed (and remain employed) after their release, thus reducing the pressures that lead to recidivism. Although this belief appears sensible and we have nothing to indicate that it is unfounded, there is no hard data to support it. Much of the evidence offered in its behalf is anecdotal only; individual success stories abound, but there is no empirical study showing lower recidivism rates among inmates who have participated in meaningful vocational training and/or prison industry programs. In short, there is little evidence that an industrial prison experience makes a difference in an inmate's post-prison life. (1984: 299)

Recently, a few investigators have attempted to determine the effect of prison industry employment on offender behavior. In 1984, the Utah Governor's Task Force on Correctional Industries examined recidivism rates of inmates released during 1983 after employment in correctional industries and the general 1983 release population. The return-to-prison rate for all releasees was 29% (as of August 1, 1984), but the prison return rate for participants in the correctional industries program was 13%.

To test for selection bias, the groups were compared on several recidivism-relevant variables; no significant differences were found on these dimensions. The researchers acknowledged that industry participants and nonparticipants may have differed on motivational factors or other dimensions that were not assessed. The task forced estimated that at an average cost of $13,350 per returned inmate, the 55% lower return rate for industry participants saved Utah taxpayers more than $1.5 million during the first 7 months of 1984.

Basinger (1985) employed a similar approach to study the effect of industry employment on recidivism among Ohio prisoners. Basinger selected stratified samples of the Ohio general prisoner population and the OPI (Ohio Prison Industries) population in early 1983. No significant differences were found between the OPI group and the general prisoner population on age, race, education level, I.Q., offense type, civilian employment history, and prior incarcerations, but the OPI group had served less time in prison than the general prisoner population.

Basinger's findings on recidivism must be regarded cautiously because the number of OPI inmates who were released and therefore at risk of recidivism for the 1-year follow-up period was quite small. Of OPI-employed inmates who met this criterion, 11% had returned to prison within a year of release. The estimated recidivism rate for all Ohio releasees was 12.5%, so Basinger concluded that "we cannot comfortably say that participation in the Ohio penal industry program independently reduces the probability of recidivism."

Johnson (1984) examined the relationship of prison industry experience and postrelease adjustment among 1,210 offenders released from the Florida Department of Corrections. Using a 2-year follow-up period, Johnson reported no significant relationships between postrelease employment and rearrest and no significant effects of prison work experience on either postrelease employment or recidivism. Inmates who participated in two programs, community work release and vocational education, were more likely to be employed after release, but such participation had no systematic effect on recidivism.

Finally, a recent study of the behavior of employed and unemployed prisoners in New York examined both in-prison and postprison behavior. After controlling for a priori intergroup differences, the researchers concluded that participation in prison industry programs may have reduced the incidence of prison rule violations among working inmates. However, as in previous studies, the postrelease recidivism rates of working and nonworking prisoners were virtually identical (Flanagan, Thornberry, Maguire, and McGarrell, 1987).

In sum, the few empirical studies that have examined the presumed beneficial effects of prison labor on inmate behavior have reached contradictory but largely pessimistic conclusions. Labor programs are certainly not alone in failing to withstand empirical scrutiny of effectiveness in the prison environment. However, existing research is neither detailed nor sensitive to the many subtle beneficial effects that may inhere to work in prison or to the vast differences that may exist between various shops. However, such findings should caution proponents of expanded prison work programs to limit their claims for the rehabilitative promise of productive labor in prisons. Expecting any single experience within the prison sentence to reverse the many factors that lead to criminal offending is an unrealistic goal, and productive work for prisoners can be supported on many other socially useful grounds.

8. CONCLUSION: THE NEW PENOLOGY, OR MORE OF THE SAME?

In *The Search for Criminal Man*, historian Ysabel Rennie reminds us of the cyclical nature of innovation in penology. She observed that

> there is very little in this field that has not at some time been tried and found wanting, forgotten for a generation or two, and then revived as the answer to the crime problem. In no other area has a history of practical failure provided a surer guarantee of ideological immortality. (1978: xviii)

Is the recent interest in rejuvenating the concept of prison labor, with the emphases on reducing costs, reforming offenders, and forging partnerships between the prison and private business just another recurrence of an old penological ghost? Or, have we learned enough from past experience to avoid the pitfalls this time around?

If we have learned anything at all, the following lessons should guide efforts to fashion more productive, cost-effective, and meaningful work programs for prisoners. First, the interest and involvement of private business can provide many opportunities to expand and modernize prison work, but this involvement, by itself, has never been and will never be a panacea for the problems of prison labor. Productive and effective prison labor has always been more of a goal than a reality for reasons that are inherent in the social histories of offenders, the environment of the prison, and the social and political environments in which these institutions exist.

Prison shops are staffed by offenders who, in many cases, are there in part because of failure to lead productive economic lives in the free economy. The constraints imposed by the inmate labor force will not vanish with the introduction of private managers; the deficiencies must be addressed via comprehensive, costly (and nonprofitable) programs of academic and vocational education.

Also, work programs in prison may always be less productive than comparable operations outside because of the many limitations imposed by the prison environment. The primary objective that our society assigns to these institutions is not, after all, production. Rather, we expect security from these institutions and will continue to judge their performance against this standard. When the goals of security and production conflict, production has (and will) give way to the requirements of security. If this imbalance deflates productivity, then we must either accept it or transform our notions about prison.

Prison labor has always been limited by our sense of what social benefits offenders should enjoy, and in an increasingly competitive economic world the benefit of productive and rewarding work will be zealously guarded. If Americans protest the farming-out of labor-intensive jobs to foreign allies because these practices cost American workers their jobs in a shrinking postindustrial labor market, will increased "farming" of manufacturing and technical positions to convicted criminals be accepted with equanimity? Thus far, the reinvolvement of private business in prison labor has not raised alarm among labor and business groups because the scale of this involvement has been very limited. Broadening the scale of private sector involvement may reignite the fears of unfair competition, the ideology of the principle of least eligibility, and other motivations to keep prison labor in its place.

For all these reasons, the goal of full and meaningful employment for all able-bodied prisoners is probably not obtainable. There may simply be an excess supply of inmate labor in a market setting where numerous factors suppress the demand for inmate labor. This does not mean, of course, that we should abandon the goal of providing meaningful employment for prisoners. Rather, it suggests that efforts to increase productive labor by prisoners should be judged against the abysmal record of the recent past rather than against the idyllic goal of full employment.

History also suggests that the renewed involvement of private business in prison labor may also *create* new problems, many of which are unanticipated in the heady atmosphere that accompanies the introduction of an "innovative" idea. Certainly the contracting and lease systems of a century ago seemed like a "good idea" to the superintendents of that era. The deficiencies and abuses associated with mixing the governmental interest in punishing lawbreakers and the entrepreneurial interest in making money quickly became apparent, to the shame of both parties. The record suggests that reestablishment of that nexus should be undertaken with great caution, administered with close supervision, and expanded only after sober deliberation of the merits and shortcomings of the relationship. Because current prison production taps only a small fraction of the restricted state-use market (Greiser *et al.*, 1984), the necessity of going outside of the governmental sector in search of broader markets for prison-made goods may be questionable and may mask a reluctance among policymakers to expand and diversify prison production with governmental resources.

History suggests that there is real danger in overselling the role of work within the prison experience. Certainly the early penitentiary designers exalted the role of work and felt that the combination of hard labor and moral training was sufficient, by itself, to overcome the many influences that lead to criminal behavior. Full employment for all prisoners makes a nice slogan, but many offenders may benefit more directly from programs designed to remedy academic and vocational deficiencies. A correctional agency that operates 10 prisons may not need 10 "industrial prisons" (Sexton, 1982) but a mixture of industrial prisons, academic prisons, vocational training prisons, geriatric prisons, and even a spartan but secure "loafers prison" for inmates who refuse to avail themselves of the opportunities available in a diverse correctional system.

Finally, history warns us not to expect too much from any of our efforts. The history of penology is replete with examples of good ideas that failed miserably, benevolent intentions that backfired, and unbridled optimism destroyed by evaluation research. Much of this research suggests that matching certain *types of offenders* with specific *types of programs* is the key to success, and conversely, that mismatches waste time, personnel, money, and effort. Thus enhancing opportunities for credible work experience may be very beneficial for *some* offenders under certain conditions. These targeted interventions are more rational than wholesale prescription of the same medicine for all. In a related vein, we need to develop meaningful criteria to determine the effectiveness of prison labor programs, and these criteria must be rationally related to a set of ordered objectives for prison work.

In summary, the renewed attention to the problem of prison labor holds promise for reducing the debilitating effects of idleness, providing meaningful ways to do time, and accomplishing many other beneficial objectives for offenders, the correctional system, and society. Improvement of prison work programs is not a panacea for all the problems of prisons, however, so efforts to reform prison work should proceed with a firm understanding of the mistakes of the past, the limitations of the present, and reasonable expectations for the future.

9. REFERENCES

American Correctional Association. *Public policy for corrections: A handbook for decision-makers.* College Park, MD: American Correctional Association, 1986a.

American Correctional Association. *A study of prison industry: History, components, goals.* College Park, MD: American Correctional Association, 1986b.

Association of the Bar of the City of New York, Committee on Corrections. Can our prisons become factories with fences? *The Record of the Association of the Bar of the City of New York*, 1985, 40(4), 298–312.

Auerbach, Barbara. New prison industries legislation: The private sector reenters the field. *The Prison Journal*, 1982, *62*(2), 25–35.

Barnes, Harry Elmer, and Teeters, Negley K. *New horizons in criminology* (3rd ed.). Englewood Cliffs, NJ: Prentice-Hall, 1959.

Basinger, Aaron. Are prison work programs working? The impact of prison industry participation on recidivism rates in Ohio. Columbus, OH: Ohio State University School of Public Administration, 1985.

Burger, Warren E. More warehouses, or factories with fences? *New England Journal on Prison Law*, 1982, *8*(1), 111–121.

Calkins, Kathy. Time: perspectives, marking and styles of usage. *Social Problems* 1970, *17*(4), 487–501.

Coffey, Osa. T.I.E.: Integrating training, industry and education. *Journal of Correctional Education*, 1986, *37*(3), 104–108.

Conrad, John P. News of the future: Research and development in corrections. *Federal Probation*, 1986, *50*(3), 74–77.

Cullen, Francis, and Travis, Lawrence F. Work as an avenue for prison reform. *New England Journal on Criminal and Civil Confinement*, 1984, *10*(1), 45–64.

Flanagan, Timothy J, Thornberry T. P., Maguire, K. D., and McGarrell E. F. *The effect of prison industry employment on offender behavior: Final report of the Prison Industry Research Project*. Albany: Hindelang Criminal Justice Research Center, State University of New York at Albany, 1987.

Flynn, Frank. The federal government and the prison labor problem in the states, *Social Service Review*, 1951, 24(1 and 2), 19–40, 213–236.

Funke, Gail S., Wayson, Billy, and Miller, Neal. *Assets and liabilities of correctional industries*. Lexington, MA: D. C. Heath Company, 1982.

Gallup, George. *The Gallup Poll*. Princeton, NJ: The Gallup Poll, March 31, 1982.

Greiser, Robert C., Miller, Neal, and Funke, Gail S. *Guidelines for prison industries*. Washington, DC: National Institute of Corrections, 1984.

Guynes, Randall, and Greiser, Robert C. Contemporary prison industry goals. Chapter 2 in American Correctional Association, *A study of prison industry: History, components, goals*. College Park, MD: American Correctional Association, 1986.

Hawkins, Gordon. Prison labor and prison industries. In Michael Tonry and Norval Morris (Eds.), *Crime and justice: An annual review of research* (Vol. 5). Chicago: University of Chicago Press, 1983.

Johnson, Candace M. *The effects of prison labor programs on post-release employment and recidivism*. Doctoral dissertation. Tallahassee, FL: Florida State University, 1984.

Legge, Karen. Work in prison: The process of inversion. *British Journal of Criminology*, 1978, *18*(1): 6–22.

Lipton, Douglas, Martinson, Robert, and Wilks, Judith. *The effectiveness of correctional treatment*. New York: Praeger, 1975.

McKelvey, Blake. *American prisons: A study in American social history prior to 1915*. Montclair, NJ: Patterson Smith Publishing Co., 1972, original copyright 1936 by the University of Chicago Press.

New York State Assembly Standing Committees on Codes and Government Operations. *Joint Public Hearings on Correctional Industries*. Albany, NY: New York State Assembly, 1985.

Rennie, Ysabel. *The search for criminal man: A conceptual history of the dangerous offender*. Lexington, MA: Lexington Books, D. C. Heath Company, 1978.

Rothman, David. *The discovery of the asylum: Social order and disorder in the new republic*. Boston: Little Brown, 1971.

Schaller, Jack. Normalizing the prison work environment. In D. Fogel and J. Hudson (Eds.), *Justice as fairness: Perspectives on the justice model*. Cincinnati: Anderson, 1981.

Schaller, Jack. Work and imprisonment: An overview of the changing role of prison labor in American prisons. *The Prison Journal*, 1982, *62*(3), 3–12.

Sexton, George. The industrial prison: A concept paper. *The Prison Journal*, 1982, *62*(2), 12–24.

U.S. Department of Justice, Federal Prison System. Inmate employment record in Unicor. *Monday Morning Highlights*, September 28, 1987, p. 2.

U.S. Department of Justice, National Institute of Law Enforcement and Criminal Justice. *Study of the economic and rehabilitative aspects of prison industry, analysis of prison industries and recommendations for change*. Washington, DC: U.S. Government Printing Office, 1978.

U.S. Department of Justice, National Institute of Justice. *Private sector involvement in prison-based businesses: A national assessment*. Washington, DC: U.S. Government Printing Office, 1985.

U.S. General Accounting Office. *Improved prison work programs will benefit correctional institutions and inmates*. Report to the Attorney General, GAO/GGD-82-37. Washington, DC: U.S. General Accounting Office, 1982.

U.S. House of Representatives Industrial Commission. *Prison labor*. Washington, DC: 56th Cong., 1st sess., Doc. 476, 1900.

Utah Governor's Task Force on Correctional Industries. *The challenge of correctional industries*. Salt Lake City: State of Utah, 1984.

Chapter 9

PRISON CLASSIFICATION
The Management and Psychological Perspectives

DORIS LAYTON MacKENZIE

1. INTRODUCTION

The recent change in correctional theory and practice has been argued to represent a revolutionary-type paradigm shift (Kuhn, 1962; Mac-Kenzie, Posey, and Rapaport, 1988). As has happened in all areas of corrections, this philosophical change has had an impact on correctional classification. Historically, prison classification has moved from merely separating types of offenders to complex, empirically derived systems focusing on a variety of issues.[1] Risk predictions, needs assessments, etiologies of criminal behavior, and optimizing treatment are just some of the goals of recently developed classification systems. This diversity in the goals of prison classification may be indicative of the paradigm shift.

Although there are diverse goals of classification, a review of the

---

[1] This chapter examines prison classification for males. Classification for female prisoners is very different. The interested reader should see *Female classification: An examination of the issues*, 1984 (College Park, MD: American Correctional Association) for information on the classification of female prisoners.

DORIS LAYTON MacKENZIE • Louisiana State University, Baton Rouge, Louisiana 70803, and National Institute of Justice, U.S. Department of Justice, 633 Indiana Avenue NW, Washington, DC 20531.

historical development of prison classification for males makes it obvious that classification research, theory, and practice have recently been developing from two perspectives: management and psychological. Work from these two perspectives has been progressing in parallel with little exchange of information. Whole journals devoted to one perspective hardly allude to the other perspective (e.g., see *Crime and Delinquency*, Vol. 32, 1986).

The management perspective is a relatively new perspective in classification. It emphasizes the use of objective prison classification systems as a management tool. These systems are designed to increase the equitability, consistency, and fairness of the treatment of inmates. Such "objective" classification systems are also expected to result in a reasonable distribution of resources. Evaluating risk is a high priority in these models. Litigation, disappointment in rehabilitation programs, the rise of the justice model, and problems related to overcrowding and disillusionment with "expert-based" systems are some of the major reasons for the increasing interest in management models.

With the present overcrowded prisons in the United States, most jurisdictions have felt the need to develop some type of objective classification system. The factors to determine placement or need vary, depending upon the purpose for which the system was designed. Decisions about which factors to include in the models are chosen based on either a consensus of correctional personnel or the factors' prediction ability. The majority of the objective systems in use today are based on consensus, and, depending upon the goal of the system, this may present some problems. Evaluations of management systems have focused on examining both the functioning and the validity of the systems. In the former, the focus is on the use of the system by the staff (e.g., the number of overrides), how the factors contribute to the final classification score, or if there is a change in overclassification. The validity of the system is examined by whether the factors used in the system actually do relate to escapes, aggression, misconducts, or other behavior the factors are thought to predict.

Classification systems from the psychological perspective developed out of the rehabilitation model of corrections. Emphasis is placed on treatment, prediction, and understanding the etiology of criminal behavior. Advanced statistical techniques have been used in the development of systems such as the MMPI-based classification of Megargee and his colleagues (Megargee and Bohn, 1979) and Quay's (1983) behavioral classification system. Other models such as the I-level classification systems are deduced from developmental theory.

Although both the management and the psychological perspectives agree that all prisoners are not alike, they put different issues in the forefront in designing classification systems. To reject either perspective at this point in time may be damaging to the progress of our understanding of criminal behavior, the protection of the public, our ability to successfully treat offenders and/or the realization of fair, consistent, and equitable treatment for inmates.

2. A HISTORICAL PERSPECTIVE

Classification within prisons in this country can be divided into three distinctly different phases: an early separation of types, a time of emphasis on rehabilitation, and a later period of diversity. Before the beginning of the penitentiary movement, in the late eighteenth century, prisons or jails were essentially warehouses. One of the goals of the penitentiary movement, led by the Quakers, was to begin more humane treatment for prisoners (Fox, 1982). A part of the movement involved the initiation of a rudimentary classification system (Hippchen, 1982; Flynn, 1982; Hippchen, Flynn, Owens, and Schnur, 1978; Tetters, 1955). The basis of this system was the separation of types of offenders. Women were separated from men, juveniles from adults, first offenders from hardened criminals, and the mentally ill and retarded from others.

The next major change in classification arose during the reformatory movement in the post-Civil War period in the United States (Clear and Cole, 1986). Prison classification in the early reformatory movement was the process of determining how "criminal" the offender was. An offender's initial level of immorality and deprivation was determined. Offenders could then "progress" to less restrictive programs as they proved themselves worthy, until eventually they were released. This emphasis on rehabilitation was further elaborated in the progressive era beginning in the early twentieth century (Clear and Cole, 1986). The goal of treatment programs was the identification of the problem and the treatment of the offender according to his or her own individual needs. Classification was the process of deciding the offender's problem and the appropriate treatment.

2.1. The Medical Model and an Emphasis on Psychology

In the early twentieth century, reflecting the zeitgeist of the times, the philosophy of corrections emphasized the scientific study of people. The underlying concept of this "medical model" was that prisoners are sick. If treated appropriately, they could be "cured" or rehabilitated. The goal of corrections, then, was to "cure" the offender. This cure would differ depending upon the problem. Theoretically, classification took on a major role in the correctional system. The illnesses of offenders had to be diagnosed before they could be treated. Offenders were sent directly to reception and diagnostic centers where the process of classification (or diagnosis) could begin (Flynn, 1982; Fox, 1982). Once an offender's problems were diagnosed, he or she could be sent to the appropriate treatment program in an institution. Philosophically, classification became the keystone of the correctional process (Hippchen *et al.*, 1978). Appropriate treatment of the offender's problem was expected to flow naturally from the identification of the problem. Thus the diagnostic function of classification took priority.

Professional staff located at classification centers were responsible for the diagnosis. Interest in the etiology or cause of the individual's problem and treatment for the antisocial behavior were combined. That is, the diagnosis was assumed to depend upon an understanding of the cause of the sickness, the antisocial behavior. Thus appropriate diagnosis and treatment depended upon understanding the cause. Causal analyses almost totally focused on the intrapsychic problems of offenders (Flynn, 1982). Classification systems followed the same pattern by combining causal taxonomies with a focus on intrapsychic problems. It was assumed that successful treatment of the offender required an extensive modification of attitudes and changes in the basic faulty personality structures (Hippchen *et al.*, 1978).

The formalized classification process that was most practical and efficient was debated. Early large classification committees made up of various prison officials gradually gave way to smaller and more professional classification teams (Fox, 1972). The early emphasis on diagnosis gave way to an increased emphasis on the treatment program.

2.2. A Theoretical Revolution in Corrections

In the last decade, there have been major changes in classification and its use in prisons. These changes have been attributed to various influences. One of the first changes to occur was a move away from the psychological treatment model of rehabilitation to a reintegration model. Rather than treating the offender within the prison wall, the reintegration philosophy emphasized the importance of adjustment in the community. The risk assessment role of classification took on increased importance as these programs placed the inmate in the community and thereby increased the danger to the public.

Other changes quickly followed this new reintegration philosophy, and the result was what might most aptly be called a period of diversity in classification. Whether this represents a continuing diversity in methods and purposes of classification or a type of "paradigmatic revolution" a la Kuhn (1962) is unclear. On the one hand, classification activities are presently being used for such diverse purposes that we might expect each to continue to develop and be important for the specific purpose for which the system was developed. On the other hand, a quick examination of the recent past of correctional philosophy suggests that there may have been a period of "normal science" when the medical model of treatment was almost universally accepted. This normal science period may have given way to a scientific revolution. A revolution such as this is characterized by various competing theories, but there is no one accepted and agreed-upon paradigm. Correctional theory may now be in a stage of revolution, and the diversity in classification may reflect these competing paradigms (cf. Cullen and Gilbert, 1985).

2.3. Diversity in Classification

Institutional classification today is asked to fulfill numerous purposes, purposes as varied as protection of the public, inmates, and staff; assessing inmate needs; matching inmates with appropriate programs; determining efficient resource allocation; management planning; protection from liability; predicting inmate adjustment; maintaining institution order; reducing discipline problems; and equitable, fair, and consistent treatment of inmates (Brennan, 1987a). An understanding of a classification system must begin with an examination of the purpose for which it was designed, and the purpose is determined by theory or philosophy (Alexander, 1986; Brennen, 1987b). Thus one reason for the numerous purposes of classification today is the diversity in correctional philosophy. For example, disappointment in rehabilitation and retribution and incapacitation as goals of corrections appear to have led to classification models emphasizing management issues such as maintaining order, financial planning, and resource allocation.

Systems emphasizing equity, fairness, and consistency appear to have been developed in response to the rise of the justice model and recent federal court orders and consent decrees. A consequence of overcrowding and limited resources in many prison systems has been litigation that challenged classification procedures (Austin, 1983; Clements, 1981, 1985). The courts emphasized the need for inmates to be treated in a humane, fair and equitable manner (National Institute of Corrections [NIC], 1982). Traditional classification systems were found to be capricious, irrational, or discriminatory.

There are, however, other reasons that have been proposed to explain changes in classification. For one, overcrowding in prison has meant shrinking resources (Clements, 1982; Toch, 1981). There is no longer time for the luxury of intensive interviews and in-depth analysis of an inmate's behavior and personality. Even if there is time for such lengthy examinations of individual inmates, there are seldom sufficient programs or facilities available once the desired program is identified.

Instead, in many of the new classification systems, custody and security decisions are emphasized. The pressure on the line staff is such that they must make fast and efficient decisions with limited information.

Another reason for the change in classification systems used in prisons appears to be disappointment with the prior systems (Toch, 1981). Frequently classification systems were "expert-based." That is the classification experts were the only ones who could interpret the system used. The resulting classification did little to enlighten others as to what kind of person might be expected nor how the person might respond to various environments. The systems appeared to be "privileged files guarded by oracles waving the flag of confidentiality" (Toch, 1981). Little wonder that once the person was given the proper label, the label was virtually ignored by those who matter—the inmate and the staff.

Although the purposes of prison classification systems vary, most of the research and development work today is subsumed by one of two classes of models: psychological-based models and management models. Models based on psychology, often called classification for treatment models, grew out of the rehabilitation emphasis in corrections. The second, a relatively newer line of work, focuses on management issues within the prison.

3. THE MANAGEMENT PERSPECTIVE

Overcrowded prisons, new philosophies and goals of corrections, disappointment with earlier systems, and litigation are some of the influences that have led to the need for new classifications models. In these new generation models or as they are frequently called, objective classification models, classification is viewed as a management tool. Although the definition of "objective classification models" varies somewhat, most definitions refer to systems that employ standardized decision-making criteria to determine inmate placement in facilities, housing, and programs (see Clements, 1981, for a good review of standards and guidelines for classifications systems). The importance of using valid and reliable instruments is emphasized. Usually these systems incorporate risk assessment instruments to determine security (architectural constraints) and custody (supervision) and various scales to assess inmate needs. The expectation is that the system can be used to classify almost all offenders with few overrides and that the decisions are explicit and understood by both staff and offenders.

3.1. The Process

Today classification in most prison systems begins at reception and diagnostic centers where inmates first undergo a series of evaluations at initial classification. These centers typically identify immediate, critical problems and needs and second, provide summary reports of more intense evaluations. Theoretically objective systems include methods of summarizing the most pertinent information so that it can be forwarded with the inmate and used by classification staff to make decisions in the future.

An important decision made at this stage is the determination of the appropriate security level for the inmates. Security refers to the type of barriers that separate an inmate from the community (Levenson and Williams, 1979). This includes such features as perimeter barriers (e.g., razor wire), detection devices (e.g., TV cameras), and gun towers. The models distinguish between security and custody. Security is considered to relate to architectural features that are apt to reduce escapes. These decisions can be thought of as system-level choices, involving selection of the institution to which to send an inmate. In contrast, custody refers to the degree of surveillance of the offender. It is related to factors such as movement for meals or during the day, or leaving institutional grounds.

Internal classification, the next stage of classification, focuses on (1) the degree of supervision required by the inmate—the custody level, and (2) the type of programs or work assignment the inmate requires—the needs assessment. This stage occurs within the institution or program to which the inmate has been sent. Using the summary form from the original assessment and new assessments if necessary, classification offenders must decide upon which housing, work assignments, and programs incoming inmates will be assigned.

On the practical level, there are many problems that prohibit easy and efficient decision making throughout this process. One of the primary problems is the flow of information. If the initial assessment of the inmate's risk and needs are not explicit and understandable in the initial summary, staff at future locations must reevaluate inmates. This is both costly and time consuming.

The review and monitoring of an inmate's progress is done through reclassification. This adds a dynamic component to the process. The inmate is evaluated for appropriate changes in custody, security, or needs. At reclassification, behavior in the institution begins to be weighted more heavily in the decision-making process. Frequently, the inmate's custody levels are changed based on institutional behavior (Baird and Austin, 1985).

3.2. Use of Objective Systems

Many correctional systems have developed or are developing objective systems. In a recent national survey of state correctional systems, the District of Columbia and the Federal Prison System, 39 jurisdictions reported the use of some type of objective system (Buchanan, Whitlow, and Austin, 1986). The most frequently used objective system models were the NIC Custody Determination Model (11 jurisdictions); the Federal Prison System Security Determination/Custody System (9 jurisdictions); the Correctional Classification Profile (5 jurisdictions); the Florida Department of Corrections Decision Tree Approach (3 jurisdictions including Florida). The remaining five jurisdictions reported using a model original to their system (Buchanan, 1986; see also NIC, 1982).

3.3. Custody and Security Decisions

3.3.1. Objectivity and Choice of Factors

Objectivity in the objective classification systems can be defined in two ways. One meaning seems to refer to the ability of these systems to reflect the actual or real situation, not just the mind of the classifier. This definition refers to whether the system is valid or truly reflects the real world. From this perspective, interest focuses on whether an inmate classified into maximum security really is a threat to the public. A second meaning of the term *objective* refers to whether the system is unbiased, detached, or impersonal. The issue from this perspective is whether the system is explicit, understandable, and consistent in contrast to decisions that are individualistic and vary from classifier to classifier.

The factors used in the various objective classification systems vary greatly. Listed in Table 1 are some of the initial classification factors used in one or more of the following objective classification models: NIC model; Federal Prison System; Correctional Classification Profile; Illinois; Florida; California; and Wisconsin. Almost all of the models use escape history, detainers, prior commitments, criminal history, prior institutional adjustment, extent of violence in the current offense, and length of sentence (Buchanan *et al.,* 1986; Buchanan, 1986; NIC, 1982). At reclassification, there is an emphasis on behavior in the institution. Most systems consider major disciplinary violations, time to release, institutional adjustment, program participation, and time in the present security/custody level as important to consider during reclassification.

3.3.2. Developing the Model

Two methods of choosing the factors to be used in objective systems are (1) consensus, and (2) prediction. Consensus models use criteria based on what staff believe to be important in decisions. Most of the jurisdictions responding to the Buchanan (1986) survey reported using

TABLE 1. Factors Used in One or More of the Prison Classification Models
in Use Today

Current offense	
Length of sentence[a]	Weapon used
Expected time served	Nature of sexual offense
Seriousness of offense	Type of offense
Violence of offense[a]	Type of sentence
Detainers and warrants[a]	
Type of detainer	
Criminal record	
Prior escapes[a]	Prior assaultive offenses
Prior juvenile incarcerations[a]	Severity of prior offenses
Prior adult incarcerations[a]	Prior burglary/theft
Prior convictions	
Previous correctional behavior[a]	
Negative/positive institutional behavior	
Negative performance on community supervision	
Social factors	
Age	Military record
Education	Alcohol/drug abuse
Employment	History of violence
Marital status	
Overrides	

[a] Considered important in most systems.

consensus methods. Systems developed through consensus attempt to model the behavior of staff in making decisions. What had previously been tacit is now made explicit. Staff are asked to report how they make decisions, and these choices are included in the model. Frequently this is done by asking the staff to rank a large number of items in terms of their importance in the classification process. The items with the highest rankings are incorporated into the system.

The second type of objective system is developed through use of statistical tests predicting future behavior. These models, called *prescriptive* by Rans (1982), seek to improve upon traditional practices by validating new criteria using empirical data. This is the preferred method; however, a base of pertinent, valid, and reliable data is needed. This is seldom available.

Once criterion variables are identified, using either consensus or prediction, a decision is made as to how each variable will be weighted, and each inmate is given a total score. In some models, the weights are summed (additive), in others, points are assigned at a final node in a decision tree, and in still others a profile identifies the score (Buchanan, 1986; Buchanan *et al.*, 1986; Clements, 1986; NIC, 1982). In some models, multivariate statistical techniques have been used to help determine the weights (Brennan, 1987a; Glaser, 1987). Once the inmate is given a score, the score is compared to a scale to identify the appropriate security, custody, or need designation. There are large variances in the factors (number and type) and the weighting of the factors from system to system.

3.3.3. Evaluating the System

One of the first things that must be done in evaluating a classification system, or any system for that matter, is to identify the goals or purposes of the system. If the goal is consistency, equality, and explicitness, then consensus-based systems that are essentially descriptive may be adequate (Alexander, 1986; Clements, 1982; Rans, 1982). However, if prediction is an important element in the system, as it often is, then a system based on consensus is no guarantee of improvement over subjective systems. Thus consensus-developed models can meet the criterion of being without bias or prejudice toward the inmate but may not meet the criterion of being valid predictors.

Several benefits accrue from using consensus to build the objective system. First, because the system uses the staff's own criteria, the resulting system feels comfortable to the staff. Second, the system can be developed without an existing data base. The problem of course is that the criteria that the staff use to make decisions can be faulty in terms of the goals of the system; if consensus is the basis of the model, the decisions will also be in error. In the words of Clements (1982), we have "a more explicit version of the same questionable assumptions" (p. 77). One way this has been remedied is to develop the system using the consensus method and then to carefully evaluate the system as it operates. The benefits are that a data base is built while the system is operating and the criteria used in the system can be evaluated.

Austin (1986) proposes a method of examining classification systems using statistical analysis to identify what factors are having the most influence on the scoring. Many jurisdictions adopt systems developed elsewhere, and the choice of factors and also the weights are often chosen through consensus. Thus there may be a lack of knowledge of how the system operates in actual practice. In examining the California system, Austin (1986) found inmates' initial classification scores were almost totally determined by the sentence-length item. Yet scores had been thought to be based on a summation process using 24 variables. In another study, comparing three different models on one set of data, Austin (1983) found a wide variance in the contribution of different items. These results point out the necessity of examining the actual functioning of objective systems in the environment in which they will be used.

Another evaluation issue involves the process of classification or how the system is used by the staff. For example, if inmates are not actually placed in the security location identified as appropriate by the classification system, then changes in the number of escapes or violent episodes can hardly be attributed to the classification system. One way the classification process has been examined is through the number of overrides that occur in the system. There may be various causes for overrides. Crowding may prohibit placement according to classification level (Clements, 1982), or staff may be uncomfortable with the system. In any case, substantial overrides essentially negate any conclusions that can be drawn about the functioning of the classification system. Research examining the number of overrides suggests that this can be a substantial problem in evaluating the functioning of objective systems (Austin, 1986). In some cases, as many as 50% of the classification scores were overridden (Buchanan et al., 1986).

3.3.4. Overclassification

The primary reasons given by the jurisdictions surveyed by Buchanan, et al. (1986) for developing objective systems were, first, perceived overclassification by staff and, second, litigation by the courts. In the overcrowded prisons of today, overclassification has important consequences for management (NIC, 1982). Primarily, it is an issue of resource allocation. Overclassification is costly. The higher the level of security and custody the larger the cost of keeping an inmate. Not only is overclassification a problem in terms of cost-effectiveness, but also it is generally accepted that fairness to inmates requires classification at the least restrictive level possible, considering the safety of inmates, staff, and public (Clements, 1981, 1982).

In order to examine what would happen if a correctional department adopted one of three commonly used objective systems, Austin (1983) ran simulations using data from Nevada's correctional system. He found that use of any one of the systems had a substantial impact on the numbers of inmates classified at various security or custody levels. The shift was in the direction of designating an increased percentage of the population in lower security levels. For example, 19% of Nevada's inmate population was originally classified as maximum/close security, whereas use of the NIC classification model reduced this percentage to 2.1. In addition, the 13.5% classified by Nevada into minimum security changed to 56.6% when the NIC model was used. Similar results have been found in other state correctional systems (Buchanan, 1986) and in the Federal Prison System (Levinson, 1980).

There are at least two ways that objective systems are thought to have an impact on overclassification. First is in regard to responsibility for decision making (Alexander, 1986). In subjective systems, classification officers were expected to make decisions about inmate placement, and they also had to take responsibility for the results of their decisions. This was essentially a no-win game for the classifier. A reduction in custody or security meant increasing the danger to colleagues; a failure to reduce the classification status meant pressure from the administration. In contrast, objective systems give definite criteria to be used in decision making. If the system is accepted by the administration, the classification officer can made decisions in terms of the criteria. It can be assumed by the officer that the administration accepts these criteria. Thus, in a sense, the administration accepts more of the responsibility for decisions. Overrides are almost always available for protection; however, if the classification officers follow the standard procedure of classification, they can argue that this was appropriate should problems arise later.

The second way objective systems are expected to reduce overclassification is to improve decision making so that each inmate can be placed at the appropriate security and custody level. From this perspective, it is assumed that the instruments used in objective systems can reliably and validly identify who will be less "risky" to place in less secure facilities.

3.3.5. Validity and Risk Assessment[2]

Examinations of the validity of objective systems have focused on three issues: (1) Do the items predict the incidents they are expected to predict? (2) Do the total scores predict the incidents they are expected to predict? and (3) Are there system-level changes in incidents in the expected direction when the new objective systems are introduced? Examinations of the ability of items to predict incidents resulting in misconducts have found only moderate correlations between the items and misconducts (Baird and Austin, 1985; Buchanan et al., 1986), which is in agreement with other studies examining correlations of such items

---

[2] Assessing risk in release decision making will not be discussed here because the focus of this chapter is on classification within prisons. There is a large body of work on risk assessment in parole decisions that the interested reader should pursue (Gottfredson and Gottfredson, 1986). Some of this work is relevant to prison classification, particularly decisions in regard to work release programs, furloughs, and the like.

with institutional disciplinary adjustment (Chapman and Alexander, 1981). Buchanan *et al.* (1986) did find some evidence that total system scores divided inmates in terms of the number of misconducts. However, overall there appears to be a large difference in correctional systems in the predictive power of the total scores.

The third method of examining how well the classification system is working is to examine the number of incidents that occur over time using a quasi-experimental design. If serious incidents are found to decline when the classification system is introduced, it might be concluded that the system is the cause of the reduction in incidents. Studies of different correctional jurisdictions using various objective systems have produced mixed results. In two of the three jurisdictions examined by Buchanan *et al.* (1986), there were increases in incidents after the new system was introduced; in the third jurisdiction there was a sharp decline in incidents. In his study of the Federal Prison System, Levinson (1980) found no significant increase in assaults and escapes when security levels were substantially reduced with a new classification system.

It is generally accepted that objectivity in decision making can reduce risks in comparison to subjective decision making. The problem now is to determine what objective system works, how to choose items, and how to determine total scores. The instability of the items, low accuracy, the base rate problem, and the interaction of factors combine to make risk assessment a statistical challenge (Brennan, 1987a; Glasser, 1987).

3.3.6. Matching Inmates with Capabilities

An important element in security decisions is the matching of the security needs of the offender with the security levels of facilities in the system. In order to make this match, a method is needed to rate the security needs of the offender. And recently, researchers have noted the importance of also objectively rating facilities for security, if successful matches are to be made (Levinson and Gerard, 1986). Although the majority of jurisdictions in the Buchanan *et al.* (1986) survey reported using some type of assessment of security, custody, and program capabilities, there is little standardization of this process (Levinson and Gerard, 1986). Often staff are unsure about what is available at other institutions (Buchanan and MacKenzie, 1987). The classification of institutions is an area where there has been little work and yet, as Levinson and Gerard point out, it matters little how well the inmates are classified if they are then placed in situations unrelated to their security needs. Sending inmates to facilities that are more secure than necessary wastes resources; sending inmates to facilities that are not secure enough endangers the public. Thus, the matching of inmates and institutions on security level and objective methods of measuring both is an important topic for future researchers.

3.4. Needs Assessment

The third area of assessment in objective systems focuses on examining the needs of the inmate. The needs assessed usually fall in one of three categories: critical needs; needs related to a pattern of criminal behavior or possible difficulties at release; and needs related to management and adjustment in prison (Clements, 1986). Critical needs are those that require immediate attention such as health, mental health, and protection. These are the needs that have had the most legal attention. Examples of needs related to adjustment to the outside and criminal behavior are academic skills, intellectual functioning, substance abuse, job skills, personal-social skills (money management, leisure time, hygiene, interpersonal skills), and vocational aptitude and interests. Management and adjustment needs overlap with the preceding, particularly in regard to protection, but also, adjustment factors might include the inmate's style of interacting with others and the type of supportive networks (family) available.

Needs are usually treated as multidimensional, in that different needs are evaluated and rated separately. In a national survey, Clements (1986) found most of the 33 jurisdictions responding assessed health, psychological/mental health, intellectual ability, and academic education. A fourth of the states did this in only a present/absent or yes/no fashion. Another 30% of the states assessed additional areas such as substance abuse and vocational aptitude. The rest of the states reported using these dimensions along with several more. There are large differences in how standardized the assessment instruments are. Systems also differ in the position of the needs assessment in comparison to the security and custody decisions. The early systems emphasized the latter. More recently, Correctional Services Group has developed an objective system using a profile (Correctional Classification Profile), which considers risks as dimensions integrated with assessment of needs (Buchanan and Irion, 1983). In this way, the needs of the inmates can be considered along with risk when a decision is made as to where to send the inmate.

4. THE PSYCHOLOGICAL PERSPECTIVE

All prisoners are not alike. Different methods are needed to deal effectively with various categories of offenders. This is true from both the management and the psychological perspectives. However, there are differences in the two perspectives. Some are a manner of degree, such as how important prediction is to the models or how strongly rehabilitation is stressed. Other differences between the perspectives are larger; for instance, the causes and etiology of criminal behavior are important aspects of the psychological models but are not addressed by the management models.

From the psychological point of view, the important differences among people are personality and behavior characteristics. Appropriate classification is assumed to lead to relevant treatment that, in turn, is expected to result in a reduction in criminal behavior. The classification system also is intended to identify a suitable method of handling an offender during confinement so that treatment is maximized and problems are minimized. That is, treatment with corrections can be maximized if the inmate is in an optimal situation given his or her characteristics. The optimal situation may be a preferred environment (Toch, 1979) or appropriate staff–inmate match.

There are two types of psychological models of classification in use in prison today: developmental models and problem-area models. These models differ in theory and also in the method of development. The developmental models have been designed in a theoretical fashion (MacKenzie and Rapaport, 1988). That is, development was initiated from a theoretical perspective, and from this theory deductions were made about what would be expected empirically. Most of the classification systems of this type in use in prisons today are based on the I-level theory developed by Warren and her colleagues (1971, 1983). In contrast, the empirical models begin with the data and develop a theory based on the structure of the data.[3] Two systems in use today were developed using empirical data: Quay's Behavioral Categories (Quay and Parsons, 1971; Quay, 1983) and Megargee and Bohn's MMPI types (1979).

There are several other classification models that have been developed and tested with offenders. For example, there are a group of models exemplified by Gibbon's role career typology and Clinard and Quinney's criminal behavior systems that are based on offense types. These are not discussed here for two reasons. First, they have seldom been used within prisons to classify offenders. Second, they have essentially been rejected by Gibbons (1988) because of the recent research demonstrating evidence of crime switching and variability in the social-psychological characteristics of offenders.

---

[3] This distinction is similar to the heuristic and empirical distinction made by Magargee and Bohn (1979). We have difficulty with the term *heuristic* used in this manner.

Another group of models are presently being examined with offender populations. In particular, there is some interesting work examining typologies, using Kohlberg's stages of moral judgment (Kohlberg, 1966, 1969; Van Voorhis, 1984, 1986). Other work has focused on matching offenders and environments based on the conceptual level of the offender and the structure of the environment. This research makes use of the Conceptual Level Matching Model (Reitsma-Street, 1984) based on conceptual systems theory (Harvey, Hunt, and Schroder, 1961). However, there has been limited research with adult offender populations using moral judgment scales or conceptual-level matching, and also, these typologies have seldom been used in an applied setting. For these reasons, this work will not be reviewed further.

4.1. Developmental Models

4.1.1. I-Level Models

The integration level or I-level work began as a general theory of personality development combining aspects of developmental, psychoanalytic, Lewinian, phenomenological psychology, and social perception theories (Sullivan, Grant, and Grant, 1957; Warren, 1976). Originally it was a theory of normal personality development emphasizing interpersonal interaction. According to this theory, individuals are thought to pass through progressive stages as they mature. Each stage entails increased complexity in interacting with other people, environments, and events.

There are seven stages of I-levels in the theory. The stages represent increasing levels of perceptual complexity and interpersonal maturity. Stage 1 represents the least mature, the stage of the newborn infant. Stage 7 is the most mature and is seldom reached. Critical problems must be confronted and mastered at each level before the person can progress to the next level.

Most delinquents test at I-levels 2 through 4, few test beyond level 5. Level 2 represents a stage typical of very young children; at this stage the person focuses on his or her own needs. Other people are judged only in regard to gratification of one's needs. In contrast, youths at Level 3 are interested in power issues. They view rules as rigid and absolute. Upon reaching Level 4 an individual has internalized values. They become aware of what others expect. Level-5 individuals are less rigid in the application of rules to self and others. They can take viewpoints different from their own, and they understand different perspectives. Few offenders reach this stage of development. Continued development through Levels 6 and 7 involve increasing perceptual complexity and understanding (see Harris, 1983; Sechrest, 1987).

Within each stage, different subtypes have been identified. These are not developmental but instead represent patterns of adaptations. The subtypes have been labeled for the delinquent types at each level. For example, at Level 2 there are two subtypes: *asocial passive* and *asocial aggressive*. At this level of development, the person responds in terms of one's own needs. Each subtype differs in how persons adapt. The asocial passive withdraws or complains; the asocial aggressive is aggressive. There are three level three subtypes: *immature conformists* who conform to whoever has power, *cultural conformists* who conform to their peer group, and *manipulators* who fight conformity with anyone. Level 4 subtypes are the *neurotic acting-out* who are internally conflicted and have a negative self-image; the *neurotic anxious* who have the same self-image problems but who respond with guilt and anxiety; the *cultural identifier* who has failed to internalize socially acceptable values; and *situation-emotional reactors* who are responding to a particularly stressful situation.

There are two methods of classifying offenders as to I-level. One, the standard method, is done through an intensive interview that takes approximately 90 minutes. The interview is done by trained interviewers using open-ended questions covering specific content areas. The interviews are taped and are then rated by a second trained observer. Classifications of both stage and subtype are based on the results of the ratings of both interviewers.

There have been two major complaints in regard to I-level. First is the cost. The training of the observers, the time taken for the interview, and the fact that an observer and another rater are necessary combine to make the evaluation extremely costly. Most likely, this would be prohibitive in many prison systems. The second criticism of I-level classification has been in regard to the reliability of the evaluation. The interview method is criticized as being subjective and, therefore, lacking in consistency. In response to these criticisms, proponents of I-level respond that the interview method has a variety of advantages, particularly in regard to a more complete understanding of the individual. It is also argued that the interview sets the state for a trusting relationship between the offender and the staff. The use of a second rater for each interview is an attempt to control for reliability.

4.1.2. The Jesness Inventory

A second method of measuring I-level, the Jesness Inventory (JI), is a paper-and-pencil test designed to solve the time and objectivity problems (Jesness, 1974, 1976; Jesness and Wedge, 1984). Additionally, Jesness and his colleagues have proposed alternative terminology to eliminate the strong maladaptive nomenclature of the previous labels for the subtypes at each developmental level. The system was originally designed for juveniles but was later modified for use with adults. There are 155 true-false items yielding age-normed T scores on 11 personality/attitude scales. The subtype is determined from these scores (Jesness and Wedge, 1985).[4]

Due most likely to criticisms of the interview methodology, I-level researchers have been concerned with the reliability of the classifications. Reviews of both the interview methods and the JI indicate fairly high reliability coefficients (Jesness, 1974, 1983; Jesness and Wedge, 1984; Palmer and Werner, 1972).

There are relatively few validity tests of I-level. Van Voorhis (1984) is presently examining I-level and comparing the levels to Hunt *et al.*'s (1978) Conceptual levels, Magargee and Bohn's (1979) MMPI-based system, Quay and Parsons' Taxonomies (1971), and Kohlberg's Stages of Moral Judgment (1969). I-level has been found to correlate moderately with age, and there are differences among subtypes in such factors as academic aptitude, demographic characteristics, and self-reported behavior (Jesness, 1983).

Research using I-level with correctional populations has focused mostly on delinquents. Proponents argue that its advantage is in the use of differential treatment and matching the staff with the offender. There is some evidence of success with differential treatment (Palmer, 1974). However, the situations have been limited, and a few subtypes seem to be sufficient for distinguishing treatment methods (Palmer, 1978, 1984; Sechrest, 1987).

The reasons for the failures when matching I-level and treatment have been attributed to two possible causes. First, it may be that the treatment was "weak" and therefore had little effect on the inmate (Sechrest and Redner, 1979). Or second, as Sechrest argues, it may be a problem with specification of what is expected for the different subtypes and I-levels (Sechrest, 1987). From this perspective, there need to be clear hypotheses about what matches should optimize treatment and what results are expected (MacKenzie, Posey, and Rapaport, 1988). For example, it might be expected that juveniles would benefit from treatment that is designed to enable them to move to a higher I-level. They might not be expected to have reached their highest level of maturity and complexity. Therefore such treatment programs would help them to move to higher levels. On the other hand, adult offenders might be thought to have reached a plateau in their development. In such cases,

---

[4] The most recent editions of the JI do not classify the I-level stage, and this has led to criticism from proponents of the original I-level classifications using interview methods.

rehabilitation might be best if directed at methods of helping them to adjust at their current level of development. Overall, the results of the I-level classification appear to be promising for the development of a theory for understanding some criminal behavior, but at this point the evidence in support of differential treatment and staff–offender matching is not strong (Sechrest, 1987).

4.2. Problem-Area Models

The second area of focus within the psychological perspective is what might be called problem-oriented. These models are based on problem areas or the lack thereof. The two models representing this orientation that are being used in prisons today are Quay's behavioral categories and Megargee and Bohn's MMPI-based classification.

4.2.1. MMPI-Based Model

The MMPI is one of the psychological tests most frequently used in corrections. It contains 566 items in a true–false format. Originally it was designed to diagnose psychopathology in psychiatric settings. The items form 14 scales: 10 measure different personality dimensions (hypochondriasis, depression, hysteria, psychopathic deviate, masculinity–femininity, paranoia, psychasthenia, schizophrenia, hypomania, social introversion), and 4 are included for validity purposes (cannot say, lie, frequency or infrequency, and correction). The rationale of the test is that an individual who answers the test items similar to someone who is in a clinical population (e.g., depression) will most likely have other behavioral characteristics similar to the clinical population. For example, if someone responds with strongly depressive responses, it is assumed that the person will act like a depressed person in other aspects of his or her life. Magargee and his colleagues used the profiles of the 10 scales to develop the classification system. The researchers argued that the MMPI was an excellent measurement because there is a uniform data base, it is widely used in prisons, it is easy to quantify, the data is collected in an objective format, it has been used with adults, and it can easily be readministered to examine changes over time (Megargee and Bohn, 1979).

The classification system was developed empirically based on the profiles of scores from the 10 scales. A set of essential and accessory rules is used to identify the group to which a profile belongs. In order to insure that the groups were determined by the empirical data not by subjective identification of types, the groups were given neutral alphabetical names.

Once the groups were empirically determined, they were compared on a large variety of behavioral and psychological characteristics. The groups were found to differ on a large number of these variables.

Examinations of the interrater reliability of the classification of different profiles indicated fairly high agreement (Carey, Garske, and Ginsberg, 1986; Zager and Megargee, 1988). There are mixed test–retest reliability results and some uncertainty about what conclusions to draw from these results. There have been a series of studies examining test–retest reliability (Johnson, Simmons, and Gordon, 1983), but in a review of these studies, Zager (1983) rejects the conclusions of most of the studies due to methodological flaws. However, there is some question of how consistent the results should be over time. On the one hand, the system was expected to be dynamic and to be sensitive to changes occurring with the passage of time. On the other hand, too frequent changes lead to questions as to the consistency of the measures.

Another issue that has been studied in regard to the MMPI-based system is whether the system can be empirically replicated with other groups (Zager, 1988). Again this presents a dilemma. If the groups can be assumed to be similar to the original group, then replication would be expected. However, there is little in the way of theory to tell researchers what to expect with different groups. For example should women fall into the same 10 groups, or would a classification system for them look very different.

Investigations of the ability of the MMPI-based system to predict future behavior have produced mixed results. Some have found the system valuable in reducing institutional violence (Bohn, 1979); others conclude that the system is not highly predictive of adjustment in a prison setting (Hanson, Moss, Hosford, and Johnson, 1983). The results of an exploratory study by Wright (1986) suggest that prison adjustment, including aggression, may be reduced if matches are made between MMPI types and characteristics of the environment.

4.2.2. Quay's Behavioral Categories

The second problem-based model was also developed through empirical methods. Originally, the Quay system was developed for juveniles using a self-report questionnaire. It is based on early work by Jenkins, which was extended by Quay and his colleagues (Quay and Parsons, 1971). More recently, Quay has developed the Adult Internal Management System (AIMS) to be used to classify adults (Quay, 1983; Levinson, 1988). In this system, five different types of individuals were identified through the use of factor-analysis techniques: the aggressive psychopath, the manipulator, situational, inadequate-withdrawn, neurotic-anxious.

Individuals are classified using checklists completed by institutional staff. Two checklists are used: the Correctional Adjustment Checklist and the Correctional Adjustment Life History. The former is completed by a trained correctional officer after there has been sufficient time to observe a newly admitted offender. The life history checklist is completed by a caseworker who makes use of the presentence report, interviews with the offender, and any available record data.

The Quay system was developed using a large number of items reflecting past history information and present behavior. It is the most behavioral-type scale of the psychological classification systems. Theoretically, it is dynamic in that the behaviors in the checklist would be assumed to vary over time. The life history variables would not be expected to change. Examination of the construct validity by Quay (1983) indicated that the groups differ on external criteria such as age, race, academic achievement, income, and criminal justice experience.

Levinson (1988) studied the Quay system in combination with unit management. Inmates were classified into three groups: the aggressive (aggressive psychopaths and manipulators), the situational or normals, and the weak (inadequate-withdrawn and neurotic-anxious). He found that use of unit management and the Quay classification in combination resulted in fewer problems in the institution. In this system, inmates were assigned to units based on their classification within the three groups. Each group spent most of their time together, at work and recreation, but no group was denied access to any programs.

One of the major criticisms of the Quay system is that it is costly in regard to staff training and administration time (Margargee and Bohn, 1979). The staff must learn how to complete the checklists. There also has to be sufficient time for the staff to get acquainted with an offender before the behavioral checklist can be completed. Additionally, the case history information must be available and of high quality if an analysis of the life history of the offender is to be made.

5. A COMPARISON

Psychological classification within objective systems is part of the needs assessment. Mental health is assessed as a critical need early during the evaluation process. Almost all jurisdictions responding to the Clements (1986) study said they performed mental health evaluations. However, many did this in a *yes* or *no* fashion, meaning that either the inmate was identified as needing immediate mental health attention or not. Thus, it appears that serious problems would be dealt with but not much would be offered in the line of counseling for those with less serious problems.

Classification for treatment from the management perspective is very different from what has traditionally been the realm of psychologists. Specialists in many fields (education, vocational education, social services) all are asked to evaluate the inmate. The emphasis is not helping the offender to adjust to prison or life on the outside but rather to identify specific targets for change.

It has been proposed that the change from rehabilitation models (psychology-based models) to needs assessment is partially a function of the change in the philosophy of corrections. The justice model moves offenders' problems and desires for self-improvement to the status of rights. Equity, consistency, and fairness may be primary goals of classification in the new models. Prediction is important in terms of dangerousness. From the psychological perspective, offenders differ in personal and behavioral characteristics, and these are precursors to dangerousness. In comparison to the management perspective, rehabilitation and treatment take priority in psychological classification models. The psychological approach focuses on understanding the causes and etiologies of criminal behaviors.

The major practical difference in the management and psychological perspectives occurs during internal classification. At this time, decisions must be made as to housing, programs, and work assignments. Management models are used to evaluate the inmate for custody and needs. In contrast, at internal classification (or earlier), psychological models are used to evaluate and classify the inmate in terms of personality/behavioral characteristics, and then placement decisions are made. Although at first this difference seems minor, a more complete examination of the difference makes it obvious that this difference carries large implications. How difficult it is to integrate the two perspectives is shown in a recent excellent book on needs assessment by Clements (1986). Psychological/mental health problems are examined as one of the needs of offenders. This is done from the perspective of a diagnostic procedure. Clements proposes that an adequate assessment should embrace more than just acute crises and that other needs, for example, counseling for sex offenders, should also be identified. Interestingly, no mention is made in this section of the psychology-based classification systems. The latter are mentioned only under recommendations to determine victimization potential. The original goals of the psychology-based systems appear to be wider than just victimization needs.

There has been some research that attempts to integrate the psychological and management perspectives (Hanson et al., 1983; Wright,

1986). Predicting recidivism has been shown to be successful using some of the probation and parole risk assessment instruments (Gendreau and Ross, 1987). These instruments have two components: static variables such as age and previous convictions and dynamic variables reflecting personal needs such as substance abuse or antisocial thinking. Many of these variables overlap with variables used in making custody and security decisions. Gendreau and Ross argue that the dynamic variables may represent constructive methods of developing treatment programs for these offenders. Thus by integrating the two lines of research, the success of risk assessment, although developed from the management perspective, may enable us to identify problem areas that can be addressed through treatment programs. They caution, however, that these programs must be developed with a knowledge of principles developed in previous treatment research. For example, some of the moral reasoning research has illustrated the need to intervene at the appropriate level of cognitive capacity if treatment programs are to be successful.

Objective classification systems used for management have many advantages, not the least of which is the method of development—consensus. This results in a system that appears to have face validity. Although staff must be trained in the use of the systems, they appear reasonable and, because they are frequently developed through consensus, they are comfortable to the staff. But is this initial infatuation with these systems based on our beliefs about what should be and not on what actually is? There are as yet a limited number of studies examining the reliability and validity of these systems. In contrast, the psychological systems have been examined much more thoroughly. It may not be that the new objective systems are more successful in fulfilling their goals but rather that the psychological systems have been studied enough for us to know where the "soft" spots are. Objective systems are new; overall there is no more evidence in support of their reliability and validity in comparison to psychological systems. Rather they may be less well tested.

Certainly on the positive side for the objective systems is the attempt to involve inmates and line staff in the classification decision making as has been advocated by Toch (1981). The attempt to develop a system that will result in equitable and consistent treatment for inmates is also a major advantage of these models from the perspective of fairness. The courts have emphasized the necessity of such systems if there is to be a fair allocation of resources.

An examination of needs assessment also suggests that these models may incorporate more of the theoretical perspective of sociologists. That is, in contrast to the individual-level and internal focus of the psychological models, these models appear to be compatible with a perspective emphasizing social problems such as lack of educational and employment opportunities.

There are many advantages to the objective systems. But do we want to drop the psychological perspective so quickly? The emphasis on rehabilitation seems important to most of us. However, the most important issue, and the reason we cannot drop the development of the psychological models, is that this perspective is directed to understanding criminal behavior and the etiology of such behavior. If we drop our interest in understanding and theory, where will we be 10 or 20 years from now? An even greater fear is that our work on theoretical issues will become separate from the prison environment. We will benefit most if we continue, as we have until recently, with our close interaction between practice and theory. Our recent "separate-but-equal" work threatens this closeness. Will the results be disastrous for one perspective? Are we experiencing a paradigm shift? Will the new paradigm in some sense incorporate the old? These are the questions that must be addressed in our future work in classification.

6. REFERENCES

Alexander, J. Classification objectives and practices. *Crime and Delinquency*, 1986, *32*, 323–338.

American Correctional Association. *Female classification: An examination of the issues.* College Park, MD: American Correctional Association.

Austin, J. Assessing the new generation of prison classification models. *Crime and Delinquency*, 1983, *29*, 561–576.

Austin, J. Evaluating how well your classification system is operating: A practical approach. *Crime and Delinquency*, 1986, *32*, 302–322.

Baird, C. S., and Austin, J. *Current state-of-the-art in prison classification models: A literature review for the California Department of Corrections.* San Francisco, CA: NCCD, 1985.

Bohn, M. J., Jr. Management classification for young adult inmates. *Federal Probation*, 1979, *43*, 53–59.

Brennan, T. Classification for control in jails and prisons. In D. M. Gottfredson and M. Tonry (Eds.), *Prediction and classification: Criminal justice decision making.* Chicago: The University of Chicago Press, 1987a.

Brennan, T. Classification: An overview of selected methodological issues. In D. M. Gottfredson and M. Tonry (Eds.), *Prediction and classification: Criminal justice decision making.* Chicago: The University of Chicago Press, 1987b.

Buchanan, R. *Evaluation of model prison classifications.* Kansas City, MO: Correctional Service Group, 1986.

Buchanan, R. A., and Irion, J. G. *The correctional classification profile.* Paper presented at the 113th Annual Congress of Correction of the American Correctional Association, 1983.

Buchanan, R., and MacKenzie, D. L. *An evaluation of classification in the Louisiana Department of Corrections.* Report to the Louisiana Department of Corrections, 1987.

Buchanan, R. A., Whitlow, K. L., and Austin, J. National evaluation of objective prison classification systems: The current state-of-the-art. *Crime and Delinquency*, 1986, *32*, 272–290.

Carey, R. J., and Garske, J. P., and Ginsberg, J. The prediction of adjustment to prison by means of an MMPI-based classification. *Criminal Justice and Behavior*, 1986, *13*, 347–365.

Chapman, W., and Alexander, J. *Adjustment to prison: A review of inmate characteristics associated with misconduct, victimization and self-injury in confinement*. Albany: New York State Department of Correctional Services, 1981.

Clear, T. R., and Cole, G. F. *American corrections*. Monterey, CA: Brooks/Cole Publishing Co., 1986.

Clements, C. B. The future of offender classification: Some cautions and prospects. *Criminal Justice and Behavior*, 1981, *8*, 15–38.

Clements, C. B. The relationship of offender classification to the problems of prison overcrowding. *Crime and Delinquency*, 1982, *28* 72–81.

Clements, C. B. Towards an objective approach to offender classification. *Law and Psychology Review*, 1985, *9*, 45–55.

Clements, C. B. *Offender needs assessment*. College Park, MD: American Correctional Association, 1986.

Cullen, F. T., and Gilbert, K. E. *Reaffirming rehabilitation*. Cincinnati: Anderson Publishing Co, 1985.

Flynn, E. E. Classification systems: Community and institutional. In L. J. Hippchen (Ed.), *Holistic approaches to offender rehabilitation*, Springfield, IL: Charles C Thomas, 1982.

Fox, V. B. *Introduction to corrections*. Englewood Cliffs, NJ: Prentice-Hall, Inc., 1972.

Fox, V. B. History of offender classification. In L. J. Hippchen (Ed.), *Holistic approaches to offender rehabilitation*. Springfield, IL: Charles C Thomas, 1982.

Gendreau, P., and Ross, R. Revivification of rehabilitation: Evidence from the 1980s. *Justice Quarterly*, 1987, *4*, 349–408.

Gibbons, D. C. Some critical observations on criminal types and criminal careers. *Criminal Justice Behavior*, 1988, *15*, 8–23.

Glaser, D. Classification for risk. In D. J. Gottfredson and M. Tonry (Eds.), *Prediction and classification: Criminal justice decision making*. Chicago: The University of Chicago Press, 1987.

Gottfredson, S. D., and Gottfredson, D. M. The accuracy of prediction models. In A. Blumstein, J. Cohen, J. A. Roth, and C. A. Visher (eds.), *Research in criminal careers and "career criminals."* Vol. 2. Washington, DC: National Academy Press, 1980.

Hanson, R. W., Moss, C. S., Hosford, R. E., and Johnson, M. E. Predicting inmate penitentiary adjustment. *Criminal Justice and Behavior*, 1983, *10*, 293–309.

Harris, P. W. The interpersonal maturity of delinquents and nondelinquents. In W. S. Laufer and J. M. Day (Eds.), *Personality, moral development and criminal behavior*. Lexington, MA: Lexington Books, 1983.

Harvey, O. J., Hunt, D. E., and Schroder, H. M. *Conceptual systems and personality organization*, New York: Wiley & Sons, Inc., 1961.

Hippchen, L. J. *Holistic approaches to offender rehabilitation*. Springfield, IL: Charles C Thomas, 1982.

Hippchen, L. J., Flynn, E. E., Owens, C. D., and Schnur, A. C. *Handbook on correctional classification*. Washington, DC: American Correctional Association, 1978.

Hunt, D. E., Butter, L. F., Noy, J. E., and Rosser, M. E. *Assessing conceptual level by the paragraph completion method*. Ontario: Ontario Institute for Studies in Education, 1978.

Jesness, C. F. *Classifying juvenile offenders: Sequential I-level classification manual*. Palo Alto, CA: Consulting Psychologists Press, 1974.

Jesness, C. F. *The Jesness Behavior Checklist*. Palo Alto, CA: Consulting Psychologists Press, 1976.

Jesness, C. F. *The Jesness Inventory* (rev. ed.). Palto Alto, CA: Consulting Psychologists Press, 1983.

Jesness, C. F., and Wedge, R. F. Validity of a revised Jesness inventory I-classification with delinquents. *Journal of Consulting and Clinical Psychology*, 1984, *52*, 997–1010.

Jesness, C. F., and Wedge, R. F. *Jesness Inventory Classification System: supplementary manual*. Palo Alto: Consulting Psychologists Press, 1985. Johnson, D. L., Simmons, J. G., and Gordon, B. C. Temporal consistency of the Meyer-Megargee inmate typology. *Criminal Justice and Behavior*, 1983, *10*, 263–268.

Kohlberg, L. Moral development in the schools: A developmental view. *School Review*, 1966, *74*, 1–30.

Kohlberg, L. State and sequence: The cognitive-developmental approach to socialization. In D. Goslin (Ed.), *Handbook of socialization theory and research*, Chicago: Rand McNally, 1969.

Kohlberg, L., Colby, C. A., Gibbs, J., Speicher-Dubin, B., and Candee, D. *Standard form scoring manual*. Cambridge: Harvard University, 1979.

Kuhn T. *The structure of scientific revolutions*. Chicago: University of Chicago Press, 1962.

Levinson, R. Research proposal: Internal management classification system. Washington, DC: Federal Bureau of Prisons, July 1980.

Levinson, R. Developments in the classification process. *Criminal Justice and Behavior*, 1988, *15*, 24–38.

Levinson, R. B., and Gerard, R. E. Classifying institutions. *Crime and Delinquency*, 1986, *32*, 291–301.

Levinson, R. B., and Williams, J. D. Inmate classification: Security/custody considerations. *Federal Probation Quarterly*, 1979, *43*, 37–43.

MacKenzie, D. L., Posey, D., and Rapaport, K. R. A theoretical revolution in corrections: Varied purposes for classification. *Criminal Justice and Behavior*, 1988, *15*, 125–136.

Megargee, E., and Bohn, M., Jr., with Meyer, J., Jr., and Sink, F. *Classifying criminal offenders: A new system based on the MMPI*. Beverly Hills, CA: Sage Publications, 1979.

National Institute of Corrections. *Prison classification: A model systems approach*. Washington, DC: National Institute of Justice, 1982.

Palmer, T. B. The youth authority's community treatment project. *Federal Probation*, 1974, *38*, 3–14.

Palmer, T. *Correctional intervention and research: Current issues and future prospects*. Lexington, MA: D. C. Heath, 1978.

Palmer, T. Treatment and the role of classification: A review of basics. *Crime and Delinquency*, 1984, *30*, 195–226.

Quay, H. C. *Technical manual for the behavioral classification system for adult offenders*. Washington, DC: U.S. Department of Justice, National Institute of Corrections, 1983.

Quay, H. C., and Parsons, L. B. *The differential behavioral classification of the juvenile offender*. Washington, DC: Federal Bureau of Prisons, 1971.

Rans, L. *Inmate classification design and validations study*. Springfield, IL: Illinois Department of Corrections, 1982.

Reitsma-Street, M. Differential treatment of young offenders: A review of the conceptual level matching model, *Canadian Journal of Criminology*, 1984, *26*(2), 199–212.

Sechrest, L. Classification for treatment. In D. M. Gottfredson and M. Tonry (Eds.), *Prediction and classification: Criminal justice decision making*. Chicago: The University of Chicago Press, 1987.

Sechrest, L., and Redner, R. Strength and integrity of treatments in evaluation studies. In *How well does it work?* Washington, DC: National Academy of Sciences, 1979.

Sullivan, C. E., Grant, J. D., and Grant, M. Q. The development of interpersonal maturity: Applications to delinquency. *Psychiatry*, 1957, *20*, 373–385.

Tetters, N. *The cradle of the Penitentiary*, Philadelphia: The Pennsylvania Prison Society, 1955.

Toch, H. *Living in prison: The ecology of survival*. New York:Free Press, 1979. Toch, H. Inmate classification as a transaction. *Criminal Justice and Behavior*, 1981, *8*, 3–14.

Van Voorhis, P. *Psychological classification of the adult, male, maximum security inmate: Applications of the MMPI, I-level, conceptual level and moral judgement*. Paper presented at Annual Meeting of the American Society of Criminology, Cincinnati, November 11, 1984.

Van Voorhis, P. A cross classification of five offender typologies: Results of the pilot study. *The Differential View (Proceedings).*, 1986, *15*, 126–127.

Warren, M. Q. Classification of offenders as an aid to efficient management and treatment. *Journal of Criminal Law, Criminology and Policy Science*, 1971, *62*, 239–258.

Warren, M. Q. Intervention with juvenile delinquents. In M. Rosenheim (Ed.), *Pursuing justice for the child*. Chicago: University of Chicago Press, 1976.

Warren, M. Q. Applications of interpersonal maturity theory to offender populations. In W. S. Laufer and J. M. Day (Eds.). *Personality theory, moral development, and criminal behavior*. Lexington, MA: Lexington Books, 1983.

Wright, K. N. An exploratory study of transactional classification. *Journal of Research in Crime and Delinquency*, 1986, *23*, 326–348.

Zager, L. D. Response to Simmons and associates: Conclusions about the MMPI-based classification system's stability are premature. *Criminal Justice and Behavior*, 1983, *10*, 310–315.

Zager, L. D. The MMPI-based criminal classification system: Do proposed subgroups of type "How" differ in their behavior? *Criminal Justice and Behavior*, 1988, *15*, 39–57.

Zager, L. D., and Megargee, E. I. The MMPI-based criminal classification system: A review, current status, and future directions. *Criminal Justice and Behavior* (in press).

Chapter 10

PRISON GUARDS AS AGENTS OF SOCIAL CONTROL

JOHN R. HEPBURN

The fundamental task of prison guards is to maintain control over prisoners, thereby assuring that the prison will operate in a smooth and orderly fashion. Their ability to do this depends on the types of control available within the prison and on their position within the control structure of prisons. We shall examine the control structures available to guards, recent trends in altering the tasks of the guards, and how these relate to the principal task of maintaining control over prisoners.

Although they now are frequently referred to as correctional officers, such job titles rarely reflect a substantive alteration in the duties of the traditional prison guard. Just as the conditions of confinement within the large, maximum security fortresses erected in the nineteenth century are unaffected by whether they are titled *prison, penitentiary,* or *correctional institution,* the duties and responsibilities of the line staff today are *primarily* those of rule enforcement and custody. These personnel are, then, guards—regardless of the rhetoric.

But is it possible to move beyond the narrow limitations of these duties and responsibilities and still maintain control over prisoners? It is apparent that prison guards must cope with an environment of uncertainty and dependency and that they rely on the control structure of the prison to maintain order. It also is apparent, however, that these conditions create great dissatisfaction among prison guards. Our pur-

JOHN R. HEPBURN • School of Justice Studies, Arizona State University, Tempe, Arizona 85287.

pose here is to review the issues involved in maintaining control within American prisons and to examine the feasibility that social control can be maintained, or even enhanced, by a broad redefinition of the duties of prison guards.

1. WORKING IN AN ENVIRONMENT OF UNCERTAINTY AND DEPENDENCY

With little preparation or training, guards find themselves in a precarious position within the prison organization. Immediately, they confront occupational problems for which there is no ready and standard solution. Together, these occupational problems create an environment of uncertainty and dependency.

Uncertainty arises from three major sources, one of which is the fact that guards and prisoners are in a relationship of *structured conflict* (Jacobs and Kraft, 1978). Prisoners do not want to be confined, obviously, and they have little interest in either the security goals of the institution or the welfare of the guards. Placed in an extremely subordinate position in these castelike organizations, prisoners are likely to challenge a guard's authority at any time, over any issue. Consequently, guards must enter any encounter with prisoners cautiously and be prepared to deal effectively with uncooperative and resistant prisoners.

The second, and related, source of uncertainty is *danger*. Prisons have a great potential for violence and physical harm, and guards working inside the prison are unarmed and greatly outnumbered by prisoners. The danger may be in the form of a direct attack on the guard by one emotionally disturbed or hostile prisoner, in the risks involved in breaking up a fight between prisoners, or in being taken hostage in an escape or a riot. The threat of harm to guards has become even more salient in recent years as the prisoner populations in most prisons have swelled dramatically and become increasingly comprised of younger and more violent persons. In fact, available data suggest that the incidence of assaults on prison guards has increased in recent years, as has the level of concern by guards with the dangerousness of the job (Crouch, 1980b; Fox, 1982; Lombardo, 1981a).

Third, uncertainty is a result of the *role ambiguity* or role strain that characterizes the guard's duties (Cressey, 1959, 1965; Johnson, 1987). One source of role ambiguity occurs when guards are expected to perform divergent roles, as when they are expected to serve both treatment and custodial needs simultaneously. Treatment goals call for personal relationships, discretionary rule enforcement, and helping behaviors, for example, whereas custody goals require impersonal relationships, full and uniform rule enforcement, and controlling behaviors. Another source of role ambiguity arises when the role itself contains vague or contradictory directives. Prison guards generally are expected to exercise professional judgment and flexibility in performing their job, yet they are subject to disciplinary action if they violate, or permit the prisoners to violate, the many official rules and procedures of the prison.

Dependency refers to the fact that prison guards are dependent on prisoners. The elements of uncertainty—especially the structured conflict and danger inherent in the job—create a working environment in which guards are dependent on prisoners for their own physical safety. In addition, however, dependency refers to the structural situation by which guards must depend on prisoners for the successful completion of their own duties. Forms of prisoner resistance to the guard's control, such as a work slowdown or an increase in disciplinary problems, call to the administration's attention the guard's inability to perform assigned duties and maintain control over prisoners.

The level of control over subordinates is important in any organization, but it acquires greater significance in prisons where, as Cressey (1965: 1024) observes, "Guards manage and are managed in organizations where management is an end, not a means." Guards are caught in the middle because their superiors, on whom guards are dependent for recognition and promotion, assess the guards' work performance on how well they manage prisoners, yet these superiors often fail to provide the guards with either adequate controls or clear rules for managing a resistant prisoner population. As a result, guards often find themselves in the position of depending on the cooperation of prisoners in order to satisfy their superiors and keep their jobs.

It is somewhat ironic that those who are asked to maintain order and predictability within the prison find themselves working from a position of uncertainty and dependency. Indeed, it is because guards must work in an environment of uncertainty and dependency that the formal and informal structures of control are so important.

2. THE FORMAL STRUCTURE OF SOCIAL CONTROL

Historically, the formal structure of social control within American prisons provided guards with a great deal of power over the prisoner population. Organizational control was so decentralized that prison guards were authorized to supervise prisoners, isolate troublemakers, and discipline deviants. The administrative structure required prisoners to rely heavily upon guards for recommendations to new work areas or housing units, for protection from other prisoners, for permission to move about from one area of the prison to another, and for assistance with everyday problems and complaints. In short, guards were granted the professional autonomy to intervene in a broad range of prisoner activities and to allocate privileges and sanctions.

2.1. Challenges to the Traditional Structure of Control

Several events have changed the formal structure of control in the last 20 years, however. The movement toward humanitarian reform and rehabilitation has weakened the guards' authority (Carroll, 1974; McCleery, 1961). Treatment professionals espouse contrary objectives for prisons and call for the abolition of many rules and procedures upon which guards have relied to maintain control. Treatment professionals also dispense many privileges previously controlled by guards.

In addition, many states have moved toward increasing prison bureaucratization (Jacobs, 1977, 1983). Autonomous departments of corrections have been created, and the authority of the local warden has been transferred to central office administrators. An increased emphasis has been placed on rational legal authority, formalization, centralized decision making, and professionalization in prison administration and control (Crouch, 1986; Johnson, 1987). Simultaneously, the courts have abandoned their policy of not becoming involved in the internal affairs of prisons and have intervened to set limits on guard discretion and authority (Irwin, 1980; Marquart and Crouch, 1985). Finally, inmates have become more politicized and are more likely to collectively express discontent by both violent and nonviolent confrontations.

These and other changes have altered the guards' authority. Decisions affecting the prisoners' progress through the prison are now shared with, or completely relinquished to, treatment specialists and administrators. Prisoner councils represent prisoner interests in policymaking and disseminate information. Counselors, ombudsmen, and institutionalized grievance procedures address prisoner complaints and problems. Quasi-judicial, due process procedures have been introduced as a means of making decisions in disciplinary, classification, revocation, and grievance hearings. All staff are more accountable now than ever before; their actions are subject to systematic review and possible rebuke if they fail to conform to policies and procedures.

2.2. Loss of Control and the Bases of Power

These changes in the formal structure of control lead many guards to believe their control has eroded to a point that the routine performance of their job is impeded (Carroll, 1974; Crouch, 1986; Duffee, 1975;

Hawkins, 1975; Jacobs, 1983; Stastny and Tyrnauer, 1982). One survey of guards in Illinois indicates that over 80% feel prisoners have so many rights that it is difficult to maintain discipline (Jacobs and Kraft, 1978). Similarly, Irwin (1980) reports that 85% of the Calfironia guards surveyed agreed that prisoners had too much influence in decisions about prison policies and procedures. More recently, Fox (1982:46) found an intense concern among guards at five maximum security prisons "over the expansion of personal freedoms of prisoners arising from an increase in special privileges, program opportunities or court-mandated rights."

It is the view of many guards that their level of control within the formal structure of the prison is actually surpassed—and not merely threatened—by the prisoners' level of control. A survey of guards at four prisons found that guards felt they had significantly less control than did their prisoners over the operations of the prison (Hepburn, 1987). These guards, if given the opportunity, would redistribute power by decreasing the prisoners' level of control to a point below that of the guards' current control *and* increasing their own level of control to a point equal to what they now perceive as the prisoners' level of control.

As if to exacerbate this feeling of a loss of control, guards also feel they are not receiving the necessary recognition, support, and cooperation from departmental and local administrators to do their job effectively (Crouch, 1986; Fox, 1982; Lombardo, 1981a, 1981b; Marquart and Crouch, 1985). Duffee's (1975:168) conclusion that guards hold values "antagonistic to the successful implementation of managerial desired correctional policy" is consistent with the finding of Bartollas, Miller, and Dinitz (1976) that guards subscribe to a normative system that stresses distrust and cynicism toward administration.

It seems clear that this sense of powerlessness among guards is related to the recent reforms and changes that have altered the prison's structure, values, and goals. After all, the power of guards is related to their centrality in the administration's pursuit of organizational goals and to the bases of power available to them. The nature of the guards' loss of control, therefore, can be examined in light of the five traditional bases of power in the formal structure of control.

The structural position of guard provides its incumbent with the formal authority to command, or *legitimate power*. The guard has the right to exercise control over prisoners by virtue of the structural relationship between the position of guard, which confers the right to be obeyed, and the position of prisoner, which conveys the duty to obey. The guards' power resides in "mere incumbency in office," according to Cressey (1965): Orders are obeyed simply because they are issued by guards, and prisoners comply simply because they are prisoners.

Lombardo (1981a) reports that nearly half of the guards surveyed at New York's Auburn prison believe their power over prisoners derives from their lawful position to enforce the rules, and Hepburn (1985) finds that guards from five prisons located in four states are more likely to attribute their ability to control prisoners to legitimate power than to any other source of power. Yet, legitimate power exists only to the extent that prisoners view guards as having a legitimate right to give orders and be obeyed, and prisoners may accept the guards' right to give orders but feel no obligation to obey.

Coercive power, the second basis of power, resides in the prisoners' perception that guards have the ability to punish disobedience. One might expect the coercive power of guards to be great. After all, guards are the coercive unit within a coercive organization that relies on coercive compliance to achieve its goal of coercive containment (Etzioni, 1961). Yet recent reforms have limited the utility of coercion as a means of control (Crouch, 1980a; Marquart and Crouch, 1985). Today, many prisoners feel that the punishments that can be imposed do not differ materially from the punishment they endure by being incarcerated. Moreover, guards who rely solely on coercive power to gain compliance risk retaliation by prisoners and questions by their superiors about their inability to control the prisoners by other means. Consequently, very few guards rely on coercive power.

Nor do many guards rely on reward power, or the ability to issue rewards and privileges to prisoners. Formerly, guards made the decisions affecting such matters as the prisoners' assignment to housing and work areas, participation in programs, accumulation of "good time," and release on furlough or parole. The formal rewards of parole, good time, and program participation have been taken for granted by prisoners, however, and bureaucratic and judicial reforms have reduced or totally eliminated the guards' ability to influence these and many other decisions. Consequently, guards have few formal privileges and benefits to allocate.

Compliance is based on expert power when prisoners obey because they believe guards have some special skill, knowledge, or expertise. Cressey (1965) suggests that power based on technical competence and judgment is more characteristic in treatment-oriented prisons where guards become a component of the total therapeutic milieu than in those that are oriented solely to custody. In a therapeutic environment, the guard's professional judgment of the needs of each prisoner is the basis on which control is exercised. Yet guards are likely to feel that competence, professional judgment, and expertise in doing one's job characterize all prison guards, even though the nature of the job responsibilities may differ in custody-oriented prisons.

Bureaucratic administrative procedures tend to limit the scope of expert power, however. The professional autonomy of guards is threatened by the routinization of tasks and technical procedures and by the centralization of decision making. Given less latitude, guards have fewer opportunities to demonstrate or use their expertise. Nonetheless, the reduction in coercive and reward power has increased the guards' reliance on expert power.

Finally, a guard can exercise *referent power* over prisoners to the extent that they respect and admire the guard. Some time ago, Schrag (1961) observed that a guard's control over prisoners depends primarily on the guard's persuasive skills and leadership. More recently, Lombardo (1981a) reports that the more experienced guards view their power as derived from their manner of working with the prisoners. Lombardo refers to this as "personal authority" and suggests that prisoners comply because they respect the conduct of the guards. Guards who are fair and even-handed in their relations with prisoners, who display a degree of respect to the prisoners, who fulfill their promises to the prisoners, and who exercise their legitimate authority with impartiality and without malice gain respect among prisoners. Yet it is difficult to develop a basis for referent power when guards have withdrawn from routine involvements with prisoners in response to bureaucratic and legal reforms.

Of these five bases of power, legitimate power is the most crucial. It is essential to the stability of any bureaucratic organization. Legitimate power also is capable of gaining compliance by the largest number of prisoners, over the widest scope of prisoner activities, and over the greatest amount of time and effort devoted to those activities. As Pfeffer (1981:366) notes, "the acceptance of authority is critical in the management of large formal organizations . . . ; authority, legitimated power, is important in being able to make choices in a fashion that approximates the rational model."

Bureaucratic and legal reforms in American prisons have altered the formal structure of control. Coercive and reward power are inconsistent with the prison administration's new values and goals, and those guards who have relied on these bases of power for compliance by prisoners are experiencing a loss of control. Those guards who have been around long enough to remember "the good old days" may have trouble adapting, but any felt loss of control should be only temporary as each new cohort of prison guard learns governance by position and expertise.

3. THE INFORMAL STRUCTURE OF SOCIAL CONTROL

As with any organization, an informal structure of control arises within the prison. Unlike the formal structure of control, which is imposed from above by administrators, legislators, and jurists, the informal structure of control is constructed by guards and their prisoners. Within the boundaries established by the formal rules and procedures, and occasionally extending beyond those boundaries, a network of working agreements and informal relationships emerges to create another, equally important, control structure. In prisons, the informal control structure is shaped by the dependency relationship between guards and prisoners.

A dependency relationship between prison guards and their prisoners has been observed for quite some time (Carroll, 1974; Cloward, 1960; Irwin, 1980; Jacobs, 1977; Sykes, 1958). As already noted, guards are locked into structured conflict with prisoners. They feel they lack both the formal bases of power and the administrative support necessary to control a resistant and threatening prisoner population. Consequently, guards are dependent on prisoners for their own personal safety and for the successful completion of their duties. It is this ability of the prisoners to influence the safety and goal attainment of the guards that creates the guards' dependence on the prisoners (Hepburn and Crepin, 1984).

Dependency relationships are characterized by tension and tolerance. A web of commitments develops, drawing each party further into the dependency relationship. Through a continuous process of give-and-take, imposition, and bargaining, a set of working agreements, arrangements, or "understandings" is negotiated between guards and prisoners. These agreements may take various forms.

3.1. Repression as a Means of Informal Control

One response by guards to their perceived loss of control over prisoners is to resist the dependence relationship and (re)gain control by repressive tactics (Lombardo, 1982). Guards become more custodial and more punitive toward prisoners, and relationships with prisoners are more detached, contractual, and formal as guards strive to lessen their dependence on prisoners. Insults, obscenities, and other forms of verbal abuse are commonly used to denigrate the prisoners and assert the authority of guards, but repression is rooted in the guards' willingness to use physical violence.

Marquart (1986), for instance, details how verbal assaults and varying degrees of physical violence were employed as a "socially structured tactic of prisoner control" in a Texas prison. Intimidating verbal threats and assaults were used to humiliate, ridicule, and demean prisoners. Moreover, three distinct types of physical coercion existed. Minor offenses resulted in an "attitude adjustment" or "counseling" session, in which the prisoner was shoved, kicked, and/or slapped. More serious infractions, such as failure to show respect to guards or questioning the authority of guards, resulted in "ass whippings," but the most severe beatings were reserved for those prisoners who physically attacked guards, incited other prisoners to mob action, or tried to escape.

All prisons require a measure of repression and coercion, but very few are characterized by routine verbal and physical assaults by guards on prisoners. Attempts by guards to maintain control by asserting what limited power they possess create relatively unstable conditions. Repression can destroy the cohesion that exists and undermine the guards' legitimate authority. Indeed, the use of repression to gain control over prisoners may have the opposite effect, producing rebellious prisoners and an extremely unsafe working environment for guards.

3.2. Accommodation as a Means of Informal Control

Another response to the dependence relationship is accommodation, a working agreement between guards and prisoners to assist in meeting one another's needs. It is a reciprocal relationship in which favors are exchanged: Prisoners submit to the guards' authority, and the guards tolerate minor rule infractions by the prisoners.

In a relationship of accommodation, guards maintain stability and order among prisoners by granting special favors and permitting minor violations, in exchange for which prisoner leaders are expected to maintain control over other prisoners. By selectively regulating the flow of contraband (e.g., drugs and alcohol) and other activities (e.g., gambling and sex) that comprise the underground economy of the prisoners, selectively recognizing informal leaders of religious, racial, or other groups, and selectively attempting to influence the housing and work assignments of prisoners, guards are able to satisfy the material, power, and status interests of the prisoners.

The use of prisoners to control prisoners is a widespread practice (Marquart and Crouch, 1984). There are instances of formal accommodation, as in the use of prisoner trustees as supervisors of prisoner labor and the formation of prisoner governmental councils to represent prisoner interests, but informal accommodations predominate. Prisoner informants, or "snitches," are cultivated for both the information they can provide and the divisiveness they represent. Gang leaders receive privileges and status in exchange for maintaining control over the members of their gangs.

This practice of dispensing scarce commodities, bits of information, and prized assignments to those prisoners who could dominate other prisoners assures the guards of greater cooperation from prisoners. Referring to this reciprocity as a "corruption of authority," Sykes (1958) claims that guards actually enhance their authority over prisoners by allowing that authority to be corrupted. The effect of the guards' use and abuse of authority is to create such a degree of prisoner dependency on the guards that prisoner initiative, activism, and protest are regulated by the guards.

Informal control, in summary, is based on working agreements between guards and prisoners that become routinized over time and are institutionalized into normative expectations (Thomas, 1984). Resources are invested in the relationship, and boundary rules are negotiated to circumscribe and delimit the focus of this reciprocal relationship. In this manner, the informal structure of control emerges, tenuous and fragile, from the daily negotiations between guards and their prisoners. It provides alternative strategies by which guards can exert control and increase predictability.

The greatest degree of control over prisoners flows from the informal control structure. Predictability is possible when relationships are structured, and uncertainty is reduced when relatively stable working agreements exist. Whether by repression or accommodation, the informal control structure removes a great deal of the uncertainty from the working environment and produces order and change within the prison. This is not to argue that the formal control structure is irrelevant to the question of control and order. On the contrary, the formal control structure sets the broad parameters of control within the prison and serves as the ultimate mechanism of control when complete disorder threatens. Yet, the formal control structure is not adequate to manage the daily activities of the prison; nor is it able to resolve the uncertainties of the guards' working environment.

4. JOB SATISFACTION, SERVICE DELIVERY, AND SOCIAL CONTROL

Studies of a wide range of organizations report that the degree of uncertainty and the level of control exercised over one's work are related to stress, alienation, and cynicism. It is not surprising, therefore, to note that prison guards who experience the greatest uncertainty and feel the least able to control prisoners are found to have the highest levels of stress, alienation, and cynicism (Cullen, Link, Wolfe, and Frank, 1985; Hepburn, 1987; Poole and Regoli, 1981, 1983; Whitehead and Lindquist, 1986). Further, high levels of stress, alienation, and cynicism are associated with negative attitudes toward co-workers, demoralization, and dissatisfaction with the job.

Job dissatisfaction and worker burnout create problems for prison administrators. One problem is the instability caused by high rates of turnover. National surveys report turnover rates among guards of 25% annually in most states, with some states reporting an annual turnover rate of nearly 40%; Louisiana experienced an annual turnover rate of 75% (Corrections Compendium, 1984; May, 1976). Among those who remain on the job, however, the problem is one of indifference, or even hostility, toward the job.

One approach to the problem has been to focus attention on the individual attributes of the guards. Although some effort has been made to identify desirable work histories and personality traits, the major emphasis has been on increased education. A part of a general call for the professionalization of correctional personnel (National Advisory Commission on Criminal Justice Standards and Goals, 1973; Task Force on Corrections, 1967), increased education among prison guards was advocated as a means to improve job performance, address problems of prison management and control, and enhance morale. Increased education, in the absence of any other changes, does not improve job satisfaction among prison guards, however (Jurik and Musheno, 1986). Indeed, a number of studies find that job satisfaction is lowest among the better educated guards (Cullen et al., 1985; Jurik, Halemba, Musheno, and Boyle, 1987).

Job satisfaction is largely a result of the extrinsic and intrinsic rewards available in the job. Extrinsic rewards include such factors as the amount of pay, job security, fringe benefits, and opportunities for advancement. Similarly, each job offers varying degrees of intrinsic rewards, such as the freedom to plan one's own work activities and schedule, the chance to use one's skills and talents, the opportunity to acquire new skills, and the likelihood of personal growth in the job. Better educated workers expect more extrinsic and intrinsic rewards in their jobs, and, therefore, better educated workers become more dissatisfied when their jobs lack these rewards.

It is apparent, then, that increased emphasis on education in the absence of substantial changes in the nature of the guard's job will not resolve the problem; in fact, that approach is likely to have the unintended consequence of actually increasing the degree of dissatisfaction, burnout, and turnover among prison guards. A more promising approach to the problem is that of improving the guards' intrinsic rewards by redefining the role and duties of the prison guard.

4.1. Service Delivery as Job Enrichment and Control Enhancement

One suggestion for improving the guards' attitudes toward their work is participatory administration, by which the prison administration grants guards an active and formal role in making decisions regarding prison policies and procedures (Fox, 1982; Lombardo, 1982). Such participation improves communication by providing guards with a forum for voicing their concerns to administrators and, equally important, by improving the communication to guards of a decision's administrative purpose or rationale. And if it actually increases the relative influence of guards within the prison, participatory management is a means of empowerment.

Another suggestion for increasing the job satisfaction of prison guards calls for more far-reaching changes in the actual duties and responsibilities of the job. Toch (1978), Lombardo (1981b), and Johnson (1987) are among those who propose that the guards' role be redefined in terms of human service workers. These "support-oriented guards" would assist prisoners with institutional problems and act as referral agents or advocates with the prison bureaucracy. With the proper training and support systems, each guard would be expected to be not only a rule enforcer but also a lay counselor, a dispute mediator, an administrative ombudsperson, a treatment aide, and a social worker.

There are strong arguments on behalf of service delivery (see, for example, Johnson, 1987; Jurik and Winn, 1987; Jurik and Musheno, 1986; Lindquist and Whitehead, 1986). First, because more highly educated guards prefer human services delivery to strict custody and control duties, the redefinition of the job should attract more educated applicants, especially among those educated in the human services disciplines (e.g., social work, psychology, criminology, and sociology). Second, human services delivery is assumed to provide variety, autonomy, a sense of accomplishment, and other important intrinsic rewards that, it is reasoned, will increase job satisfaction and reduce burnout and turnover. Third, it is believed that human services delivery provides a more favorable orientation among guards toward prisoners: There is less social distance between guards and prisoners, and guards are less punitive in their attitudes and behaviors toward prisoners.

A fourth argument on behalf of human services delivery can be made in terms of how such activities strengthen the existing structure of social control. Formal control is likely to be enhanced because human services delivery creates opportunities for guards to develop alternative bases of power. Legitimate power provides guards with control over the largest number of prisoners and the widest range of prisoner activities, but control over prisoners is maximized when guards can exercise multiple and disparate forms of power. Human services delivery should permit guards to develop expert and referent bases of power, thereby extending and diversifying their formal control over prisoners.

Informal social control also is thought to be enhanced by human services delivery. The activities by which guards render services and help prisoners with personal problems and institutional needs, it is argued, will alter the balance of reciprocity between guards and prisoners. Prisoners will become more dependent on guards for meeting daily needs, providing routine services, and resolving frequent disputes, thereby producing a new and different pattern of accommodation as an informal control structure within the prison.

4.2. Service Delivery and Role Ambiguity

The transformation to service delivery appears promising, but can it deliver on these promises? There are strong reasons for believing that it can not. One formidable obstacle is implementation. To succeed, service delivery requires that corrections departments (1) substantially increase the amount, and therefore the costs, of preservice and in-service training; (2) drastically increase the number of persons employed, because the broad range of services and duties to be provided to the prisoners will necessitate a much lower ratio of prisoners per human services worker than currently exists with prisoners per guard; and (3) assure that the new duties and responsibilities are completely communicated and supported throughout the entire correctional system, especially at the upper administrative ranks within each prison. Funding for increased training and more employees always is problematic, and it is even more questionable at a time when most of the available funds are being poured into the construction of additional prisons. Administrative and supervisory support must come from persons who have worked within prisons for a long time, many as prison guards, and who may resist the transformation of the guard's duties. Yet these and other impediments to successful implementation must be overcome if there is to be a transformation to human services delivery.

Should the problems of implementation be resolved, service delivery then must confront a second major obstacle. As noted earlier, there is a relationship of structured conflict between guards and prisoners. One implication of this structured conflict is that prisoners attempt to manipulate guards for their own purposes, and the broader the range of involvements by guards in the activities of prisoners, then the greater the manipulative pressure by prisoners on guards. Another implication is that prisoners know that custody and control are the primary duties of the guard and that a guard by any other name (e.g., "correctional officer" or "human services worker") and with any other duties (e.g., counselor, mediator, aide) is still a "cop," a "screw," or a "hack" whose primary function is rule enforcement. Similarly, guards recognize that they cannot get too close to the prisoners if they are to avoid (even the appearance of) favoritism and maintain discipline.

The obstacles of implementation and structural conflict raise the possibility that the movement to services delivery actually may decrease, rather than increase, job satisfaction. As noted earlier, there is a growing research literature (see Philliber, 1987) that indicates that role ambiguity arises from ambiguous or ill-defined role expectations and from inadequate supervisory guidance and support, both of which are possible outcomes of an inadequate implementation. An additional source of role ambiguity occurs when the job requires quite diverse and contrasting roles, as when the duties of services delivery urge the development of personal, warm relationships with prisoners but the structural conflict that exists calls for an impersonal, detached relationship. For the same reasons that role ambiguity is greater among guards in treatment-oriented prisons than among guards in custody-oriented prisons or that treatment staff have greater levels of role ambiguity than custody staff, the expectations of human services delivery will increase role ambiguity among prison guards charged with the primary responsibility of custody and control. As role ambiguity increases, uncertainty in the working environment increases and job satisfaction decreases.

5. CONCLUSION

Prisons are coercive organizations. Locked into a relationship of structured conflict with prisoners, and dependent on prisoners for both their personal safety and their occupational success, prison guards must rely on formal and informal controls to assure predictability and order within the prison. Any expansion of the duties and responsibilities of the guard, such as is suggested by proponents of a human services delivery model, must be consistent with the formal and informal control structures. Whatever else they may be, guards are primarily agents of social control.

6. REFERENCES

Bartollas, C., Miller, S., and Dinitz, S. *Juvenile victimization: The institutional paradox.* New York: Halsted Press, 1976.

Carroll, L. *Hacks, blacks and cons: Race relations in a maximum security prison.* Lexington, MA.: Lexington Books, 1974.

Cloward, R. Social control in the prisons. In R. Cloward *et al.* (Eds.), *Theoretical studies in social organization of the prison.* New York: Social Science Research Council, 1960.

Corrections Compendium. *National survey of correctional staff turnover.* Lincoln, NB: Contact, 1983.

Cressey, D. Contradictory directives in complex organizations: The case of the prison. *Administrative Science Quarterly,* 1959, *4,* 1–19.

Cressey, D. Prison organizations. In J. March (Ed.), *Handbook of organizations.* Chicago: Rand-McNally, 1965.

Crouch, B. M. The book vs. the boot: Two styles of guarding in a southern prison. In B. Crouch (Ed.), *The keepers.* Springfield, IL: Charles Thomas Publishers, 1980a.

Crouch, B. M. The guard in a changing prison world. In B. Crouch (Ed.), *The keepers.* Springfield, IL: Charles C Thomas Publishers, 1980b.

Crouch, B. M. Prison guards on the line. In K. C. Haas and G. P. Alpert (Eds.), *The dilemmas of punishment.* Prospect Heights, IL: Waveland Press, Inc., 1986.

Cullen, F., Link, B., Wolfe, N., and Frank J. The social dimensions of correctional officer stress. *Justice Quarterly,* 1985, *4,* 505–533.

Duffee, D. The correctional officer subculture and organizational change. *Journal of Research in Crime and Delinquency,* 1975, *12,* 155–172.

Etzioni, A. *A comparative analysis of complex organizations.* New York: Free Press, 1961.

Fox, J. *Organizational and racial conflict in maximum security prisons.* Boston: D. C. Heath, 1982.

Hawkins, G. *The prison: Policy and practice.* Chicago: University of Chicago Press, 1976.

Hepburn, J. R. The exercise of power in coercive organizations: A study of prison guards. *Criminology,* 1985, *23,* 146–164.

Hepburn, J. R. The prison control structure and its effects on work attitudes: The perceptions and attitudes of prison guards. *Journal of Criminal Justice,* 1987, *16,* 49–64.

Hepburn, J. R., and Crepin, A. E. Relationship strategies in a coercive institution: A study of dependence among prison guards. *Journal of Social and Personal Relationships,* 1984, *1,* 139–157.

Irwin, J. *Prisons in turmoil.* Boston: Little, Brown, 1980.

Jacobs, J. B. *Stateville: The penitentiary in mass society.* Chicago: University of Chicago Press, 1977.

Jacobs, J. B. *New perspectives on prisons and imprisonment.* Ithaca, NY: Cornell University Press, 1983.

Jacobs, J. B., and Kraft, L. Integrating the keepers: A comparison of black and white prison guards in Illinois. *Social Problems,* 1978, *25,* 304–318.

Johnson, R. *Hard time.* Monterey, CA: Brooks/Cole Publishing Co., 1987.

Jurik, N., and Musheno, M. The internal crisis of corrections: Professionalization and the work environment. *Justice Quarterly,* 1986, *3,* 457–480.

Jurik, N., and Winn, R. Describing correctional security dropouts and rejects: An individual or organizational profile. *Criminal Justice and Behavior,* 1987, *14,* 5–25.

Jurik, N., Halemba, G., Musheno, M., and Boyle, B. Education, working conditions and the job satisfaction of correctional officers. *Work and Occupations,* 1987, *14,* 106–125.

Lindquist, C., and Whitehead, J. Guards released from prison: A natural experiment in job enlargement. *Journal of Criminal Justice,* 1986, *14,* 283–294.

Lombardo, L. X. *Guards imprisoned.* New York: Elsevier, 1981a.

Lombardo, L. X. Occupational stress in correctional officers: Sources, coping strategies, and implications. In S. Zimmerman and H. Miller (Eds.), *Correction at the crossroads: Designing policy.* Beverly Hills, CA: Sage, 1981b.

Lombardo, L. X. Stress, change and collective violence in prison. In R. Johnson and H. Toch (Eds.), *The pains of imprisonment.* Beverly Hills, CA: Sage, 1982.

McCleery, R. Policy changes in prison management. In A. Etzioni (Ed.), *Complex organizations: A sociological reader.* New York: Holt, Rinehart & Winston, 1961.

Marquart, J. W. Prison guards and the use of physical coercion as a mechanism of prisoner control. *Criminology*, 1986, *24*, 347–366.

Marquart, J. W., and Crouch, B. M. Coopting the kept: Using inmates for social control in a southern prison. *Justice Quarterly*, 1984, *1*, 491–509.

Marquart, J. W., and Crouch, B. M. Judicial reform and prisoner control: The impact of *Ruiz v. Estelle* on a Texas penitentiary. *Law and Society Review*, 1985, *19*, 557–586.

May, E. Prison guards in America. *Corrections Magazine*, 1976, *6*, 48.

National Advisory Commission on Criminal Justice Standards and Goals Corrections. Washington, DC: Law Enforcement Assistance Administration, 1973.

Pfeffer, J. *Power in organizations*. Marshfield, MA: Pitman, 1981.

Philliber, S. Thy brother's keeper: A review of the literature on correctional officers. *Justice Quarterly*, 1987, *4*, 9–37.

Poole, E. D., and Regoli, R. M. Alienation in prison: An examination of the work relations of prison guards. *Criminology*, 1981, *19*, 251–270.

Poole, E. D., and Regoli, R. M. Professionalism, role conflict, work alienation, and anomia: A look at prison management. *The Social Science Journal*, 1983, *20*, 63–70.

Schrag, C. Some foundations for a theory of correction. In D. Cressey (Ed.), *The prison: Studies in institutional organization and change*. New York: Holt, Rinehart & Winston, 1961.

Statsny, C., and Tyrnauer, G. *Who rules the joint?* Lexington, MA: Lexington Books, 1982.

Sykes, G. M. *The society of captives*. Princeton: Princeton University Press, 1958.

Task Force on Corrections. *Task force report: Corrections*. Washington, DC: The President's Commission on Law Enforcement and Administration of Justice, 1967.

Thomas, J. Some aspects of negotiated order, loose coupling, and mesostructure in maximum security prisons. *Symbolic Interaction*, 1984, *7*, 213–231.

Toch, H. Is a 'correction officer' by any other name a 'screw'? *Criminal Justice Review*, 1978, *3*, 19–35.

Whitehead, J. T., and Lindquist, C. A. Correctional officers' job burnout: A path model. *Journal of Research in Crime and Delinquency*, 1986, *23*, 23–42.

Part IV

LIVING IN PRISON

Chapter 11

NONCOPING AND MALADAPTATION IN CONFINEMENT

HANS TOCH and J. DOUGLAS GRANT

Ned Nolan (not his real name) was sentenced to prison for an attempted robbery. His disciplinary dossier contains entries such as:

> While counting out inmates for breakfast, I checked his cell and found him still in bed.
> He cut his right forearm with a razor blade.
> He started hollering at the teacher. I told him to be quiet because the class was in session, and he became argumentative.
> While watching movies he stood blocking the view of several inmates. He refused to move, claiming that it was his spot and he wasn't moving.
> He left his cell and went to the slop sink and got buckets of water. I told him he was interfering with the count, and he got mad and started yelling.
> He threw hot water at an officer, soaking his shirt.
> He refused to continue working in the kitchen.

There are also charges such as:

> A disturbance occurred on the gallery. An officer rushed to the scene and found an inmate lying on the floor bleeding. A check of the company revealed that you had left the gallery and went to the hospital school area. It was discovered that you had a bloody kleenex in your hand. When you were questioned by the sergeant, you admitted that you had cut the inmate because he owed you cigarettes. You said, "I wanted to kill him. I tried to cut his throat but he put his arm up."
> You were involved in a fight with another inmate. You refused several

HANS TOCH • School of Criminal Justice, State University of New York at Albany, Albany, New York 12222.   J. DOUGLAS GRANT • Nicasio, California 94946 (Formerly of the Social Action Research Center).

direct orders given by facility members to break it up, making the use of force necessary to stop this fight. . . . When a pat frisk was done on you, it was discovered that you were in possession of a homemade weapon. When you appeared before the facility adjustment panel concerning these charges you informed the panel that you intended to kill the other inmate and that it wasn't over yet.

At the time of his arrest, Mr. Nolan reports that he has been sleeping in an abandoned building and has been hungry much of the time. He also explains that he is unemployed because work makes him dizzy. His probation officer writes that

> the defendant impresses as a marginal person of limited intelligence who has eked out a living mostly by menial low-paying jobs. He claims a physical disability and showed the probation officer what appeared to be a malformed large toe. . . . He indicated he has a metal plate in his head. . . . He describes severe pain in his feet, headaches, and general aches throughout his body as well as dizziness. . . . He seems to be of limited intellectual ability.

After Mr. Nolan arrives in prison he signs himself into protection,[1] claiming that he "is in fear of his life," and announces that "he does not want to be released into any part of the population." Mr. Nolan is consequently assigned to a program for victim-prone prisoners,[2] but the staff of this unit object to his presence. They write:

> He impresses as a very unstable and confused person who is probably, at the least, a schizoid personality. . . . He first impressed as of limited intelligence, paranoid, lacking social skills and a malingerer who is unable to accept responsibility for his actions. His actions over the past several months have positively reinforced this impression. His disciplinary record is terrible. He has numerous misbehavior reports of a serious nature (fights, possession of a weapon); he has mutilated himself to obtain attention; his ability to get along with inmates is nil. He can best be described as infantile in his dealings with staff. . . . It is easy to discuss the resident's strengths, he doesn't have any. . . . He is not prepared to function in any program where responsibility is required, mainly because he does not know what the word means.

A year later, staff still complain about Mr. Nolan. They observe that "his program participation has been nil, and he has been a distinct disciplinary problem."

Mr. Nolan is released from prison, but he is returned for absconding

---

[1] Prisons and detention systems make provision for inmates at risk in their prison population by permitting inmates to sign themselves into protective segregation. Formal protective settings require trade-offs, in that they offer safety but restrict physical freedom and program involvement (Toch, 1977).

[2] The New York prison system has pioneered the use of settings for inmates who are deemed lacking in resilience or adjudged to have "victim attributes." Such settings provide low-pressure social environments but encourage participation in educational and vocational activities.

from parole. Soon after reentering the prison, he comes to see a staff member requesting protective custody. He explains that he is apprehensive and upset. He also surrenders a homemade weapon that he sees as a tool of self-defense and offers detailed information about illegal activities of other inmates. In a second incident, Mr. Nolan throws a tantrum because he objects to a cereal that is served to him for breakfast.

It is obvious that one problem with Mr. Nolan is that he functions at a very primitive level, which among other things makes him an exemplar of the frustration aggression theory in action. One reason why Mr. Nolan is very frequently frustrated is because he resents circumscription and structure (he explodes when he is not permitted to wander about the institution or to express himself in a loud voice), and on the other hand, he becomes disturbed when his rigid routines are interfered with—such as when people invade space he feels he has preempted. Mr. Nolan also has a penchant for feeling persecuted and attacks those of his peers whom he fears.

When Mr. Nolan first arrives in prison, he experiences considerable anxiety, but any claim he has to being considered a mental health client diminishes over time because his complaints are overshadowed by his acting out, including the tantrums he throws in which staff members are targets. These assaults paradoxically occur despite the fact that Mr. Nolan regards prison staff as parental figures who reliably protect him after he has surrounded himself with enemies.

1. THE MULTIPROBLEM INMATE

Ned Nolan illustrates one of the most serious problems shared by prison administrators and society, which has to do with the residual or bottom-line function prisons are called upon to perform. It has been said that prisons are the "garbage pails" of society; what this intends to suggest is that persons are often swept into prison after other social agencies have unsuccessfully tried to address their difficulties. Many prison clients, in other words, have been "discarded" by other human service staff, who view them as hopeless cases.

Though it is true that a person must be sentenced for a crime to be committed to prison, this requisite for confinement is often not a very informative feature, in the sense that the person usually has more salient attributes than the fact that he is an offender. This point holds for a great many more offenders than one would suspect because most crimes are casually committed and involve limited skills. In dealing with inmates, therefore, we must realize that we can be distracted from assessing all sorts of liabilities they have by centering on their criminal histories.

Ned Nolan illustrates the need for an uncontaminated perspective. Nolan is technically a robber, but he is more prominently a man relegated to a life of vagrancy by a combination of real and perceived handicaps, which continue to manifest themselves in the prison, making Nolan an irrepressible and annoying inmate. Neither the causation nor the consequences of Nolan's difficulties are easy to describe: Nolan can be labeled as a *multiproblem* individual, meaning that an extended list of his personal deficits, liabilities, and handicaps can be presented. Such a list would include the fact that Nolan has been reliably diagnosed as brain damaged and that his measured intelligence is low. The list might also include Nolan's low self-esteem and his limited aspirations, and it could describe traits such as high impulsivity and low frustration tolerance and clinical states such as bouts of depression.

A list of measurable deficits, however, at best provides *clues* to problems and offers reasons why problems might arise if they arise. This sequence is suspect, in that postdiction is easier than prediction. The fact that an offender is diagnosed as brain damaged does not portend prison misbehavior nor foreordain difficulties for the offender in the community. A diagnosis for a recalcitrant person, however, beckons as an explanatory formula because it saves inconceivable trouble implicit in the question, "Why does this person do what he does?", which is invariably difficult to answer. The formula may also allow for simple remedies, such as medication that suppresses misbehavior by lowering energy levels or inducing depression. What the formula does *not* do is "explain," and this is so *even where a deficit contributes to behavior*, because explaining means not only answering the question "what?" but also responding to "how?" and "why?" questions. This enterprise would entail specifying the role Nolan's brain lesions play in producing his misbehavior, a task that no one can undertake. Deficits, moreover, are ingredients that must be combined, with different combinations yielding different, frequently contrasting, products. There are men with IQ scores comparable to Nolan's, for instance, who have gentle, sweet, and angelic dispositions and are congenial as clients. Even impulsivity (which looks like a behavior propensity) can lead to divergent outcomes, depending on the forms that impulse release takes, the efforts a person makes to use supports to supplement poor controls, and the effects of anticipated and/or experienced reactions from others.

Impulsivity-related prison misbehavior such as Nolan's thus ranges from serious to nonserious and from lighthearted to grim. Some "impulsive" inmates pose danger to other inmates, in that they regard others as objects of need satisfaction and use violence to intimidate, extort, expropriate, or strongarm those susceptible to intimidation. Other high-impulsivity prisoners are amusingly minor league and inconsequential miscreants. They may play "Russian roulette" with prison rules, taking risks in the casual pursuit of short-term goals, seemingly oblivious to predictable repercussions. Other such inmates have a propensity to "jail" (Irwin, 1970): In operationalizing their personal definition of the "good life"—which consists of accumulating illicit amenities—such inmates engage in *sub rosa* activities (including hustling), viewing the "official" prison as an irrelevant sideline.

Impulse management issues can also pose more serious problems for the offender than they for others. Stress-aggression and frustration-aggression patterns sometimes have this attribute in that the stimulus experiences (frustration or stress) can be incredibly painful. Where a frustration-aggression pattern obtains, the inmates, whenever they are disappointed or obstructed in the pursuit of goals (which may be a frequent experience), become disgruntled and react with bursts of blind and irrational rage. In stress-aggression patterns, the inmates tend to feel that situations close in on them, whereupon they experience panic and anxiety and blow up under pressure with tantrums that express a sense of helplessness. Impulsivity-related games also often turn sour: In examining chronic misbehavior in prison, we encounter inmates who engage in nonreflective, childlike, self-serving, and short-sighted behavior that brings boomerang effects, leaving the inmate despondent and suffused with self-pity.

Mr. Nolan's outlook makes him operate at a level of infancy, satisfying his needs in a direct and primitive fashion. Prison officials would say that Nolan is a chronic, serious management problem. Statistically, they can make a strong case. The average inmate records two to four disciplinary violations per year, and many inmates are never (or hardly ever) charged with misbehavior, whereas Nolan has continuous disciplinary charges pending. This means that authorities must subject Nolan to many sanctions, which have no deterrent consequences. As a result, both Nolan and the system have insoluble problems, a point that also holds for other inmates who engage in considerable misbehavior.

2. RESPONDING TO THE NONCOPING INMATE

Like most maladaptive inmates, Nolan represents a checkered problem. He at times acts out, subjecting other persons (both inmates and staff) to assaults; but Nolan is also a redundant victim, who must often seek protection. Ought Nolan to be sequestered with other predatory inmates, or does he belong in a low-pressure setting for victim-prone inmates? We find that Nolan has his version of prison routine, which conflicts with that of the prison. Whereas this appears to be a "mainline" management issue, Nolan's motives are hardly standard motives. We have noticed, for example, that at times Nolan appears lost, aimlessly perambulating about, whereas at other times he can be rigid, and at such times he seems unable to tolerate deviations from private rituals. Is Nolan a disturbed or disordered inmate? Mental health staff have seen Nolan after suicide gestures and have certified that he is not disturbed. But what this means is that Nolan does not reach the threshold of "disturbedness" that qualifies him for mental health services, and this threshold is relatively stringent because prison mental health resources are scarce (as they are in the community) and must be rationed.

As it happens, Nolan has been sentenced to a prison system (New York's) that has settings for unusual inmates. Nolan is assigned to such a setting, but he strains its hospitality, contaminates its climate, and is only retained, against staff advice, because no place can be found that more appropriately fits Nolan's needs.

This type of dilemma is not accidental. Persons who fail in the community also fail in prison because prisons, like other settings, test personal coping skills and adaptive resources. Of course, in some ways prisons are more protective than the community, so that Nolan's capacity to earn his keep—which is minimal or nonexistent—is not tested. But prisons have accentuated stressful features, such as ever-present guards who demand compliance with rules and dominant peers who feel that fear calls for exploitation, and these are features that produce disproportionate difficulties for some imprisoned persons. Adolescents who have unresolved resentments against parental figures, for example, may feel unable to cope, or at least cope dispassionately, with the presence of prison guards.[3] Such chips-on-the-shoulder patterns can produce dependency-related misbehavior in prisons. Sensitized inmates may alternate between dependent and rebellious behavior, depending on whether they feel their needs are met or frustrated. Others expect rejection from guards, and invite it, by behaving in obnoxious, challenging ways. Still others take a straightforward rebellious, defiant, and

---

[3] Glaser (1977) thus points out that "those familiar with correctional institutions soon learn that punishment of disobedient inmates tends to be much more extreme in juvenile and youth facilities than in prisons for adults. . . . This attitude develops because stubborn rebelliousness, as an assertion of autonomy and of what is perceived by them as their manly or womanly strength of character, is more common among younger offenders than it is among older ones. . . . Hostility between offenders and criminal justice personnel reaches passionate levels whenever the most actively and compulsively alienated offenders enter into escalating exchanges of hostile gestures with the most actively and compulsively conformist members of the staff (p. 312).

challenging stance or feel that no one has a right to tell them what to do and react angrily to perceived infringements of their autonomy. Disciplinary sanctions can make such situations even worse, in that some inmates cannot accept sanctions, which conflict with their versions of adulthood.

In sum, prisons offer tests of resilience that nonresilient persons, of the kind who disproportionately inhabit prisons, cannot pass, and the disciplinary process thus becomes overloaded with the results of coping failures. Not surprisingly, inmates on mental health case loads have higher disciplinary violation rates than do other inmates (Toch and Adams, 1986), and disturbed inmates appear disproportionately among chronic disciplinary violators; the same point holds for inmates who have low measured intelligence, such as Nolan. If accurate information were available on more diverse predictors of poor coping competence—such as data about learning disabilities or language deficits—these measures would no doubt be equally predictive of high disciplinary violation rates and of chronicity of violations.[4]

Disciplinary sanctions, by default, become standard responses to maladaptive behavior, though formal sanctions are supplemented at times with other responses, such as Nolan's placement in the special (protective) setting. Such responses, however, can be deployed for only a small number of inmates, and they are often—as in Nolan's case—compromise resolutions. These options also are—with rare exception—exercised independently of disciplinary proceedings and address different aspects of the same behavior. Dramatic examples are the careers of psychotic inmates who are alternately hospitalized and penalized. Such inmates often disrupt prison routine because they withdraw from their surroundings, living seclusively in private worlds, and at extremes, neglecting self-care and hygiene to the discomfort of other inmates. Disturbed inmates can also engage in seemingly unmotivated attacks on others, or against themselves, at times responsive to hallucinations, delusions, cumulating anxiety or tension and self-hate. Such inmates may also feel extremely persecuted and explode at persons they imagine wish them ill or want to harm them. They can manifest mixed disruptive patterns in which they alternately withdraw and explode.

---

[4] In a New York prison cohort, 3.7% of inmates could be described as "chronic violators," defined as sustaining a rate of eight or more violations over 75% (or more) of their prison careers. The proportion of chronics becomes 5.7% for inmates who have low measured intelligence, 6.3% for prison mental health outpatients, and 7.3% for outpatients with low intelligence. Chronicity translates into a serious management problem in that the 3.7% chronics (who overrepresent short-termers and whose "time at risk" is thus understated), account for 15% of prison violations and 18% of violent infractions committed by the cohort.

3. DISCIPLINARY RESPONSES TO ECCENTRIC VIOLATIONS

The responses of prison staff to behavior that violates prison rules range from unrecorded and informal to legalistic and very formal. When behavior that comes to the attention of authorities is marginally disruptive, particularly when it consists of nonpublic, one-time offenses, the response the behavior receives is often limited to rebukes or sermons, which are called "counseling" by guards (Lombardo, 1981). More serious or more patterned misbehavior invites formal dispositions and sanctions, and serious violations, such as acts of violence and destruction of property, lead to major disciplinary hearings and heavy penalties.

Though there are observers (e.g., Fox, 1958; Glaser, 1964, 1977) who argue for flexible and individualized discipline, most favor a "just deserts" system that allots standard dispositions to equivalent offenses. Such a system is advocated on the grounds that it provides equity and fairness (Fogel, 1975), but it is also sometimes defended as a way of instilling a sense of responsibility in miscreants for their reprehensible acts.

In a survey of mental health problems in New York prisons, staff of the New York Correctional Association discovered that emotionally disturbed inmates "are subject to the same disciplinary procedures as other inmates" (Steelman, 1987: 36), and the survey staff found that

> most mental health personnel feel quite strongly that it would not be a good idea to treat the mentally ill as if they were different from their fellow prisoners when it comes to disciplinary matters. Many [mental health] unit chiefs said they believe most inmates do know right from wrong, that it is important for them to have to take responsibility for their actions, and that they should not come to feel that they can "use" their mental illness as a way to avoid disciplinary measures. Therefore, there was little argument on the principle that even prisoners with lengthy psychiatric histories should be sent to the SHU (segregation units) when the corrections' disciplinary process mandates it.

In an unrelated survey of federal prison staff, respondents volunteered comments such as "behavior, regardless of its intention, needs to have some consequences." Some noted that if we exculpate the idiosyncrasies of disturbed inmates, we run the risk of encouraging manipulativeness. Other staff felt that *"sickness*, whether it is physical or mental, should never, for any reason, be an *excuse* for hurting or injuring anyone" (Toch and Adams, 1987: 131). The prison staff did not, however, favor rigidity or indifference, in that they recommended dealing with irrationally motivated minor violations by referring inmates to mental health staff (Toch and Adams, 1987). A parallel survey in New York showed that mental health personnel did demur in classifying some acts (such as serious suicide gestures or refusals to eat "poisoned" food) as legitimate disciplinary infractions. These same staff members also opted to "refer for treatment" rather than discipline inmates whose bizarre behavior (e.g., lapses in self-care and fear-inspired self-insulation) could have been technically punishable. (Toch and Adams, 1988).

Where the impact of dispositions on the inmate has to be considered, because the inmate is in very poor shape, a legalistic stance becomes hard to sustain, even for those who favor mainstreaming (the emphasizing of normalcy) as a goal. The New York survey group notes that an inmate who breaks down with a psychotic episode in a disciplinary confinement setting may be removed "for crisis intervention" but is later returned to serve the rest of his time, with predictably adverse results (Steelman, 1987: 39). The problem is one of inflexibility of a system which has

> no alternative currently available but for the prisoner to be returned to punitive segregation until his term there expires, no matter what the costs may be in terms of his mental and physical well-being, or the financial burden born by the State for his frequent terms of psychiatric treatment. (pp. 41–42)

The sponsors of the New York prison survey suggest that "any inmate who has received [mental health] services be screened [by mental health staff] prior to being placed in punitive segregation" and argue that "alternative housing arrangements" should be provided for inmates for whom segregation is deemed "seriously detrimental" (p. 86). This solution is based on the supposition that the inmates' level of suffering and their reaction to stresses of confinement can be predicted by the staff, which is not the case. Moreover, such a system gives mental health staff the de facto power to administer or withhold punishment, a responsibility that has elsewhere provided heart-wrenching ethical dilemmas to prison medical personnel (Smith, 1984).

There are other issues in the disciplining of disturbed inmates that raise even more fundamental questions. In the New York survey report, a retarded inmate is described who is frustrated by an officer, sets his cell on fire, is locked up, and ends up weeping unconsolably. In connection with another case, staff learned of "instances where inmates had been sentenced to time in punitive segregation *as punishment for having attempted to kill themselves*" (Steelman, 1987: 41; emphasis in the original). The survey staff report that:

> In one instance, an inmate at Coxsacke [a youth prison] was sent to SHU for a term of 18 months: twelve months for attempting to escape, and six months for attempting suicide after being recaptured. The hearing officer at the disciplinary proceeding stated that, although the inmate was clearly in need of

mental health services, he was being sent to SHU as an example to the other
prisoners, and [he] would simply have to learn to "face his problems."

Given the system in which the hearing officer exercises his function,
this statement represents the most humane position he can take, recognizing the irrationality of the inmate's motives. What the officer does
is to restate the premise of the disciplinary process, which is designed
for punishment and deterrence. Penalties are meant to discourage disruptive acts, which include suicide attempts, presupposing that inmates
possess sufficient rationality of motive to make punishment plausible
and deterrence possible. In his capacity as a client of the mental health
system, the inmate may be a panic-stricken youth who embarks on an
unthinking, fantasy-imbued effort at escape, followed by an ambivalent
gesture of self-destruction; in his capacity as target of discipline, the
same inmate becomes sturdier; we assume he can learn to "face his
problem" after a protracted term of enforced solitude. In his capacity
as disciplinary client, the inmate also serves as object lesson to those
who (unlike himself) premeditatedly contemplate jailbreaks or suicide
attempts.

The point is not that such an inmate is inappropriately disciplined
(though 18 months of segregation is a gargantuan sentence that may be
disproportionate to the offense) but that the inmate looks different from
the stereotypic offender for whom the system is intended. It is to the
latter sort of inmate—to the mythical "no-prison-can-hold-me" type of
escapee—that the hearing officer's admonitions are plausibly addressed.

The problem is that the system contains an insufficient number of
options (essentially two: disciplinary and mental health), and has no
way of combining these options other than through a mental health
referral "on the side."[5] Standard responses must thus address nonstandard problems, and the outcome is often strained and ill-fitting.

---

[5] Glaser (1977) is one of few observers who argues against a pristine conception of discipline. He writes that "a deliberate effort to integrate discipline with counseling is appropriate . . . discipline rehabilitates inmates providing that the rules become internalized as their personal opinions. Also, habits are best extinguished if they are not merely
punished, but if alternative behavior is reinforced by reward" (p. 308).

Fox (1958) suggests that "within the system of rewards and punishments, the prison
administrator must maintain a treatment center or adjustment center, which is a 'therapeutic community' without the sanctions of reward and punishment which the incor-
rigible offenders have already demonstrated by their incorrigibility that they are not
prepared to take. . . . The custodial personnel who attempt to maintain discipline in a
prison must be prepared to understand human behavior, rather than trying to judge the
amount of pressure necessary to keep a man in line" (p. 326).

4. SUPPLEMENTING DISCIPLINARY RESPONSES

Hearing staff use mental health referrals but do so infrequently, and mostly in conjunction with other formal dispositions. The fact is understandable, not only because the point at which inmates have been charged with offenses seems the wrong time to make referrals, but also because mental health staff are reputed to be inhospitable to clients whose behavior problems are salient, unless they show symptoms of formally diagnosable disorders.

Nonetheless, priceless opportunities may have been missed at such junctures because disciplinary hearing officers make ideal referral agents. This is so because they have data about inmate behavior that enables them to identify problem inmates. Most importantly, they have data about past transgressions that permit them to think about patterned chronicity. Incident descriptions in disciplinary dossiers provide clues as to whether the motivational pattern of the inmate is nonroutine, in the sense that his or her behavior reflects low maturity level, emotional problems, intellectual limitations, or social ineptness. The hearing officer routinely knows about any sanctions that have been tried in the past without success, in efforts to break cycles of misbehavior. Finally, the officer is in a position to decide whether sanctioning the inmate makes sense, not only in terms of what sanctions have accomplished but in terms of whether the personality and behavior pattern of the offender corresponds to the offender stereotype (volitional, deliberate, and malevolent) for which the sanctioning process is designed (Fox, 1958).

If, *in the disciplinary officer's mind*, standard punitive dispositions sit uneasily when applied to an inmate, the officer should have nonstandard options that he could use to supplement the options he now has. This means that the prison system should provide the officer with tools that have rehabilitative potential as an adjunct to purely disciplinary sanctions, where these do not make sense. Such tools should be available to the officer *and* the inmate in that the inmate must ultimately decide whether he prefers to see himself as *being* a problem and/or as *having* a problem, provided he does not contest his culpability. One would hope that *some* inmates might consider the appropriateness of self-appraisal, particularly at a career juncture—such as having been caught with the goods for the umpteenth time—that links their conduct with an impending undesired fate. Even more tangible incentives could be provided, of course, such as the hearing officer suspending his disposition to permit the inmate to try a new or different program.

Resocialization options one can consider vary, and though we shall delineate an option to show how it would work, many others come to mind. Therapeutic communities of all kinds have been successfully tried (Toch, 1980; Whiteley, Briggs, and Turner, 1973), and one model, the Just Community (Hickey and Scharf, 1980), offers moral education as its modality and looks particularly germane. Expanding mental health services could cover adjustment and coping problems, provided mental health staff decided they were willing to deal with mental health, as opposed to mental illness, concerns. Behavioral and social learning approaches also have relevance to maladaptive behavior, but given the history of the deployment of behavior modification in prisons (to which we shall return), such approaches must be designed to meet the highest standards of ethics and humaneness.

No matter what referral or program options are considered, one must face the basic question of whether a socialization or rehabilitative effort can be grafted or appended onto the disciplinary process. The latter, after all, serves the prison's interest, whereas the former's goal is to assist people to lead happier, fuller, and more productive lives. We now turn to this question:

5. IMPROVING COPING SKILLS: THE ETHICAL DILEMMA

An intervention that centers on the coping deficits of persons in any setting such as a prison must parcel out attributes of the setting. This is so because one cannot treat an individual as a "noncoper" should the demands that are made on him be inhumane, unreasonable, or unfair. If a person fails to conform to conditions to which no one should be expected to conform— or if he stands out because he is "sane in insane places" (Rosenhan, 1973)—his conduct may indeed be descriptively maladaptive, but the cause of his problem—and the solution to his problem—lie in reforms of the environment.

The same point does not hold in most settings, where the environment and the person are both imperfect and where maladaptive behavior may be sparked by constraints and pressures but where it is also disproportionate, destructive, or self-destructive and/or harms both the person and the environment. Although there may be no excuse for stultifying educational settings, for instance, one can legitimately center attention on persons who engage in vandalism, predation, or disruptiveness in such settings on the grounds that these persons' behavior (1) is not a corollary or consequence of imperfections of the setting, and (2) would make the person a substantial liability in any setting, to himself and to others. Moreover, there is the fact that inside the setting, maladaptive behavior (3) worsens the quality of the environment even further, both for the noncoper's contemporaries and those whose follow in his wake.

These considerations, on the other hand, only make it doubly necessary that any interventionist's goals be uncompromisingly clear and that such goals unambiguously translate into details of program design. The demise of behavior modification in 1974 after its shortlived introduction into adult prisons is a case in point. As noted in an authoritative overview sponsored by NIMH (Brown, Wienckowski, and Stolz, 1975):

> Persons using behavior modification procedures have been particularly criticized for their attempts to deal with rebellious and nonconformist behavior of inmates in penal institutions. Because the behavioral professional is often in the position of assisting in the management of prisoners whose antagonism to authority and rebelliousness have been the catalyst for conflict within the institution, the distinctions among his multiple functions of therapy, management, and rehabilitation can become blurred, and his allegiance confused. (p. 16)

The NIMH authors conclude that

> behavior modification should not be used in an attempt to facilitate institutionalization of the inmate or to make him adjust to inhumane living conditions. Further, no therapist should accept requests for treatment that take the form "make him 'behave,'" when the intent of the request is to make the person conform to oppressive conditions. (p. 17)

Given this proscription, it is clear that early prison interventionists, who had operated a program called START in a federal institution from 1972 to 1974, had invited some of the disapproval they had generated. One member of the group (Scheckenbach, 1984) maintains that inmates could be given no choice about participating in START and notes that "the basic argument for involuntariness arises from the original idea of such a program as START" (p. 468). This "original idea" was expressed by a friendly witness at a START-inspired trial who pointed out that "a voluntary program could be expected to be used by those prisoners who find themselves distressed by their situation, not by those who are causing extreme distress to others but are little inconvenienced themselves" (p. 468). The mutually exclusive view that "distress to self" and "distress to others" poses a choice of goals is resolved in favor of a custody-related concern. Scheckenbach (1974) recalls that "the task which was presented to the START staff was to develop a program to establish and/or increase what the institution and society deems as [sic] adaptive, appropriate behavior" (p. 463).

The problem lies in the fact that *only* the prison but *never* the inmate enters this sort of equation. What did not occur to Scheckenbach and his colleagues is that punitively dealt with inmates might "deem" some behaviors maladaptive themselves if given the opportunity to review the data from their own perspective. It might be relevant to the inmates, for example, to discover that they had "spent an average of 49% of their institutional time in segregation status where they continued to be destructive of property, assaultive towards other inmates, and verbally and physically abusive towards staff, including throwing food, urine, and feces at them" (p. 463).

The issue for the inmates, of course, would be different than that for staff, whose concern revolves around the bankruptcy of custodial alternatives that leaves the system no recourse but to place men in perpetual lockup. But the inmates, as it happens, have ended up equally resourceless, as reflected in the impotence of the blind rage with which they express their helplessness and their inability to extricate themselves from escalating confrontations.

This means that interventions could solve the prisons' problem while solving that of the inmates. One at least could solve the problem of inmates who might consider having a problem after mature deliberation, under circumstances that show respect for them as responsible, self-determining adults. Given the exercise of such options—followed by program participation providing opportunities for self-examination— the inmates could preserve their dignity and the prison could also benefit, without need for the interventionist to wallow in the question— "Which master do I serve, and who is my client?"

It can be argued, in fact, that one cannot help the inmate without helping the prison, in that *no coping problems can be addressed without attending to contemporary behavior,* which means that when one addresses the maladaptive behavior of persons *who happen to be in prison,* one's subject matter must be behavior *in the prison,* which is of necessity maladaptive *to the prison,* or some aspect of prison. If the inmate is to review and try to change his behavior, there is no way in which one can obtain data for the inmate to analyze and no way of rehearsing and testing his new behavioral options other than by centering on management-relevant facts and expecting to see improvements of which prison officials would approve.

6. A REGENERATIVE APPROACH TO THE CHRONIC OFFENDER

There are several somewhat interrelated behavior change strategies that could provide a supplement to disciplinary approaches to managing the chronic offender. One strategy is that suggested by studies of dependent populations other than offenders.

Langer (1983) has reviewed such studies and has described a sense of power that comes from participating in decisions that contribute to mastering one's internal and external environment. Her work suggests that if a person can evolve a formula that extricates him from a dilemma he poses to himself or others, such regenerative problem solving can increase the person's feelings of self-esteem and his feelings of mastery in addressing problems of social living. By sharing a review of one's patterned problem with one's peers and then sharing with such peers an accountability strategy for modifying one's pattern, a person can move through cognitive problem solving, to what Maxwell Jones (1953) called "emotional social learning." In this modality, a great many feelings can be explored and experienced beyond whatever insight is derived from engagement in creative thinking.

Social learning of the sort discussed by Jones centers on feedback about a person's maladaptive behavior, particularly, maladaptive behavior that causes problems, which provides "live" learning content for social learning (therapeutic) groups. It is a short step from this view to envisage a group that centers on each member's *pattern* of maladaptive behavior, which can be deduced from a series of incidents in which the person has encountered difficulties and produced problems for others. This approach has not yet been attempted with prison disciplinary incidents but has been deployed in peer review panels that centered on arrest reports filed by problem police officers. (Toch, Grant, and Galvin, 1975). The review panel process consisted of the following stages:

(1) *The necessity for the panel is documented.* Typically, the process would be initiated when an officer reaches a threshold number of incidents on an up-to-date inventory of violent involvements.

Other ways of mobilizing the review panel would include requests by supervisors or by the subjects themselves. In such cases, however, the record would have to bear out the man's eligibility by showing a substantial number of recent involvements.

(2) *A preparatory investigation for the interview* is conducted. Data relating to the subject's performance on the street is obtained from available secondary sources. This includes interviews with supervisors, reports by peers, and all information on record. The investigation culminates in a planning session in which panelists formulate hypotheses and draft questions that streamline the panel session.

(3) Then comes the interview itself, which can be divided into three stages:

(a) *Key incidents are chronologically explored,* including not only actions taken by all persons involved in the incident, but also their perceptions, assumptions, feelings and motives.

(b) *The summation of these data in the form of common denominators and patterns* is undertaken primarily by the subject, with participation by the panelists. An effort is made to test the plausibility and relevance of the hypothesized patterns by extrapolating them into other involvements.

(c) *The discussion of the pattern* occurs last, and includes tracing its contribution to violence. This stage features the exploration of alternative approaches that might be conducive to more constructive solutions. (Toch *et al.*: 246–247)

In transposing this model into a prison context, one could assume for simplicity's sake that the program can be developed as a component of an ongoing therapeutic community. The administrative entities involved would then be the disciplinary panel of the prison and the therapeutic community's membership. The disciplinary staff could nominate participants, and the inmate who is nominated would have the choice of volunteering or not for participation. The therapeutic community staff could have the final say about whether they would accept the volunteer. For at least the initial effort, it would seem reasonable that if the therapeutic community staff would not want to accept an inmate because they feel that he poses a disruptive potential for the rest of the community, it should be up to the disciplinary staff to make another decision as to appropriate action. A disciplinary pattern, however, should not be grounds for rejection from the program because the nominated inmate would have to be a chronic disciplinary offender facing the disciplinary board's action following a specific formal incident charge.

Though intake screening poses a risk of creating interface problems (through accusations of "dumping" countered by charges of excessive intake selectivity), there are countervailing advantages. For one, the step provides staff with the opportunity to study the inmate's folder, to formulate hypotheses, and to plan social management approaches; for another, staff (and possibly inmates involved in screening) would have a chance to make a public commitment to take risks of their own devising, which is a powerful means of reducing resistance in planned change experiments (Lewin, 1947).

The core of an inmate-centered intervention could consist of a group comprised of four or five review candidates, and the staff team could consist of a mental health and a custodial staff member and an inmate peer counselor. The latter role could evolve as the program matures, in that the peer staff member could then be selected from a pool of successful program graduates, and he could be picked for having charisma and demonstrated problem-solving competence.

Sequences of events in the groups's operation could vary, but a plausible sequence could consist of four stages or phases. Phases 1, 2, and 3 could be scheduled for 2 hours a day over 5 consecutive days each week. In the first part of Phase 1, the group would review with each of its members his recorded formal incidents over his entire career thus far, as they appear in his record. Following an analysis in which themes and patterns are hypothesized, the inmate could be allowed to add additional information to expand and/or modify the initial formulation. All members of the group would be expected to participate in sharing ideas and questions in an effort at mutual problem solving, the goal being to reach a consensus as to patterns that describe each individual's incident sequence and account for his repetitive nonadaptive behavior.

Phase 2 would consist of role playing and reverse role playing by participants for pattern clarification and understanding. In such role playing, the inmate would play himself and assorted opponents (fellow inmates or staff) in characteristic personal encounters. Other means could also be used to ensure that the inmate internalizes the results of his pattern analyses. This task, moreover, is not confined to pattern definition, in that once the pattern is defined, cues must be identified that set off incidents. These cues could be a suspected putdown, a guilt feeling, a sense of crowding, anger, and pangs of loneliness, and direct and/or imagined threats from others.

Once incident cues have been surfaced, the strategy calls for self-control routines, actions that the person derives from the role playing and shared thinking of the group about just what sets him off when. These self-management responses to incident cues could be breathing and muscle-flexing routines, a "time-out" session, a memorized talk to oneself (counting to 10 or its equivalent), contacting a previously identified supportive other, working out, counseling, sharing with peer–inmate counselors, involvement in program development or conflict negotiation or mediation, AA-type procedures such as apology and seeking a fresh start in one or more relationships, scheduled and/or emergency group meetings. Such techniques would make up Phase 3 of the process, which would consist of the development of a change strategy for each of the offenders, with the crucial requisite being the participation of the person in developing his own strategy for self management.

Phase 4 would consist of quality control reviews. At some point following the termination of Phase 3 (possibly after several months), the panel would meet to check on the progress of each offender, reviewing critical benchmarks that would be included in the inmate's plan of action. This review would be followed by a discussion of possible strategy modifications. Additional progress reviews could occur after reasonable intervals, leading to further modifications of coping strategies for the inmate.

7. OBSTACLES AND RESOURCES

Some major concerns must be addressed in proposing a program such as that outlined above. For openers, how much staff, inmate, and organizational resistance must we anticipate? Beside initial resistance to letting any new program be established, what are the probabilities that an effort such as this would become an "innovation ghetto," with its operation, whether successful or not, seen as a competing not-part-of-the-regular-program irritant? After top-level legitimating, it would seem in order to spend considerable time addressing the concerns of the multioverlapping reference groups of the organization—very much including employee unions. Custody, mental health, and disciplinary staff would have to be represented in organizational meetings in which the program is discussed.

A second consideration is how the target group of chronic offenders would be perceived by significant and general others as a result of their participation. Will they be flooded with problems of being seen as "snitches," "crazies," or "manipulators," as opposed to people with a real problem who are engaging in a legitimate effort at problem solving?

Conducting a program as a component of an established therapeutic community would obviously help to get it under way. Having the inmate participate in lieu of a suspended sentence is a possible motivator, but this context raises the specter of blackmail. On the other hand, it might help the offender justify his program participation and help him to provide a rationale to others as to why he is participating.

Putting aside the possibility of participation as an alternative to a suspended sentence or to punitive custody, what might be "in it" for the participating chronic offender? Most critical, it would seem, is the opportunity provided for the inmate to gain support and recognition of his ability to change, a rare commodity within the prison culture in general and for chronic offenders in particular. Another major benefit to the participant is the chance he would get of solving a difficult problem for himself. Although it is certain that any self-respecting chronic offender will experience a sense of injustice during and following repeated disciplinary encounters, he will also perhaps have experienced moments of doubt. It is axiomatic that no one—including the chronic problem inmate—is bad, mad, or deviate all of the time. The appeal one could offer such a person, therefore, is one of redemption and of escape from a seemingly insoluble problem at a time of personal crisis.

ACKNOWLEDGMENTS. The research on which this chapter is based was supported by the National Institute of Mental Health under Grant #7RO-IMH39573-01 ("Careers of Disturbed and/or Disruptive Inmates"). We are indebted to Raymond Broaddus, assistant commissioner of Health Services, New York State Department of Correctional Services, for facilitating access to the prison records on which this chapter is based. Opinions expressed are ours, however, and do not reflect views of sponsoring agencies.

8. REFERENCES

Brown, B. S., Wienckowski, L. A., and Stolz, S. B. *Behavior modification: Perspective on a current issue.* Washington, DC: Department of Health, Education and Welfare, NIMH, 1975.

Fogel, D. "*We are the living proof. . .*" *The justice model for corrections.* Cincinnati: Anderson Publishing, 1975.

Fox, V. Analysis of prison disciplinary violations. *Journal of Criminal Law, Criminology and Police Science,* 1958, *49,* 321–326.

Glaser, D. *The effectiveness of a prison and parole system.* Indianapolis: Bobbs-Merrill, 1964.

Glaser, D. Institutional disciplinary action and the social psychology of disciplinary relationships. In R. M. Carter, D. Glaser, and L. T. Wilkins (Eds.), *Correctional institutions* (2nd ed.). Philadelphia: Lippincott, 1977.

Hickey, J. E., and Scharf, P. L. *Toward a just correctional system: Experiments in implementing democracy in prisons.* San Francisco: Jossey-Bass, 1980.

Irwin, J. *The felon.* Englewood Cliffs, NJ: Prentice-Hall, 1970.

Jones, M. *The therapeutic community: A new treatment method in psychiatry.* New York: Basic Books, 1953.

Langer, E. J. *The psychology of control.* Beverly Hills, CA: 1983.

Lewin, K. Group decision and social change. In T. M. Newcomb and E. L. Hartley (Eds.), *Readings in social psychology.* New York: Holt & Company, 1947.

Lombardo, L. X. *Guards imprisoned: Correctional officers at work.* New York: Elsevier, 1981.

Rosenhan, D. On being sane in insane places, *Science,* 1973,. *179,* 250–258, *180,* 365–369.

Scheckenbach, A. F. Behavior modification and adult offenders. In I. Jacks and S. G. Cox (Eds.), *Psychological approaches to crime and its correction.* Chicago: Nelson-Hall, 1984.

Smith, R. *Prison health care.* London: British Medical Association, 1984.

Steelman, D. *The mentally impaired in New York's prisons: Problems and solutions.* New York: The Correctional Association of New York, 1987.

Toch, H. *Living in prison: The ecology of survival.* New York: Free Press, 1977.

Toch, H. *Therapeutic communities in corrections.* New York: Praeger, 1980.

Toch, H., and Adams, K. Pathology and disruptiveness among prison inmates. *Journal of Research in Crime and Delinquency,* 1986, *23,* 7–21.

Toch, H., and Adams, K. In the eye of the beholder? Assessments of psychopathology among prisoners by federal prison staff. *Journal of Research in Crime and Delinquency,* 1987, *24,* 119–139.

Toch, H., and Adams, K. Punishment, treatment and prison infractions. *Journal of Offender Counseling and Rehabilitation,* 1988, *12,* 5–18.

Toch, H., Grant, J. D., and Galvin, R. T. *Agents of change: A study in police reform.* Cambridge, MA: Schenkman Publishing, 1975.

Whiteley, S., Briggs, D., and Turner, M. *Dealing with deviants: The treatment of antisocial behavior.* New York: Schocken Books, 1973.

Chapter 12

INMATE ADJUSTMENT TO PRISON

LYNNE GOODSTEIN and KEVIN N. WRIGHT

1. INTRODUCTION

Since the publication of *The Prison Community* (Clemmer, 1940) virtually thousands of books and articles have been published on prison life and the adjustment of prisoners to their confinement. Most authors depict prison life as destructive to inmates who reenter community life with increased knowledge concerning the mechanics of crime and a reserve of bitterness toward "the system." In recent years, researchers have recognized that whereas incarceration impacts adversely on some prisoners, others cope relatively well with the stresses of confinement. Researchers have begun to identify factors, both external to the prison environment and internal to the inmate, as well as combinations of these factors that may influence the type of adjustment an inmate makes.

This chapter reviews work produced within the past several decades on inmate adjustment to prison, focusing on conditions of incarceration and individual inmate characteristics found to influence adjustment patterns. It pays special attention to environmental conditions, personality factors, and behavioral responses that may mediate against the potentially adverse effects of incarceration.

LYNNE GOODSTEIN • Administration of Justice Department, The Pennsylvania State University, University Park, Pennsylvania 16802.   KEVIN N. WRIGHT • Center for Education and Social Research, State University of New York at Binghamton, Binghamton, New York 13901.

2. MODELS OF PRISONER ADJUSTMENT

Scholars of prisoner reactions to incarceration have primarily focused on mechanisms that allow or promote antisocial prisoner behavior
and attitudes. Two perspectives have been proposed to account for the
presumed negative influences of prison life, one centering upon features
of the prison environment, the other on characteristics of the prisoner
population itself.

3. RESEARCH ON PRISONER SUBCULTURES: THE
DEPRIVATION MODEL

Early research on inmate adjustment focused on unique characteristics of the prison environment that influenced inmate behavior, both
within prison and after release. Researchers assumed that particular
aspects of prison life exert negative influences on inmates' attitudes,
values, modes of social interaction and self-concepts, causing prisoners
to be less capable of succeeding in the community after release than they
were upon entry. This view has become known as the deprivation model
of imprisonment.

Deprivation theorists characterized the prison as an environment
that prevents inmates from fulfilling certain basic needs. Sykes (1958;
see also Sykes and Messinger, 1960) articulated the deprivations inmates
are forced to endure as the five "pains of imprisonment" that include
the loss of social acceptance, material possessions, personal security,
heterosexual relations and personal autonomy. Inmates' responses to
these deprivations, both at the social organizational and individual levels, then become the objects of study for researchers attempting to examine the deprivation model.

3.1. Prisonization and the Inmate Counterculture

Most deprivation model researchers have focused upon the social
and organizational responses of prisoners to incarceration (Clemmer,
1940; Garabedian, 1963; McCorkle and Korn, 1954; Sykes, 1958; Tittle,
1972; Wellford, 1967). They suggest that inmates cope with their deprivations by developing a normative system that opposed the authority
exercized by institutional staff and administration. Known as the "inmate code," this system emphasizes such actions as refusing to report
inmate rule violations or to assist authorities in other matters of discipline, rejecting the value of treatment and work programs, and main-
taing loyalty to and solidarity with other inmates (Clemmer, 1940; Well-

ford, 1967). Collective adherence to this code results in an informal counterculture in which inmates could be accepted on their own terms and achieve self-respect. Conformity to this normative system, better known as "prisonization," enables inmates to "reject their rejectors" (McCorkle and Korn, 1954) and neutralize the pains of imprisonment.

To examine the validity of the deprivation model, researchers attempted to demonstrate that aspects of the inmate subculture arose in response to the unique deprivations of imprisonment itself. Presumably, as the extent of deprivation varies across institutions or among individuals, so, too, should the degree of prisonization. Thus researchers examined inmates' level of prisonization as a function of conditions and contexts of deprivation, such as length of time served and type of facility.

3.1.1. Time Served

Assuming that extended time in prison results in increased deprivation, researchers have examined the relationship of prisonization to both time served and sentence phase. In a well-known study, Wheeler (1961) found that conformity to conventional norms varies as a U-shaped function with time; inmates arrive at prison with conventional values, serve midsentences with prisonized perspectives, and then resume conventional values as they approach release. Findings of some subsequent studies support the existence of this U-shape relationship (Garabedian, 1963; Jensen and Jones, 1976), whereas the findings of others question the recurrence of conventionality (Atchley and McCabe, 1968; Hautaluoma and Scott, 1973; Troyer and Frease, 1975; Wellford, 1967). In studies that found inmate attitudes varying with time served, however, increased commitment to antisocial values accompanied more time served (Garabedian, 1963; Wellford, 1967; Wheeler, 1961), suggesting that more time in prison may lead to increasingly antisocial attitudes.

3.1.2. Facility Type

Researchers have also pointed to the deprivation model to account for the higher levels of prisonization found among inmates incarcerated in facilities emphasizing custody versus treatment (Akers, Hayner, and Gruninger, 1977; Berk, 1966; Fry, 1976; Street, Vinter, and Perrow, 1966; Sieverdes and Bartollas, 1986). However, it is also possible that these differences are the result of selection bias, as the studies cited do not control for differences in the inmate populations across institutions of varying security levels.

One study does attempt to separate the effects of institutional environment from those of the characteristics of the inmate population.

Feld (1981) examined juveniles, matched on preprison characteristics, from 10 residential placements differing across the treatment-custody continuum. Compared to treatment-oriented placements, custodial institutions foster higher levels of inmate violence and exploitation, more alienation from staff, less inmate solidarity, less trust and concern for others, the valuing of inmate leaders who filled violent and negative roles, and a general acceptance of the necessity for direct physical action and toughness. His work provides an important demonstration of the influence of organizational structure and deprivation on the development of antisocial attitudes and behavior among inmates.

3.2. Institutional Dependency

Another branch of deprivation theory targets the formal, "official" structure of the prison organization as contributing to adjustment difficulties for inmates. Beginning with the work of Goffman (1961), some scholars have argued that the prison fosters institutional dependency by infantilizing inmates, altering their self-concepts, undermining their self-esteem, and limiting their autonomy.

Scholars in this tradition describe the implications of functioning in an overregulated "total institution" on the inmate's self-concept. For example, although most prisoners consider the maintenance of their relationships with significant others outside of prison as a foremost concern (Richards, 1978), the reality of incarceration allows for only brief, infrequent, and stilted interactions with family and friends in crowded and noisy visiting rooms. Moreover, as Meisenhelder (1985) notes, the attributes of prisoners considered to be most salient by prison officials have little to do with the individuals' fundamental views of themselves as fathers, husbands, or group members. Rather, ones's offense and sentence length exert primary influence over decisions concerning one's treatment, place of residence, and eligibility for institutional benefits such as work release and furloughs. Defined by past conduct and prevented from continuing meaningful levels of contact with individuals outside of prison, prisoners perceive that time has stopped until they can resume their former identities upon release.

Institutional dependency theorists also suggest that prison life undermines inmates' abilities for autonomous decision making through providing inadequate opportunities for exerting control (Goodstein, MacKenzie, and Shotland, 1984). They argue that institutional life creates a sense of helplessness through minimizing outcome control, choice, and predictability, three mechanisms through which individuals achieve senses of control.

Life is routinized for inmates, who are given few choices to exert.

Prisoners are permitted few choices over the content or scheduling of their daily activities, their clothing and personal effects, or their living arrangements. The reality of confinement continually reinforces a prisoner's inability to exert outcome control because an inmate is not in a position to effect the outcome most desired, immediate release from prison. And although in many ways the extreme regimentation of prison life creates an ultrapredictable situation, most prisoners are not reliably provided with advance information about critical events such as furloughs, job changes, and parole release dates.

Theorists and researchers who focus on the impacts of the formal institutional organization on inmates suggest that these identity-stripping and control-limiting mechanisms undermine inmates' capabilities for coping with their environments, both within prison and later after their release. Considerable psychological research on the effects of reduced control tells us that individuals with limited control opportunities can experience such adverse impacts as depression, anxiety, and increased health risks (see Goodstein et al., 1984, for a review of this research). Although less empirical research on the consequences of "identity stripping" has been performed, ample evidence exists that many prisoners are preoccupied with, and fear, the prospect of becoming institutionally dependent (Meisenhelder, 1985).

3.3. Deprivation Effects on Postrelease Outcome

In the case of both effects of deprivation, prisonization, and institutional dependency, scholars contend that these conditions are counterproductive for postrelease success. Prisonization researchers argue that conformity to the inmate subculture decreases the likelihood of postrelease success (Clemmer, 1940; McKorkle and Korn, 1954; Thomas and Foster, 1972), although few studies have examined this relationship empirically.

Others emphasize the negative impacts of the deprivation of autonomy inherent in prison life. Morris and Morris (1962) claim that incarceration results in "the continuous and systematic destruction of the psyche" (p. 347). They and others (Goffman, 1961; Goodstein, 1979) propose that institutionalization produces prisoners who are ill-suited for life after release due to the prison's reinforcement of institutionally dependent behavior. Because prisons deprive inmates of opportunities for independence and autonomy, releasees who adjust well to institutional pressures for obedience may experience greater postrelease difficulties than inmates who resist such pressures. Four studies that have examined the relationship between institutional adjustment and postrelease outcome suggest that conformity to the rules of the formal organization may lead to greater difficulties upon release, whereas nonconformity may enhance short-term postrelease adjustment (Goodstein, 1979; Jaman, 1971; Kassebaum, Ward, and Wilner, 1971; Miller and Dinitz, 1973).

4. THE IMPORTATION MODEL: A COUNTERPOINT TO DEPRIVATION

In proposing the importation model of prisonization, John Irwin (Irwin, 1970; Irwin and Cressey, 1962) challenged the deprivation theorists' view that prisoner social behavior is purely a reflection of the unique deprivations of incarceration. He argued that inmate subcultures, norms, and roles are extensions of belief systems and norms to which prisoners had subscribed prior to entering prison and that the inmate subculture mirrors prisoners' preprison social and personal characteristics. In essence, one needed to look no further than the street for the origins of prisonization.

Jacobs (1974, 1976, 1977) and Carroll (1974) joined Irwin to further argue that the deprivation model's perspective of a unified and cohesive prisoner social organization was simplistic and inaccurate. Rejecting the assumption of widespread inmate solidarity, they viewed the prison population as comprised of multiple subgroups subscribing to different norms and values and competing with one another for power and influence.

> New analyses of prison organization must shake loose from the "total institution" model . . . with its emphasis on individual and small group reactions to material and psychological deprivations. . . . Perhaps the prison community is more fruitfully viewed as an arena where competing groups seek at each other's expense larger memberships and greater power. (Jacobs, 1976, p. 476)

Advocates of this differentiated inmate subculture model proposed that fundamental changes in prisons had resulted in a breakdown in the solidarity of the informal inmate community that had dominated prisons from the early part of this century until approximately the 1960s. Specifically, authors (Irwin, 1980; Jacobs, 1976) pointed to the rapidly increasing proportions of ethnic and racial minorities in prisons, coming particularly at a time of general societal attention to issues of racism and civil rights, as partially responsible for divisions within the inmate community.

Theorists also portrayed the inmate subculture as fundamentally altered by changes in correctional management styles introduced in many prisons during the 1960s and 1970s. As opposed to earlier periods in which correctional administrations functioned autonomously, with little surveillance and virtually no intervention from the "outside," during the 1960s a variety of external groups targeted prison conditions as issues of interest. Pressure for change, coupled with increased civil litigation aimed at improvements in prison conditions, resulted in more liberal conditions of confinement. Inmates enjoyed greater freedom of movement, more yard and recreational privileges, increased opportunities to participate in interest groups and clubs, and more relaxed mail and visitation privileges.

Ironically, the trend toward relaxation of administrative control, combined with the shifting demographics of the prisoner population, may have rendered institutions less safe and more dominated by a violent ethic than when they had been controlled by more repressive administration (Ekland-Olson, 1986; Irwin, 1980; Marquart, 1986; Marquart and Crouch, 1985; Stastny and Tyrnauer, 1982).

Investigations of the increased role of inmate violence appear to have replaced earlier preoccupations with prisonization among criminologists. More recent organizational analyses of contemporary prison life highlight the importance of the expression or threat of violence to the inmate "public culture" (Carroll, 1974; Colvin, 1982; Irwin, 1980; Jacobs, 1977; Johnson, 1987). As Johnson (1987) states in his review, "violence became the order of the day and the preferred mode of adjustment among the convicts" (p. 84). And Irwin (1980) aptly notes, "Toughness in the new hero in the violent men's prison means, first, being able to take care of oneself in the prison world, where people will attack others with little or no provocation. Second, it means having the guts to take from the weak" (p. 193).

These descriptions leave readers with an image of prison as dangerous and damaging to inmates. Within the violent culture of the new prison, inmates must become familiar with violent tactics, or at least maintain the facade. This orientation, although presumed necessary within the institutional context, ultimately leads to problems in postrelease adjustment. The case in point is Jack Abbott (1981), a long-term incarcerate who embodied the orientation toward violence described in this literature and who, shortly after release, engaged in an unprovocated act of aggression that resulted in his reincarceration.

4.1. Empirical Tests of the Importation Model

Compared to the deprivation mode, the importation model implies different hypotheses about the origins of prisoner subcultures and the determinants of prisoner behavior. If features that inmates bring with them to prison determine inmate adaptation to prison, major differences in adjustment patterns should be found among inmates with different preprison characteristics and experiences. The importation model predicts that factors such as race, sex, and area of origin constitute important determinants of prisoner adjustment.

4.1.1. Racial Differences in Inmate Adjustment

Considerable research on the association of race and inmate adjustment has been conducted in recent years. Black and white inmates have been found to differ in patterns of adjustment in areas such as ethnic/racial solidarity, expression of power and violence, experience of stress, and prisonization.

Researchers describe blacks as developing a significantly more integrated and supportive social system within prison than whites (Carroll, 1974; Johnson, 1976). This sense of solidarity derives from blacks' shared cultural background, having come primarily from low-income urban areas (Fagan and Lira, 1978). Additionally, blacks' shared experience with racism and discrimination and their identification with political, social, or religious groups may provide them with more avenues through which to experience, and express, solidarity (Jacobs, 1976; Reasons, 1974).

In studies of inmate conflict and violence, research has found that blacks are more likely to possess control and influence in daily institutional affairs (Bartollas, Miller, and Dinitz, 1976) and be aggressors in conflict situations (Fuller and Orsagh, 1977). Studies relying upon official misconduct figures find that officials charge blacks with assaultive behavior more frequently than whites (Flanagan, 1983; Poole and Regoli, 1980; Ramirez, 1984). In instances of sexual victimization, findings suggest that blacks are perpetrators and whites targets (Bartollas *et al.*, 1976; Carroll, 1974; Scacco, 1975; Wooden and Parker, 1982). For example, one study finds that compared to one-fifth of blacks, almost half of the whites in a sample of New York State prison inmates were targets of sexual aggression (Lockwood, 1980).

Whether these results accurately reflect differentials in aggressive behavior between blacks and whites is unclear because other studies find no differences (Ellis, Grasmick, and Gilman, 1974; Goetting and Howsen, 1983; Petersilia, 1983; Wright, 1987) or inconsistent results (Goodstein and MacKenzie, 1984) in the frequency of aggressive acts. Some researchers propose that apparent race differences on aggression may result from discriminatory treatment of blacks by correctional staff, thereby inflating official statistics (Poole and Regoli, 1980; Wright, 1987) and aggravating resistance among the inmates themselves (Goodstein and MacKenize, 1984).

In the areas of stress and coping, research suggests that whites have more difficulty in adjusting to prison life than blacks. Compared to blacks, white manifest a higher rate of psychological breakdowns (Johnson, 1976) and self-injury (Wright, 1987), higher levels of general mood disturbance, more depression, and more anxiety (Fagan and Lira, 1978; Oldroyd and Howell, 1977), although one study found whites to be no more anxious and less depressed (Goodstein and MacKenzie, 1984).

Ironically, little is known about the relationship of race to prisonization itself, yet available studies produce consistent results. Blacks appear to enter prison with highly prisonized attitudes and maintain them throughout their terms. In contrast, whites appear to develop prisonized attitudes after exposure to the prison culture, manifesting either a linear increase in prisonized attitudes (Alpert, 1978; Goodstein and MacKenzie, 1984) or Wheeler's U-shape function (Jensen and Jones, 1976). Evidence suggests that racial differences in prisonization result from differential exposure among blacks and whites to the world of the urban inner city. Goodstein and MacKenzie (1984) found that by controlling for area of origin, racial differences disappeared, suggesting that inmates who come from urban backgrounds enter prison equipped with prisonized attitudes. This finding would characterize the experience of proportionately more blacks than whites.

4.1.2. Sex Differences in Inmate Adjustment

If inmates import a subculture into the prison context, a logical test of the model would be a comparison of male and female prisoners. Researchers have found that in place of male prisoners' emphasis on toughness, opposition to staff, and general solidarity, female prisoners develop strong bonds with smaller groups (Giallombardo, 1966; Heffernan, 1972; Ward and Kassebaum, 1965). Many female prison inmates have been documented as forming pseudofamilies in which women play specific roles, such as husband, daughter, or cousin, providing emotional and material support to other family members (Fox, 1982). Attempts to identify a unitary inmate social structure, parallel to that which presumably dominates men's prisons, have been unsuccessful (Heffernan, 1972).

Researchers have also looked specifically at patterns of homosexuality within women's prisons. Rather than using homosexual activity as a means of expressing dominance and power, as is the case for most males in prison (Lockwood, 1980), women engage in homosexual relationships on a more consensual basis as a means of obtaining emotional security during incarceration (Giallombardo, 1966; Moyer, 1978). Recent work also underscores the greater salience for women of their relationships with their children and additional pain experienced due to this separation (Baunach, 1985).

Researchers who have focused qualitatively on the social organization of women in prison, in comparison to men, tend to attribute these variations to differential socialization patterns among women and men. Inmate subcultures in women's prisons reflect the high value women are socialized to ascribe to cooperation, nurturance, and support. As Giallombardo (1966) states, "the family group in the female prison is singularly suited to meet the internalized cultural expectations of the female role" (p. 185).

Several researchers have examined prisonization among female prisoners, seeking to determine, as they have with males, whether antistaff attitudes develop as a result of institutional deprivations or preprison factors (Jensen and Jones, 1976; Hartnagel and Gillan, 1980; Tittle, 1969). These studies have yielded findings similar to results of studies on males. Deprivation effects, such as the U-shaped function and changes over time were found by some researchers (Jensen and Jones, 1976; Tittle, 1969), whereas importation factors, such as age, prior imprisonment (Hartnagel and Gillan, 1980), race, and area of origin (Jensen and Jones, 1976) were also shown to be related to prisonization among female inmates.

5. COMPARISONS OF DEPRIVATION AND IMPORTATION MODELS

Thomas and his associates (Thomas, 1970, 1977; Thomas and Foster, 1972; Thomas, Peterson, and Zingraff, 1978) underscore the futility of an "either/or" approach to understanding factors influencing inmate adjustment by demonstrating additive relationships between the deprivation and importation approaches to prisonization. They conclude that the importation of preprison socialization experiences, the deprivational characteristics of the prison, and extraprison influences during one's prison stay share in determining individual adjustment patterns.

Others have attempted "head-to-head" comparisons of deprivation and importation factors in accounting for inmate adjustment patterns. A number of these studies include variables reflecting both prison-specific and extraprison variables in complex models designed to predict some aspect of adjustment. The results of these studies are mixed: one study (Feld, 1981) more strongly confirms the deprivation model, whereas three others support importation (Hartnagel and Gillan, 1980; Hepburn and Stratton, 1977; Poole and Regoli, 1983).

Carroll (1983) proposed a contextual approach to inmate adjustment

by suggesting that background characteristics lead to different adaptation patterns, depending upon specific institutional contexts. He hypothesized that extraprison variables more strongly influence inmate
adjustment in less secure institutions where deprivations are fewer,
whereas the harshness of more secure prisons would overshadow these
factors and influence all inmates equally. To support his case, he cites
one study of two federal youth centers that found that antisocial youths
are equally prisonized in treatment and custodial institutions, but pro-
social inmates show less prisonization in the treatment institution (Slosar, 1978). Other researchers also demonstrate differential effects by type
of prison (Hartnagel and Gillan, 1980), time in prison (Faine, 1973), and
individual characteristics such as race and criminal orientation (Alpert,
1978; Goodstein and MacKenzie, 1984).

6. PROBLEMS WITH THE PRISONIZATION CONSTRUCT

The hundreds of studies of the importation and deprivation models
provide correctional scholars with some understanding of the forces
operating on inmates and their individual and collective reactions to
these influences. However, the importance of the importation versus
deprivation debate as well as the value of the study of prisonization in
general has recently come under attack from corrections researchers.
Critics indict this body of research and theory on both methodological
and theoretical grounds.

Some critics contend that the various instruments to measure prisonization actually measure different constructs. Some studies use measures of nonconformity to staff expectations, whereas others employ
measures of conformity to the inmate normative system (Porporino and
Zamble, 1984). Moreover, researchers employing these measures rarely
test them for reliability or internal consistency (Poole, Regoli, and
Thomas, 1980).

The theoretical construct of prisonization has also been criticized as
too general and crude to be very helpful in developing a general understanding of inmate adjustment (Carroll, 1983; Porporino and Zamble,
1984). Knowing how an inmate scores on a self-report index of prisonization reveals little about how he or she will behave in a wide range
of institutional contexts. It is likely that equally prisonized inmates differ
from one another on other behavioral factors that may be at least as
important as prisonization in developing an understanding of adaptive
functioning.

A recent study also questions an underlying assumption of the theory of prisonization, that inmates and staff members comprise two sep-

arate and competing social organizations maintaining opposing value systems. Ironically, although many researchers (Garabedian, 1963; Wellford, 1967; Wheeler, 1961) considered disagreement with staff attitudes as the main indicator of prisonization, they never measured staff attitudes directly. In a study that administered prisonization instruments to samples of inmates and staff at the same institutions, Ramirez (1984) found that agreement between some staff and inmate groups was as high as, and sometimes higher than, agreement within staff and within inmate groups. Thus, neither inmate nor staff groups share uniform perspectives concerning prescribed inmate conduct; nor do staff and inmates maintain conflicting perspectives. Another study found wide within-group variation on inmates' responses to a conventional prisonization instrument, suggesting low inmate uniformity (Garofolo and Clark, 1985).

Research on guard-to-inmate interaction also questions the prevalence of inmate commitment to an antisocial belief system—be it prisonization or a violent public prison culture. The picture of a unified inmate population opposing the influence of representatives of "legitimate" society presumes antipathy toward all correctional staff. Clearly, the structural features of prison frequently place inmates and guards in conflict, and the power imbalance would reasonably lead inmates to feel resentment toward those perceived as immediately responsible for their deprivations.

In this context, it is interesting that several investigators have identified correctional officers as instrumental in providing support and critical services to prisoners. In an early study, Glaser (1964) found that releasees identified work supervisors to be more helpful in release planning than any other correctional staff member. More recently, researchers have demonstrated that many correctional officers are extensively involved in providing human services to inmates, acting as referral agents, counselors, members of formal or informal treatment teams, and crisis intervention agents (Johnson, 1979; Lombardo, 1981, 1982, 1985; Toch, 1981b; Toch and Grant, 1982; Toch and Klofas, 1982).

If one focuses on prisonization, the picture of prisoners receiving and accepting help from correctional officers might appear as incomprehensible as soliders being provided with daily rations and shelter by the enemy. The work documenting the human relations services performed by correctional officers provides an important counterpoint to the image of prison as fostering only bitterness toward authority.

If it can be assumed that some inmates do not become prisonized, would it be reasonable to infer that they have become institutionally dependent? Despite elegant theorizing about the conditions of total institutions that foster institutional dependency, available evidence casts doubt on the prevalence of this response. One study (Goodstein, 1979) attempted to identify prisoners from three institutions of varying custody levels as institutionally dependent, based upon their acceptance of the routinization and minimal demands of prison life. Less than 10% of the inmates at each prison were found to be institutionally dependent.

Selected work on self-esteem also questions the assumption that institutional life impacts negatively on inmates' self-perceptions. If the limitations of the formal organization of the prison were powerful enough to lead to the development of institutional dependency, one would expect self-esteem to decrease. This decrease would be most likely to occur during the early stages of incarceration, as one learned that one was helpless to control outcomes and make choices. Leveling off would follow as inmates adjusted to their lack of control by developing institutional dependency. However, most studies on inmate self-esteem find either an increase over the course of the sentence (Bennett, 1974; Gendreau, Gibson, Surridge, and Hug, 1973) or no change at all (Atchley and McCabe, 1968; Culbertson, 1975). Only a few studies demonstrate a decline in self-esteem (Fitchtler, Zimmerman, and Moore, 1973; Hepburn and Stratton, 1977), and these do not mirror the flattening-out pattern hypothesized by an institutional dependency model.

In summary, researchers and critics have raised questions about the generalizability of the constructs of prisonization and institutional dependency. We have presented evidence that prisoners and guards do not always maintain separate world views; indeed, prisoners and guards appear to be more similar to each other than they are to some members of their own groups. Given the fact that not all inmates manifest the types of behaviors projected to create problems for them after release, how are we to understand the effects of prison on inmates?

7. HOW HARMFUL ARE EFFECTS OF PRISON LIFE?

In looking at the effects of imprisonment, it is important to distinguish pain from harm. Harm is an outcome that has lasting negative consequences, whereas pain is an immediate aversive condition that may or may not result in extended damage. Being incarcerated is a painful experience, one that few, except for the most institutionally dependent, would voluntarily choose. Indeed, society intends for prisons to be painful; an explicit objective of the correctional system is to inflict punishment upon those who have been convicted of violating the law (Thomas, 1986).

The construct of prisonization is based on the assumption that the pains of imprisonment will be accompanied by the harms of imprisonment. It assumes that inmates who adjust according to its prescriptions will be disadvantaged in the long run, that they will leave prison worse off than when they entered, and that releasees are less capable of success than they would have been if they had not employed this adjustment strategy.

An increasing body of research on the effects of specific aspects of imprisonment on a variety of cognitive, personality, and attitudinal measures does not support the argument that prisons are particularly harmful to the majority of inmates. Studies fail to demonstrate adverse effects of confinement on cognitive, perceptual-motor, and personality functioning (Banister, Smith, Heskin, and Bolton, 1973; Bolton, Smith, Heskin, and Banister, 1976; Cohen and Taylor, 1972; Heskin, Bolton, Smith, and Banister, 1974; Heskin, Smith, Banister, and Bolton, 1973; Sapsford, 1978). Bukstel and Kilman's (1980) review of 90 experimental studies examining psychological effects of imprisonment on performance, personality, and attitude variables also supports the view that prison is not harmful to all individuals. They note that "an individual's response to confinement is determined by a complex interaction of variables" (p. 487) that results in deterioration in some prisoners, improvement in others, and no change in still others. Bonta and Gendreau (1987), focusing upon specific conditions of confinement such as crowding, protective custody, long-term imprisonment, short-term detention, and solitary confinement, support this view by concluding that these conditions do not reliably result in negative impacts. Rather,

> the empirical data questions the validity of the view that imprisonment is universally "painful." Solitary confinement, under limiting and humane conditions, long-term imprisonment, and short-term detention fail to show detrimental effects. From a physical health standpoint, incarcerates appear more healthy than their community counterparts. . . . Paradoxically, and unfortunately in a way, prisons may actually minimize the stress for an inmate by removing the need to make daily decisions . . . and controlling behaviors that may lead to increased difficulties. (p. 41)

Past work on inmate motivation for participation in correctional treatment programs further suggests that many prisoners attempt to use their time constructively to deal with problems they brought with them to prison. In their study of Canadian prisoners, Zamble and Porporino (1988) found that 80% of those surveyed indicated that they had set a goal to accomplish during their confinement, 75% involving some sort of institutionally offered training program. Half reported that self-improvement was the main objective in their attempts to adjust to prison.

Most correctional scholars had assumed that inmates engaged in program participation primarily to demonstrate to parole boards that they had expended effort for self-betterment (American Friends Service

Committee, 1971). One might expect, then, that prisoners would choose not to enroll in correctional rehabilitation programs when their participation is not linked to parole release. The implementation of determinate sentencing has served to sever that linkage, permitting researchers to distinguish between extrinsic and intrinsic motivations to engage in programs for self-betterment. Although determinate sentencing appears to reduce inmates' motivation for program participation slightly, even without external incentives, the majority of determinate sentenced prisoners continue to participate (Goodstein and Hepburn, 1985). More importantly, both determinate and indeterminate sentenced inmates rank self-improvement as the primary reason they participate in programs (Goodstein and Lutze, 1989). Another study found no difference in extent of program involvement between inmates functionally serving determinate sentences and those anticipating parole review (Goodstein, 1982).

In summary, research suggests that, contrary to the assumptions of the most prevalent models of inmate adjustment, institutional life is not particularly harmful to most inmates. Nor are most prisoners so embittered by their experience with prison authorities and the criminal justice system that they refuse to use their prison sentences constructively.

8. EXPANDING CONCEPTIONS OF INMATE ADJUSTMENT

Who, then, are these prisoners who are neither prisonized nor institutionalized? What are the characteristics of those inmates who are not harmed but may, in fact, experience some degree of growth or improvement during their terms of confinement? What attributes can we identify that may serve to mitigate against the potentially adverse effects of prison life?

-- One attribute that appears to be valuable for prisoners is a sense of efficacy, a belief in oneself as being able to get things done. In psychology, this attribute has become known as an internal locus of control (Bandura, 1977; Rotter, 1966). Theorists argue that individuals with this type of perspective, "internals," believe that events are not random or attributable to fate or chance. They believe that behaviors and subsequent events are contingent, and, specifically, they perceive that their efforts will result in desired outcomes. In the prison context, inmates who enter prison with expectations for self-efficacy would be expected to "find ways to maximize their choices, exert control over outcomes, and seek information to enhance the predictability of personally relevant future events" (Goodstein et al., 1984: 353).

The available correctional research on locus of control strongly supports this argument. Prisoners with this orientation deal more successfully with the stresses of imprisonment than externally oriented inmates. For example, researchers in one study provided reformatory inmates with a variety of information about prison life, including facts about the reformatory, future opportunities, and content relevant to obtaining parole (Seeman, 1963). Internals were found to be superior to "externals" at seeking and retaining information about parole regulations and how the reformatory was run, presumably enabling them to function more effectively, whereas the groups were similar on the acquisition and retention of less personally relevant information.

Other researchers found that compared to externals, inmates with internal loci of control manifested superior skill in working toward desired ends, such as improved living conditions and time away from the reformatory (Wright, Holman, Steele, and Silverstein, 1980). They concluded that internally oriented prisoners were more motivated toward mastery, more cognitively active in preparing for mastery, and more in control of their environment. Inmates with orientations toward self-efficacy have also been found to engage in less conflict with both guards and inmates than inmates with strong external locus of control beliefs (MacKenzie and Goodstein, 1986).

Self-efficacy also appears to mediate against the adverse effects of the inmate counterculture. Two studies suggest that greater inmate autonomy is asociated with adaptations favorable to institutional goals and inversely related to countercultural values (Osgood, Gruber, Archer, and Newcomb, 1985; MacKenzie, Goodstein, and Blouin, 1987).

Inmates with higher degrees of self-efficacy also appear to make more successful emotional and physical adjustments to prison life. For example, they appear less suceptible to anxiety and depression than inmates with higher external locus of control beliefs (MacKenzie and Goodstein, 1986). Indeed, greater personal control, originating from any source, appears to enable prisoners to adjust more successfully, as measured by reduced anxiety levels and greater participation in institutionally sanctioned activities (MacKenzie et al., 1987). A similar finding is reported by Ruback, Carr, and Hopper (1986) in a study of inmates' responses to their living accommodations. They found that prisoners who believed they were in control rated their living areas as better and experienced less stress and adverse physical symptoms than inmates who felt they were not in control. This finding, that personal control is related to more effective coping even after type of housing is held constant, further suggests the value of personal control in mediating effects of crowding on adjustment.

Although the preceding studies are correlational, one study points to the causal significance of control beliefs in reducing anxiety and depression. Porporino and Zamble (1984) demonstrated that inmates scoring higher on personal efficacy upon entering prison report lower levels of depression and anxiety 6 months later.

The studies cited suggest that prisoners who believe that they can have some impact on their environment appear to have an advantage in adjusting to the oppressive, routinized, and control-limiting climate of the prison. Through what mechanism or process do they attain this advantage? One means has been referred to as "niche" creation. Researchers who have conducted extensive observation and interviews of prisoners' daily routines have shown that some inmates are highly motivated to create or locate situations in the prison, labeled *niches*, which afford them at least some degree of comfort and control (Seymour, 1977, 1982; Toch, 1977).

Finding and occupying a niche presumably enables a prisoner to satisfy at least some of his or her needs and to function in a microenvironment that is compatible with his or her interests. Presumably, a prisoner who is able to find and inhabit an appropriate niche "fashions a round of life that will enhance his ability to negotiate the stresses of prison that are of greatest concern to him" (Johnson, 1987: 104). Niches personalize the prison experience to an extent that would not have been imagined by prisonization or institutional dependency theorists. To quote Johnson (1987), "men in niches try to live as individuals, not as role types or anonymous members of collectivities. Their goal is to find a routine that meets their basic needs and provides, as much as possible, a 'slice of home' in an otherwise alien environment" (p 104).

Although niches are potentially valuable in facilitating constructive inmate adjustment, they are unlikely to be available to everyone. This would be especially true in contemporary overcrowded prisons where administrators and staff have little leeway to assign inmates proactively to settings and programs on the basis of needs (Toch, 1981a). Some prisoners more effectively locate appropriate niches and find ways to become situated in them than do others. Niche location "relies upon the individual prisoner's ability to identify his needs, either consciously or unconsciously, and then manipulate environmental outcomes successfully so that he may situate himself in the prison—both physically and interpersonally—so that at least some of these needs can be met" (Seymour, 1977: 181). Those inmates who possess the skills and cognitive perspectives reflecting higher degrees of self-efficacy may hold the advantage in obtaining, and maintaining, niches.

9. CONCLUSION

This chapter has illustrated that modes of adjustment to confinement differ widely across individuals, groups, and prison types. In contrast to early work, which concentrated upon the adverse effects of imprisonment on inmates, we have attempted to present a balanced view of inmate adjustment. The data do not indicate widespread deterioration or criminalization as a result of confinement. Rather, most inmates desire to use their time in confinement constructively, and some, particularly those armed with personal resilience to "respond in an appropriate manner when stressed" and "react more directly to the demands of the environment" (MacKenzie and Goodstein, 1986: 221), may succeed.

Understanding the possibilities for facilitating successful adjustment among a greater number of inmates requires a shift of perspective. Rather than focusing on individual personality characteristics or group interactions, it is necessary to direct attention to more objective, physical features of the prison environment. Extensive work on identifying characteristics of the general prison environment that may lead to successful coping has been performed. The following chapter concentrates on this work.

10. REFERENCES

Abbott, J. H. *In the belly of the beast.* New York: Vintage, 1981.

Akers, R. L., Hayner, N. S., and Gruninger, W. Prisonization in five countries: Type of prison and inmate characteristics. *Criminology,* 1977, *14,* 527–554.

Alpert, G. P. Prisons as formal organizations: Compliance theory in action. *Sociology and Social Research,* 1978, *63,* 112–130.

American Friends Service Committee. *Struggle for justice: A report on crime and punishment in America.* New York: Hill and Wang, 1971.

Atchley, R. C., and McCabe, M. P. Socialization in correctional communities: A replication. *American Sociological Review,* 1968, *33,* 774–785.

Bandura, A. Toward a unified theory of behavioral change. *Psychological Review,* 1977, *84,* 191–215.

Banister, P. A., Smith, F. V., Heskin, K. J., and Bolton, N. Psychological correlates of long-term imprisonment: I. Cognitive variables. *British Journal of Criminology.* 1973, *13,* 312–323.

Bartollas, C., Miller, S., and Dinitz, S. *Juvenile victimization: The institutional paradox.* New York: Halstead Press, 1976.

Baunach, P. J. *Mothers in prison.* New Brunswick, NJ: Transaction Books, 1985.

Bennett, L. A. The application of self-esteem measures in a correctional setting: II. Changes in self-esteem during incarceration. *Journal of Research on Crime and Delinquency,* 1974, *11,* 9–15.

Berk, B. Organizational goals and inmate organization. *American Journal of Sociology,* 1966, *71,* 522–534.

Bolton, N., Smith, F. V., Heskin, D. J., and Banister, P. A. Psychological correlates of long-term imprisonment. *British Journal of Criminology*, 1976, *16*, 38–47.

Bonta, J., and Gendreau, P. *Reexamining the cruel and unusual punishment of prison life.* Unpublished Manuscript, 1987.

Bukstel, L. H., and Kilman, P. R. Psychological effects of imprisonment on confined individuals. *Psychological Bulletin*, 1980, *88*, 469–493.

Carroll, L. *Hacks, blacks, and cons: Race relations in a maximum security prison.* Lexington, MA: Lexington Books, 1974.

Carroll, L. *Towards a contextual model of inmate culture and social structure.* Paper presented at the American Society of Criminology meetings, Denver, Colorado, 1983.

Clemmer, D. *The prison community,* Boston: Christopher, 1940.

Cohen, S., and Taylor, L. *Psychological survival: the experience of long-term imprisonment.* Harmondsworth, England: Penguin, 1972.

Colvin, M. The New Mexico prison riot. *Social Problems,* 1982, *29*, 449–463.

Culbertson, R. G. The effect of institutionalization on the delinquent inmate's self-concept. *Journal of Criminal Law and Criminology,* 1975, *66*, 88–93.

Ekland-Olson, S. Crowding and prison violence: Evidence from the post-Ruiz years in Texas. *Law and Society Review,* 1986, *20*, 387–422.

Ellis, D., Grasmick, H. G., and Gilman, B. Violence in prisons: A sociological analysis. *American Journal of Sociology,* 1974, *80*, 16–43.

Fagan, T. J., and Lira, F. T. Profile of mood states: Racial differences in a delinquent population. *Psychological Reports,* 1978, *43*, 348–350.

Faine, J. R. A self-consistency approach to prisonization. *Sociological Quarterly,* 1973, *14*, 576–588.

Feld, B. C. A comparative analysis of organization structure and inmate subcultures in institutions for juvenile offenders. *Crime and Delinquency,* 1981, *27*, 336–363.

Flanagan, T. J. Correlates of institutional misconduct among state prisoners. *Criminology,* 1983, *21*, 29–39.

Fichtler, H., Zimmermann, R. R., and Moore, R. T. Comparison of self-esteem of prison and non-prison groups. *Perceptual and Motor Skills,* 1973, *36*, 39–44.

Fox, J. G. *Organizational and racial conflict in maximum-security prisons.* Lexington, MA: Lexington Books, 1982.

Fry, L. J. The impact of formal inmate structure on opposition to staff and treatment goals. *British Journal of Criminology,* 1976, *16*, 126–141.

Fuller, D., and Orsagh, T. Violence and victimization within a state prison. *Criminal Justice Review,* 1977, *2*, 35–55.

Garabedian, P. C. Social roles and processes of socialization in the prison community. *Social Problems,* 1963, *11*, 139–152.

Garofalo, J., and Clark, R. D. The inmate subculture in jails. *Criminal Justice and Behavior,* 1985, *12*, 415–434.

Gendreau, P., Gibson, M., Surridge, C. T., and Hug, J. J. Self-esteem changes associated with six months' imprisonment. *Proceedings of the Canadian Congress of Criminology and Corrections,* 1973, 81–89.

Giallombardo, R. *Society of women: A study of a women's prison.* New York: John Wiley, 1966.

Glaser, D. *The effectiveness of a prison and parole system.* Indianapolis: Bobbs-Merrill, 1964.

Goetting, A., and Howsen, R. M. Blacks in prison: A profile. *Criminal Justice Review,* 1983, *8*, 35–55.

Goffman, E. *Asylums: Essays on the social situation of mental patients and other inmates.* Garden City, NY: Anchor Books, 1961.

Goodstein, L. Inmate adjustment to prison and the transition to community life. *Journal of Research on Crime and Delinquency,* 1979, *16*, 246–272.

Goodstein, L. A quasi-experimental test of prisoner reactions to determinate and indeterminate sentencing. In N. Parisi (Ed.), *Coping with imprisonment*. Beverly Hills, CA: Sage, 1982.

Goodstein, L., and Hepburn, J. R. *Derminate sentencing and imprisonment: A failure of reform*. Cincinnati: Anderson, 1985.

Goodstein, L., and Lutze, F. E. *Prisoner program involvement and the determinate sentence: An exploration of perceived motivations*. Paper presented at the Academy of Criminal Justice Sciences meeting, Washington, DC, March 1989.

Goodstein, L., and MacKenzie, D. L. Racial differences in adjustment patterns of prison inmates—prisonization, conflict, stress and control. In D. Georges Abeyie (Ed.), *The criminal justice system and blacks*, New York: Clark Boardman, 1984.

Goodstein, L., MacKenzie, D. L., and Shotland, R. L. Personal control and inmate adjustment to prison. *Criminology*, 1984, 22, 343–369.

Hartnagel, T. F., and Gillan, M. E. Female prisoners and the inmate code. *Pacific Sociological Review*, 1980, 23, 85–104.

Hautaluoma, J. E., and Scott, W. A. Values and sociometric choices of incarcerated juveniles. *Journal of Social Criminology*, 1973, 91, 229–237.

Heffernan, E. *Making it in prison*. New York: John Wiley, 1972.

Hepburn, J. R., and Stratton, J. R. Total institutions and inmate self-esteem. *British Journal of Criminology*, 1977, 17, 237–250.

Heskin, K. J., Bolton, N., Smith, F. V., and Banister, P. A. Psychological correlates of long-term imprisonment: III. Attitudinal variables. *British Journal of Criminology*, 1974, 14, 150–157.

Heskin, K. J., Smith, F. V., Banister, P. A., and Bolton, N. Psychological correlates of long-term imprisonment: II. Personality variables. *British Journal of Criminology*, 1973, 13, 323–330.

Irwin, J. *The felon*. Englewood Cliffs, NJ: Prentice-Hall, 1970.

Irwin, J. *Prisons in turmoil*. Toronto: Little, Brown & Company, 1980.

Irwin, J., and Cressey, D. Thieves, convicts and the inmate culture. *Social Problems*, 1962, 10, 142–155.

Jacobs, J. B. Street gangs behind bars. *Social Problems*, 1974, 21, 395–409.

Jacobs, J. B. Stratification and conflict among prison inmates. *Journal of Criminal Law and Criminology*, 1976, 66, 476–482.

Jacobs, J. B. *Stateville: The penitentiary in mass society*. Chicago: University of Chicago Press, 1977.

Jaman, D. Behavior during the first year in prison. *Research Report No. 32*. Sacramento, CA: Department of Corrections, 1971.

Jensen, G. F., and Jones, D. Perspectives on inmate culture: A study of women in prison. *Social Problems*, 1976, 54, 590–603.

Johnson, R. *Culture and crisis in confinement*. Lexington, MA: Lexington Books, 1976.

Johnson, R. Informal helping networks in prison: The shape of grass-roots correctionsl intervention. *Journal of Criminal Justice*, 1979, 7, 53–70.

Johnston, R. *Hard time: Understanding and reforming the prison*. Monterey, CA: Brooks/Cole, 1987.

Kassebaum, G., Ward, D., and Wilner, D. *Prison treatment and parole survival*. New York: John Wiley, 1971.

Lockwood, D. *Prison sexual violence*. New York: Elsevier, 1980.

Lombardo, L. X. *Guards imprisoned: Correctional officers at work*. New York: Elsevier, 1981.

Lombardo, L. X. Alleviating inmate stress: Contributions from correctional officers. In R. Johnson and H. Toch (Eds.) *Living in prison: The ecology of survival*. Beverly Hills, CA: Sage, 1982.

Lombardo, L. X. Mental health work in prisons and jails: Inmate adjustment and indigenous correctional personnel. *Criminal Justice and Behavior*, 1985, *12*, 17–27.

MacKenzie, D. L., and Goodstein, L. Stress and the control beliefs of prisoners: A test of three models of control-limited environments. *Journal of Applied Social Psychology*, 1986, *16*, 209–228.

MacKenzie, D. L., Goodstein, L., and Blouin, D. C. Personal control and prisoner adjustment: An empirical test of a proposed model. *Journal of Research in Crime and Delinquency*, 1987, *24*, 49–68.

Marquart, J. W. Prison guards and the use of physical coercion as a mechanism of prisoner control. *Criminology*, 1986, *24*, 347–366.

Marquart, J. W., and Crouch, B. M. Judicial reform and prisoner control: The impact of Ruiz v. Estelle on a Texas penitentiary. *Law and Society Review*, 1985, *19*, 557–584.

McCorkle, L., and Korn, R. Resocialization within walls. *Annals of the American Academy of Political Science*, 1954, *293*, 88–98.

Meisenhelder, T. An essay on time and the phenomenology of imprisonment. *Deviant Behavior*, 1985, *6*, 39–56.

Miller, S., and Dinitz, S. Measuring institutional impact, a followup. *Criminology*, 1973, *11*, 417–426.

Morris, T., and Morris, P. The experience of imprisonment. *British Journal of Criminology*, 1962, *2*, 337–360.

Moyer, I. L. Differential social structures and homosexuality among women in prison. *Virginia Social Science Journal*, 1978, *13*, 13–19.

Oldroyd, R. J., and Howell, R. J. Personality, intellectual and behavioral differences between black, chicano, and white prison inmates in the Utah state prison. *Psychological Reports*, 1977, *41*, 187–191.

Osgood, D. W., Gruber, E., Archer, M. A., and Newcomb, T. M. Autonomy for inmates: Counterculture or cooptation? *Criminal Justice and Behavior*, 1985, *12*, 71–89.

Petersilia, J. R. *Racial disparities in the criminal justice system*. Santa Monica, CA: Rand Corporation, 1983.

Poole, E. D., and Regoli, R. M. Race, institutional rule breaking and disciplinary response: A study of discretionary decision making in prison. *Law and Society Review*, 1980, *14*, 931–946.

Poole, E. D., and Regoli, R. M. Violence in juvenile institutions. *Criminology*, 1983, *21*, 213–232.

Poole, E. D., Regoli, R. M., and Thomas, C. W. The measurement of inmate social role types: An assessment. *Journal of Criminal Law and Criminology*, 1980, *71*, 317–324.

Porporino, F. J., and Zamble, E. Coping with imprisonment. *Canadian Journal of Criminology*, 1984, *26*, 403–421.

Ramirez, J. Prisonization, staff and inmates: Is it really about us versus them? *Criminal Justice and Behavior*, 1984, *11*, 423–460.

Reasons, C. Racism, prisons, and prisoners' rights. *Issues in Criminology*, 1974, *9*, 3–10.

Richards, B. The experience of long-term imprisonment. *British Journal of Criminology*, 1978, *18*, 162–169.

Rotter, J. Generalized expectancies for internal versus external control of reinforcement. *Psychological Monographs*, 1966, *80*, (Whole No. 609).

Ruback, R. B., Carr, T. S., and Hopper, C. H. Perceived control in prison: Its relation to reported crowding, stress, and symptoms. *Journal of Applied Social Psychology*, 1986, *16*, 375–386.

Sapsford, R. J. Life sentence prisoners: Psychological changes during sentence. *British Journal of Criminology*, 1978, *18*, 128–145.

Scacco, A. M. *Rape in prison*. Springfield, IL: Charles C Thomas, 1975.

Seeman, M. Alienation and social learning in a reformatory. *American Journal of Sociology,* 1963, *69,* 270–284.

Seymour, J. Niches in prison. In H. Toch (Ed.) *Living in prison: The ecology of survival.* New York: Free Press, 1977.

Seymour, J. Environmental sanctuaries for susceptible prisoners. In R. Johnson and H. Toch (Eds.), *The pains of imprisonment.* Beverly Hills, CA: Sage Publications, 1982.

Sieverdes, C. M., and Bartollas, C. Security level and adjustment patterns in juvenile institutions. *Journal of Criminal Justice,* 1986, *14,* 135–145.

Slosar, J., Jr. *Prisonization, friendship and leadership.* Lexington, MA: D. C. Heath, 1978.

Stastny, C., and Tyrnauer, G. *Who rules the joint?* Lexington, MA: Lexington Books, 1982.

Street, D. Vinter, R., and Perrow, G. *Organization for treatment: A comparative study of institutions for delinquents.* New York: Free Press, 1966.

Sykes, G. M. *The society of captives.* Princeton, NJ: Princeton University Press, 1958.

Sykes, G. M., and Messinger, S. L. The inmate social system. In R. Cloward (Ed.), *Theoretical studies in social organization of the prison.* New York: Social Science Research Council, 1960.

Thomas, C. W. Toward a more inclusive model of the inmate contraculture. *Criminology,* 1970, *8,* 251–262.

Thomas, C. W. Theoretical perspectives of prisonization: A comparison of the importation and deprivation models. *Journal of Criminal Law and Criminology,* 1977, *68,* 135–145.

Thomas, C. W. Corrections in America: Its ambiguous role and future prospects. In K. C. Haas, and G. P. Alpert (Eds.), *The dilemmas of punishment: Readings in contemporary corrections.* Prospect Heights, IL: Waveland Press, 1986.

Thomas, C. W., and Foster, S. Prisonization in the inmate contraculture. *Social Problems,* 1972, *20,* 229–239.

Thomas, C. W., and Peterson, D. *Prison organization and inmate subcultures.* Indianapolis: Bobbs-Merrill, 1977.

Thomas, C. W., Peterson, D., and Zingraff, R. Structural and social psychological correlates of prisonization. *Criminology,* 1978, *16,* 383–393.

Tittle, C. R. Inmate organization: Sex differentiation and the influence of criminal subcultures. *American Sociological Review,* 1969, *34,* 492–505.

Tittle, C. R. Institutional living and self-esteem. *Social Problems,* 1972, *20,* 65–77.

Toch, H. *Living in prison: The ecology of survival.* New York: Macmillan, 1977.

Toch, H. Inmate classification as a transaction. *Criminal Justice and Behavior,* 1981a, *8,* 3–14.

Toch, H. is a "correctional officer" by any other name, a "screw?" In R. R. Ross (Ed.), *Prison guard/correctional officer.* Scarborough, Ontario: Butterworth, 1981b.

Toch, H., and Grant, J. D. *Reforming human services: change through participation.* Beverly Hills, CA: Sage, 1982.

Toch, H., and Klofas, J. Alienation and desire for job enrichment among correctional officers. *Federal Probation,* 1982, *46,* 35–44.

Troyer, J. C., and Frease, D. E. Attitude change in a western Canadian penitentiary. *Canadian Journal of Criminology and Corrections,* 1975, *7,* 250–262.

Ward, D., and Kassebaum, B. B. *Women's prison: Sex and social structure.* Chicago: Aldine, 1965.

Wellford, C. Factors associated with adoption of the inmate code: A study of normative socialization. *Journal of Criminal Law, Criminology, and Police Science,* 1967, *58,* 197–203.

Wheeler, S. Socialization in correctional communities. *American Sociological Review,* 1961, *26,* 697–712.

Wooden, W. S., and Parker, J. *Men behind bars: Sexual exploitation in prison.* New York: Plenum, 1982.

Wright, K. N. *Improving correctional classification through a study of the placement of inmates in environmental settings.* Binghamton, NY: Center for Social Analysis, 1987.

Wright, T., Holman, T., Steele, T., and Silverstein, G. Locus of control and mastery in a reformatory: A field study of defensive externality. *Journal of Personality and Social Psychology,* 1980, *38,* 1005–1013.

Zamble, E., and Porporino, F. *Coping behavior and adaptation in prison inmates.* New York: Springer Verlag, 1988.

Chapter 13

CORRECTIONAL ENVIRONMENTS

KEVIN N. WRIGHT and LYNNE GOODSTEIN

1. INTRODUCTION

There can be little denying that the context in which one lives and works impinges upon and shapes the individual's behavior both then and in the future. Sometimes the context of one's life may have a positive influence and will promote desirable personal change or lead to self-satisfaction. Other contexts may contribute to distress and result in the eventual deterioration of the individual's functional capacity.

Nowhere else may the importance of the environmental context be so significant as in prisons. By design, prisoners cannot escape their surroundings and through choice of people and places shape the context of their lives. Perhaps, for this reason, prison environments tend to be uniquely intense. Yet, not everyone is harmed by imprisonment: Some people deteriorate, others improve, and still others show little or no change (Bukstel and Kilmann, 1980).

Figuring out what is important within the prison context and how those attributes affect prisoners has posed a significant challenge for people who study prisons. Depending upon the researcher's purpose and disciplinary focus, conceptualizations have varied considerably. The purpose of this chapter is to review the major ways prison environments

KEVIN N. WRIGHT • Center for Education and Social Research, State University of New York at Binghamton, Binghamton, New York 13901.   LYNNE GOODSTEIN • Administration of Justice Department, The Pennsylvania State University, University Park, Pennsylvania 16802.

have been viewed and to describe the trends that appear to be developing.

Three general groups of studies are reviewed. The first focuses on the physical characteristics of the prison. This research describes the design, space, and other structural features of the prison setting. The second group of studies attempts to conceptualize what it is to live in prison by identifying those social characteristics that "press" on individuals and represent what is important to them within the unique context of prison. The final group of studies, rather than characterizing the environment, describe what happens when change disrupts traditional social structures.

2. REVIEW

2.1. Physical Characteristics of Environments

2.1.1. Structural Characteristics

Several studies have examined the relationship of physical features of the institution—cells versus dormitories, noise levels, temperature, access, visibility, and architectural aesthetics—to behavioral outcomes and attitudes of inmates. One study notes that "there is ample evidence of a vital relationship between the quality of the physical environment of any correctional institution and its administration" (Walker and Gordon, 1977: 2). Farbstein and Wener (1982) provide an excellent review of the research, much of which will be discussed here.

An evaluation conducted by the American Foundation Institute of Corrections (1968) determined that inmates, staff, and prison administrators preferred single cells to dormitories. Later research supported this conclusion and suggested that a possible reason for this preference is that private space improves inmates' perceptions of the prison setting (Goldblatt, 1972).

The most complete analysis of the effects of multiple-occupant housing analyzed archival data from more than 175,000 inmates in four facilities and questionnaire responses from more than 2,500 inmates in 12 prisons. Suicide, nonviolent and violent deaths, psychiatric commitments, inmate-on-inmate assaults, disciplinary infractions, attempted suicides, self-mutilations, illness complaints, and high blood pressure were found to occur more frequently among inmates housed in multiple-occupant units. These signs of increased pathology appear to be associated with several factors: "presence of other residents, low space per person, double-bunking, and lack of privacy" (Cox, Paulus, and

McCain, 1984: 1156). Construction of partitions within large open housing areas reduced or completely ameliorated the effects, even though the population size and space per person remained unchanged. This finding underscores the importance of privacy to successful adjustment. Other studies conducted in various settings demonstrated the association between private space and reduced adjustment problems. A behavioral analysis of residential treatment homes for juveniles discovered that residents preferred living areas with space designated for a particular purpose and private sleeping areas (Srivastava, 1978). Easy access to private rooms where inmates could not be observed by correctional officers reduced tension and violence in two federal jails (Wener and Olsen, (1980).

Related research supports the importance of access and freedom of movement within the physical environment. A study of the transition to a new women's prison determined that limited access to outdoor spaces required greater regimentation and resulted in greater dissatisfaction among staff and residents (Prestholt, Taylor, and Shannon, 1976).

In contrast to the need for privacy and freedom of movement, aspects of control are also important. Research indicates that inmates are more likely to destroy physical features that they cannot control, such as lights without switches and vents without movable louvers. Indeed, one study found that rather than preventing destruction, vandalism-resistant design provoked it (Sommer, 1972). Prisoners' inability to control even the most insignificant physical features of their environment may engender frustration that results in resistance to authority and defiance. Conversely, providing inmates with some control over their environment has a positive effect on behavior. By adding cues in a crowded setting, such as signs in a busy visitors' room, positive changes in attitudes and behavior of visitors and prisoners resulted (Wener and Kaminoff, 1983).

Prison writers often mention the ubiquity of noise in the prison environment: "Two thousand voices collected into a roar as powerful as wind from the sea. The roar moved up the cell house walls toward the sky, failed the ascent and echoed back into the pit" (Bunker, 1973: 18; see also Wright, 1985a: 164, and Braley, 1976: 155). These authors generally imply that noise has a deleterious effect, but surprisingly little research has addressed this issue. Two studies found similarly high noise levels in the Manhattan House of Detention (the "Tombs") and a new federal facility in Chicago, but neither study examined their behavioral effects (Gersten, 1977; Wener and Olsen, 1980).

Prison literature also identifies temperature as a characteristic of the physical environment of prisons that affects inmate behavior (Gould,

1980; Keerdoja, 1980; Press, 1980); yet, only one study examined its effect. A post hoc analysis found that the incidence of "uncomfortably hot days" bore no relationship to the incidence of disruptive behavior among inmates (Megargee, 1977). Related research did not support the possibility that seasonal characteristics—rainfall, temperature, seasons, or moonphase—directly affect prison violence (Atlas, 1984).

A final area of research on the physical environment of prison examines aesthetic features. Two studies found that prisoners did not vandalize spaces that were soft, colorful, and comfortable (Wener and Olsen, 1980, and preliminary work by Farbestein and Wener, 1982). Inmates and their visitors highly rated a new visiting area that used colors, carpeting, and comfortable furniture (Whiting and DeJoy, 1976). Similarly, allowing inmates to personalize their space resulted in greater satisfaction and care of the unit (Goldblatt, 1972; Srivastava, 1978).

These research findings concerning prisoners' reactions to physical environmental features consistently support the contention, discussed in the previous chapter, that environments in which inmates perceive that they possess some degree of personal control facilitate positive adjustment. Choosing to spend time in public or private spaces, functioning in comfortable surroundings, personalizing one's space, and controlling small amenities such as ventilation or lighting suggest to prisoners that their human needs for choice and control are being respected within the limitations of the prison context. "Softening" the physical environment in these ways may reduce prisoners' pains of incarceration and engender less resistance to authority.

2.1.2. Crowding

The most common research examining the physical characteristics of prison environments focuses on the effects of overcrowded facilities on inmate behavior. These studies define crowding in terms of population size, population density, and the amount of personal space and link it to such pathological reactions as stress, illness, violent and nonviolent deaths, psychiatric commitments, assaults, and other disciplinary infractions. Furthermore, other corollaries often accompany prison congestion, including social instability, diminished programming, and ascendance of custody goals. Crowding not only affects the behavior of inmates but that of the staff (Toch, 1985).

Five studies found that crowding produces physical symptoms in inmates. Living in a dormitory appears to be related to physiological measures of stress, such as pulse rate, diastolic and systolic blood pressure, and palmar sweat (D'Atri, 1975; D'Atri et al., 1981). Furthermore, illness complaints increase in crowded conditions (McCain, Cox, and

Paulus, 1976), as do rates of psychiatric commitments (Paulus, McCain, and Cox, 1978) and heart failure (Carr, 1981).

Early research findings suggested that social density rather than spatial density (the number of fellow inmates as opposed to square footage of personal space) determines satisfaction and pathological reactions. Inmates' perceived control over their environment correlates with perceptions of crowding and whether they live in single or multiple-occupant units (Paulus, Cox, McCain, and Chandler, 1975).

Later research that examined the relationship of congestion and institutional misconduct and violence failed to substantiate these findings. A study of crowding in a correctional facility for young male offenders found population size to correlate with the total number of disciplinary violations, but the rate did not increase (Megargee, 1976, 1977). The amount of personal space and population density significantly correlated with both the frequency and rate of disruptive behavior. One explanation for these discrepant findings is that the need for space and privacy may vary between youthful and older inmates or, alternatively, different dependent variables—disruptive behavior and mental health problems—relate to crowding in different ways. But because other research confirms the later results that the amount of space is more important than number of inmates, the latter explanation may be more viable (Carr, 1981; Nacci, Teitelbaum, and Prather, 1977).

One study of four Florida prisons demonstrates that crowding not only increases antisocial behavior; it also reduces prosocial behavior (Jan. 1980). Inmates and staff may deal with the increased interruptions and greater demands in carrying out their jobs by reducing the help they give to others. Furthermore, overcrowding impairs the ability of prisons to classify and treat inmates and thereby leads to their warehousing (Toch, 1985). A study of 19 federal prisons found that crowding predicted prison assault rates better than prisonization (Gaes and McGuire, 1985). A final way of viewing the effect of overcrowding examines postincarceration behavior and outcome. One study discovered that inmates released from densely populated facilities experienced higher reconviction rates than other inmates (Farrington and Nuttall, 1980).

The most extensive research regarding the effects of crowding on inmate behavior found that during the decade from 1968 to 1978, while the population of Texas prisons underwent an unprecedented period of growth without corresponding increases in facility space, deaths, suicides, and disciplinary reports rose significantly more rapidly than did the population. In comparison, when the population of Oklahoma's prisons decreased from 1973 to 1976, the rate of violent deaths fell more steeply than did the population decline (McCain, Cox, and Paulus, 1980; see also Cox et al., 1984). These findings suggest that with overcrowding, social pathologies increase at a rate that outstrips that which would be expected from the sheer numerical increase in the population. Researchers speculate that the "cognitive strain, anxiety or fear, and frustration intrinsic to most social interactions in crowded settings" cause the negative effects (Cox et al., 1984: 1148).

Several researchers have investigated the interaction of crowding and some other variable in accounting for inmate behavior. One study claims that crowding affects violence indirectly, suggesting that a cognitive process that is related to age, transiency, and need for space acts as an intervening individual-level variable. Crowding differentially causes confusion and tension in residents depending upon their cognitive-evaluative state (Ellis, 1984).

Research has produced contradictory findings regarding the need for distance and personal space and its relationship with crowding in facilitating violent and aggressive behavior. One study discovered that inmates with a greater need for interpersonal distance engaged in violent and aggressive behavior more frequently (Walker and Gilmour, 1984), whereas the second study found that inmates for whom the prison failed to meet their needs for personal space did not necessarily have greater interpersonal behavioral problems nor higher postrelease recidivism rates (Wormith, 1984).

A 1986 study compared crowding to social control in explaining violence in the Texas prison system and, in contrast to earlier conclusions, determined that disruptions in the deeply rooted prison social order resulting from the *Ruiz v. Estelle* court decision, and not crowding *per se*, led to greater violence (Ekland-Olson, 1986).

Smith's (1982) model of crowding and confinement may explain these seemingly conflicting findings. He notes that congestion does not always lead to an adverse experience and identifies research that indicates that several factors may mediate the effect. Crowding creates the potential for stress because it reduces the resources available to inmates. An individual's sense of personal control and the social group's ability to support the individual may counteract the negative potential of congestion. By bolstering their self-esteem, the traditional inmate code and culture served to support inmates' loss of autonomy. If group support is retained, as a prison becomes more crowded, then congestion may not produce negative consequences; however, when the social organization changes, as was the case in Texas, then problems may surface. Inmates may react to the frustration and tension created by crowding by becoming more aggressive, or their response may be to engage in avoidance and withdrawal.

2.1.3. New Generation Facilities

Much of the knowledge concerning the relationship between prisoners' needs and the built environment, discussed previously, has been incorporated into the design plans for a series of correctional institutions built by the federal prison system (Gettinger, 1984). Begun approximately 10 years ago, these new generation facilities incorporate a podular design allowing direct supervision of inmates at all times. Units are self-contained to restrict inmate movement and to reduce opportunities for breeches in security. Architectural features typically associated with prisons, such as bars and metal doors, are absent; the design attempts to reduce noise and promote a more humanizing setting (Zupan, Menke, and Lovrich, 1986).

Rather than depending on structural barriers and technological devices, the new facilities rely on the ability of the correctional officer to supervise and control the unit. Well-trained officers supervise approximately 40 inmates housed in each module. According to a National Institute of Corrections report: "It is the responsibility of the officer to control the behavior of the inmates in his/her unit, keeping negative behavior to a minimum, reducing tension, and encouraging positive behavior" (Nelson, O'Toole, Krauth, and Whitmore, 1984: 4). Rather than allowing inmates to assume leadership roles, the officer serves that function. Research finds lower rates of violence, graffiti, and vandalism in new generation facilities when compared to traditionally designed units (Wener, Frazier, and Farbstein, 1987).

2.2. Transactional Models of Prison Environments

Researchers who study the physical characteristics of correctional environments are generally from either of two disciplines: architecture and planning or sociology. In contrast, social psychologists approach the concept of environment differently than the structuralists; they emphasize interactions between people and events or settings and attempt to map the social ecology of these person/environment transactions. This work can be traced to the theoretical conceptualizations of Murray (1938), who argued that individuals have specific needs that vary according to strength and that these needs characterize individuals' personalities. Need works as an internal determinant of behavior, but, as Murray suggests, it does so within social environments that operate as external "presses" that facilitate or impede need satisfaction. Stern (1970; see also Pace and Stern, 1958) extended the work of Murray by mapping the needs of individuals within the same environment and exploring the effects of congruence and incongruence on individual behavior.

Recently, researchers have extended this conceptualization, suggesting that environmental demands exert forces on individuals as do internal demands, or goals, expectations, and commitments. Individuals differ in their personal adaptive resources (health, problem-solving skills, beliefs, and experiences) and their external resources (social and material support). Stress results at the point of transaction between environmental and/or internal demands and an individual's adaptive capacity (Folkman, Schaefer, and Lazarus, 1979; Lazarus, 1966, 1969; Lazarus, Averill, and Opton, 1970; Lazarus and Launier, 1978; see Porporino and Zamble, 1984, for a review).

Support for this conceptualization can be found in the prison literature. One study discovered that program participation and individual background determined inmate morale (Macht, Seidl, and Greene, 1977). Other studies detected an interaction between individual characteristics and institutionalization in determining an inmate's self-perception (Brown, 1971; Culbertson, 1975; Yarbrough, 1973). But in reality, one finds surprisingly few studies in the prison literature that investigate what has come to be known as "person–environment fit." To quote one set of prison researchers:

> Generally speaking, there are few attitudinal or behavioral dispositions that are so powerful as to totally determine actions in all situations, and few environmental events which can compel identical responses from people with varying dispositions. We would expect that the interaction between the individual and his environment would be the most powerful determinant of behavior. Yet, most previous investigations have ignored this interaction. (Porporino and Zamble, 1984: 409)

Other prison experts echo this statement when they write, "Obviously we are making a belated discovery that the interaction of the person and the situation represents an important advance in understanding the complexities of prison life" (Bonta and Gendreau, 1988: 39). Hans Toch notes, "Transaction-centered research is difficult research to do, which is why it is rarely done. It requires the charting of stimuli that impinge and of relevant reponses, with attention to psychological (coping) processes that mediate the two" (1984: 511).

2.2.1. The Social Ecology of Prison Environments

In performing transaction-centered analyses, researchers must have a mechanism to assess objectively the characteristics of the environment. Moos (1968, 1975) has pioneered this area by applying Murray's theoretical conceptualization to prison environments in a comprehensive and systematic way. He suggests that the social environment "defines what [the inmate] must cope with and clarifies for him the direction his behavior must take if he is to find satisfaction and reward within the dominant culture of the unit" (1968, p. 177). The social environment influences an individual's "attitudes and moods, his behavior, his health and overall sense of well-being, and his social, personal, and intellectual development" (Moos, 1975: 8).

Moos selected the concept of *climate* to represent the social environment of prisons. Organizational theorists generally describe social climate as the organizational analog to individual "personality" or "character" (see Moos, 1975: 4; Selznick, 1957). Climate consists of a set of characteristics that (1) distinguish organizations, (2) are relatively enduring, and (3) affect the behavior of participants in the organization (Forehand and Gilmer, 1964) and emerges from the daily experiences of organizational members. It is often conceptualized in terms of their subjective perceptions of those events. Research finds climate to be related to such organizational outcome variables as productivity and performance, satisfaction, involvement, and personal growth (Lawler, Hall, and Oldham, 1974; Sims and LaFollette, 1975; Sneider and Hall, 1972).

Moos (1975) developed the Correctional Institution Environment Scale (CIES) to measure prison climate and claims to have identified the most important environmental presses in selecting the three dimensions (relationship, personal development and growth, and system maintenance) and nine associated subscales (involvement, support, expressiveness, autonomy, practical orientation, personal problem orientation, order and organization, clarity, and control) of the questionnaire. The CIES has been used extensively to distinguish the environments of different prison units and to monitor change in a particular prison setting resulting from some administrative or programmatic modification (see Daniels, 1973; Duffee, 1975; Jones and Cornes, 1977; Skalar, 1974; Tupker and Pointer, 1975; Waters, 1977; Wenk and Frank, 1973).

Despite its relatively widespread application, critics question the theoretical and empirical validity of the nine subscales (Selo, 1976; Wright, 1979b; Wright and Boudouris, 1982). Others identify methodological problems associated with using averaged perceptions of individuals to represent an organizational main effect (Hinnings and Lee, 1971; Pennings, 1973; Tausky, 1967; see Lincoln and Zeitz, 1980, for a review). Group averages may reflect less about the organizational properties themselves than about the individuals doing the ratings (James and Jones, 1974). In addition, by relying upon averaged scores to characterize an environment, the CIES overlooks the diversity and divergence of microenvironments that exist within the larger context (Thornton, 1985). Moreover, it does not distinguish inputs of staff from those of fellow inmates.

These criticisms coincide with conclusions drawn about the concept and measurement of social climate in general. One study discovered considerable disparity in the conceptual and operational definitions of climate and concluded that the concept is extremely "fuzzy" (Guion, 1973). Another study, after an exhaustive review of the social climate literature, concludes that the concept appears to be analogous with the organizational situation and, as such, is a *catch-all* term (James and Jones, 1974).

2.2.2. The Ecology of Prison Survival

Toch (1977), like Moos, draws on the theory of person/environment interactions posed by Murray and Stern to formulate his version of prison environments. In contrast, he seeks to describe personal needs rather than environmental presses. Toch suggests that one must discover what the prison environment provides:

> If we are concerned about environmental "matches" and "mismatches" we must first classify man-environment transactions so that we can pinpoint where they are congruent and where they are incongruent. We must specify what a man requires that his environment furnishes, and what he needs that is absent from his environment.

Unlike Moos, Toch (1977, 10–16) approached the problem of identifying the important dimensions of prison environments empirically. He conducted interviews with more than 900 inmates to determine what problems prisoners face in confronting their incarceration and how they cope with these stresses. From a content analysis of the responses, he identified eight central environmental concerns: privacy, safety, structure, support, emotional feedback, social stimulation, activity, and freedom. Toch (1977; see also 1981) postulates that prisoners for whom there is a match between their salient needs and the characteristics of their immediate environments experience more comfortable and successful adjustments than will inmates for whom the person/environment match is poor. He further states that at least some inmates seek this congruence by searching out "niches" within the prison setting. Those without niches suffer greater distress.

Students of Toch have applied this theoretical perspective to describe the transactional processes that different types of inmates undergo—long-term prisoners (Flanagan, 1981), individuals detained pending the disposition of their cases (Gibbs, 1978), and victim-prone inmates (Seymour, 1982)—and have found that they adopt unique coping strategies. Toch (1975), himself, evaluated coping failures of inmates who break down in prison.

Importantly, prison policy and the actions of prison officials can affect the transactional process (Johnson and Price, 1981; Seymour, 1982; Toch, 1984). Through attempts to match "inmates with institutional programs, with staffing patterns, and client groupings" (Toch, 1977), environments can be fostered to accommodate inmates' needs and support their coping efforts. Johnson and Price call such an approach, a human service orientation.

2.2.3. Transactional Assessment

One researcher attempted to merge the theoretical conceptualization of Moos and Toch by exploring the relationship of individual and environmental characteristics to behavioral outcomes (Wright, Harris, and Woika, 1986). Because of the psychometric problems associated with Moos's CIES, the study developed a new instrument for assessing dimensions of the institutional climate, the Prison Environment Inventory (PEI), which measures Toch's eight dimensions (Wright, 1985b). Because Toch identified these dimensions empirically as the most important environmental concerns of inmates, the problem of construct validity appears to be resolved.

With this new tool, the study then investigated factors that predict successful prison adjustment. Both individual-level and organizational-level, as well as "transactional-level," factors predicted adjustment, operationalized in terms of both externally oriented acting out (e.g., aggressive and assaultive disciplinary infractions, self-reported aggressiveness) as well as what might be thought of as internally oriented acting out, in the form of emotional and psychological distress and experience of illness (Wright et al., 1985). The study examined the adjustment patterns of inmates who experienced either high or low congruence between their individual needs and their perceptions of the organizational provisions available for meeting their needs. Although the overall explanatory power of the models was not high, the results "support the claim often found in the prison literature that person/environment fit is significant in determining adjustment patterns" (Wright et al., 1985: 102). Moreover, "by assigning certain personality types to certain settings, the amount of injury, victimization, and illness can be reduced substantially" (p. 122).

2.3. Policy Changes and the Disruption of Prison Environments

The final area of research to be reviewed does not describe the prison setting directly but focuses on effects of disruption in the traditional correctional social control structures.

Most people probably view the large, maximum-security prison (colloquially referred to as the "Big House") as the typical form of incarceration. These facilities, built around the turn of century in rural areas, served as human warehouses with custody and security as their dominant day-to-day goal. Prison officials maintained rigid discipline and often used brutality to ensure social order (see Jacobs, 1977). "Serving time in a Big House meant being pressed into a slow-paced, rigid routine; cut off from outside contacts and social worlds; denied most ordinary human pleasures and stimulations; and constantly forced to contain anger and hostility" (Irwin, 1980:20). The tacit result of such authoritarian control was an environment that appeared stable and even placid (Johnson, 1987) but one in which many inmates suffered severe emotional and psychological distress (Jacobs, 1977).

Trends toward rehabilitation and court decisions concerning standards of care and custody promoted the demise of the traditional autocratic rule found in maximum-security facilities. Such events disrupted the social order and shifted the power within formal and informal prison organizations. Several studies monitored the effects of these changes.

An evaluation of the infusion of treatment programs into the Oahu prison in Hawaii during the period from 1946 to 1955 found that social disorganization resulted from the liberalization of prison policy. Because custodial staff were unable to use coercive and punitive methods to control the population as they had in the past, inmate leaders, who previously had enjoyed privilege in return for helping to maintain social order, could no longer control troublesome inmates. Disciplinary infractions soared to a level four times that before reforms were initiated. Correctional officers, treatment staff, inmates, and the administration achieved a new coalition only at the brink of anarchy (McCleery, 1961).

A similar process of disorganization led to the breakdown of order within the New Mexico prison and the riot of 1980. In 1975, prison officials severely curtailed long-standing employment and recreational programs for inmates. As a result, inmates felt a sense of deprivation, which in turn led to the escalation of violence (Useem, 1985).

Two studies conducted in the 1970s examined the effects of changes in security policy on inmate behavior. The first analyzed the consequences of a change that involved informal notification of inmates about a new practice in which prison officials would transfer disruptive individuals to a less desirable facility. A short-term drop in disruptive infractions occurred (Schnelle and Lee, 1974). The second studied the effects of a major overhaul of custody policy within a state prison system on stabbings and found that the incidence declined, but the rate of security housing increased (Bidna, 1975).

The Texas Department of Corrections has received considerable attention among penologists in recent years because it clung to the traditional punitive and coercive practices of the Big House long after other states abandoned these methods (see Johnson, 1987). Unofficial use of force by prison guards was not random nor "idiosyncratic" but "highly structured" and deeply imbedded in the complex social control system of the prison system. New guards were introduced to and rewarded for the proper use of force through an identifiable process of socialization (Marquart, 1986). A federal court case, *Ruiz v. Estelle*, handed down in 1980, disrupted this unique mixture of formal and informal controls that comprised the traditional system of discipline.

The federal hearing found the Texas prison system in violation of the Eighth Amendment: Incarceration there constituted cruel and unusual punishment. The court ordered sweeping reforms in custodial practices as well as significant changes in physical facilities, reduction in the population, and provision of basic services. This change produced a similar effect as that documented in New Mexico and Hawaii in that a marked escalation of inmate-to-inmate and inmate-to-guard violence occurred (Marquart and Crouch, 1985). One researcher attributes these outcomes to an overall loss of social control among correctional authorities and formerly powerful inmates. He observed the following changes: (1) less willingness among the staff to control inmates, (2) increased reliance on self-protection among inmates, (3) increased participation in informal cliques and gangs among inmates, (4) deeper racial divisions, (5) intragang disputes, and (6) few staff or inmates in positions to mediate conflict (Ekland-Olson, 1986).

3. CONCLUSION

The results from the research comprising all three areas—physical characteristics, transactional models, and policy change—indicate that prisons possess unique and enduring characteristics that impinge upon and shape individual behavior. Research describing the effects of policy change suggests that environments tend to be stable but that their disruption can result in the escalation of violence. The fact that policy changes, often intended to improve institutional functioning, have led to increased inmate violence contrasts sharply with research results on the effects of "new generation" prison architecture. There facilities, designed to increase correctional officer direct supervision and humanize the environment through providing prisoners with greater choice and privacy, have been found to promote positive prisoner adjustment. Violence, vandalism, and other behavioral problems appear to be less prevalent in new generation facilities.

Of course, the populations of the newly designed prisons had not

had opportunities to develop antisocial inmate subcultures prior to reform implementation, whereas the inmates of the prisons in Hawaii and
Texas functioned in "Big House" environments prior to the policy
changes. Nevertheless, the physical design features of the new generation facilities appear to have had a significant positive impacts upon
the social organization of the prison, the inmate culture, and the nature
of inmate/staff interactions.

A second theme uniting much of the research reviewed in this chapter concerns the recognition of the importance of the interaction of person and environment. The fact that objective, physical settings may be
experienced quite differently by individuals who do not share similar
characteristics is acknowledged by scholars in both the crowding and
correctional environment literatures. Researchers concerned with transactional theory share with the developers of the new generation prisons
the recognition of the importance of considering individual needs in
structuring physical and social environments in prisons. Still, this research is in its infancy. In coming years, discovery of what environmental components significantly influence different individuals will determine how well we come to understand how prisoners adjust to
incarceration, and whether they will deteriorate, improve their functional ability, or not change at all.

4. REFERENCES

American Foundation Institute of Corrections. *Philadelphia Detention Center: An evaluation
after four years use.* 1968.
Atlas, R. Violence in prison: Environmental influences. *Environment and Behavior,* 1984, *16,*
275–306.
Bidna, H. Effects of increased security on prison violence. *Journal of Criminal Justice,* 1975,
3, 33–46.
Bonta, J., and Gendreau, P. Re-examining the cruel and unusual punishment of prison
life. Unpublished manuscript, 1988.
Braley, M. *False starts.* Boston: Little, Brown, 1976.
Brown, R. L. S. *Changes in views of self and parents among a group of first time incarcerated
delinquent girls.* Doctoral dissertation, University of Oklahoma, 1971.
Bukstel, L. H., and Kilmann, P. R. Psychological effects of imprisonment on confined
individuals. *Psychological Bulletin,* 1980, *88,* 469–493.
Bunker, E. *No beast so fierce.* New York: W. W. Norton, 1973.
Carr, T. S. *The effects of crowding on recidivism, cardiovascular deaths and infraction rates in a
large prison system.* Doctoral dissertation, Georgia State University, 1981.
Cox, V. C., Paulus, P. B., and McCain, G. Prison crowding research: The relevance for
prison housing standards and a general approach regarding crowding phenomena.
American Psychologist, 1984, *39,* 1148–1160.
Culbertson, R. G. The effect of institutionalization on the delinquent inmate's self-concept
Journal of Criminal Law and Criminology, 1975, *66,* 88–93.

Daniels, D. *The Treatment Team Effectiveness Development Project.* Vol. 1. Sunnyvale, CA.: Electromagnetic Systems Laboratories, 1973.

D'Atri, D. A. Psychophysiological responses to crowding. *Environment and Behavior.* 1975, 7, 237–252.

D'Atri, D. A., Fritzgerald, E. F., Kasl, S. V., and Ostfeld, A. M. Crowding in prison: The relationship between changes in housing mode and blood pressure. *Psychosomatic Medicine,* 1981, 43, 95–105.

Farbstein, J., and Wener, R. Evaluation of correctional environments. *Environment and Behavior,* 1982, 14, 671–694.

Duffee, D. E. *Correctional policy and prison organization.* Beverly Hills, CA.: Sage, 1975.

Ekland-Olson, S. Crowding, social control, and prison violence: Evidence from the post-Ruiz years in Texas. *Law and Society Review,* 1986, 20, 387–422.

Ellis, D. Crowding and prison violence: Integration of research and theory. *Criminal Justice and Behavior,* 1984, 11, 277–308.

Farbstein, J., and Wener, R. Evaluation of correctional environments. *Environment and Behavior,* 1982, 14, 671–694.

Farrington, D. P., and Nuttall, C. P. Prison size, overcrowding, prison violence, and recidivism. *Journal of Criminal Justice,* 1980, 8, 221–231.

Flanagan, T. Dealing with long-term confinement: Adaptive strategies and perspectives among long-term prisoners. *Criminal Justice and Behavior,* 1981, 8, 201–222.

Folkman, S., Schaefer, C., and Lazarus, R. Cognitive processes as mediators of stress coping. In V. Hamilton and D. Warburton (Eds.), *Human stress and cognition: An information-processing approach.* London: Wiley, 1979.

Gaes, G. G., and McGuire, W. J. Prison violence: The contribution of crowding versus other determinants of prison assault rates. *Journal of Research in Crime and Delinquency,* 1985, 22, 41–65.

Gersten, R. *Noise in jails: A constitutional issue.* Champaign: National Clearinghouse for Criminal Justice Planning and Architecture, University of Illinois, 1977.

Gettinger, S. H. *New generation jails: An innovative approach to an age-old problem.* Washington, DC: National Institute of Corrections, 1984.

Gibbs, J. *Stress and self-injury in jail.* Doctoral dissertation, State University of New York, Albany, 1978.

Goldblatt, L. *Prisoners and their environment: A study of two prisons for youthful offenders.* Raleigh: School of Design, North Carolina State University, unpublished, 1972.

Gould, W. B. Behind the walls. *Nation,* February 23, 1980, 230, 195–196.

Guion, R. M. A note on organization climate. *Organizational Behavior and Human Performance,* 1973, 9, 120–125.

Hinnings, C. R., and Lee, G. Dimensions of organizational structure and their concept: A replication. *Sociology,* 1971, 5, 267–272.

Irwin, J. *Prisons in turmoil.* Boston: Little, Brown, 1980.

Jacobs, J. B. *Stateville: The penitentiary in mass society.* Chicago: University of Chicago Press, 1977.

James, L. R., and Jones, A. P. Organizational climate: A review of theory and research. *Psychological Bulletin,* 1974, 81, 1096–1112.

Jan, L. Overcrowding and inmate behavior: Some preliminary findings. *Criminal Justice and Behavior,* 1980, 7, 293–301.

Johnson, R. *Hard times: Understanding and reforming the prison.* Monterey, CA: Brooks/Cole, 1987.

Johnson, R., and Price, S. The complete correctional officer: Human service and the human environment in prison. *Criminal Justice and Behavior,* 1981, 8, 343–373.

Jones, H., and Cornes, P. *Open prisons.* London: Routledge & Kegan Paul, 1977.

Keerdoja, E. Tense prisoners in New Mexico. *Newsweek*, April 14, 1980, 95, 15.

Lawler III, E. E., Hall, D. T., and Oldham, G. R. Organizational climate: Relationship to organizational structure, process and performance. *Organizational Behavior and Human Performance*, 1974, 11, 137–155.

Lazarus, R. S. *Psychological stress and the coping process*. New York: McGraw-Hill, 1966.

Lazarus, R., and Launier, R. Stress-related transactions between person and environment. In L. A. Pervin and M. Lewis (Eds.), *Internal and external determinants of behavior*. New York: Plenum Press, 1978.

Lazarus, R., Averill, J., and Opton, E. Toward a cognitive theory of emotion. In M. Arnold (Ed.), *Feelings and Emotions*. New York: Academic Press, 1970.

Lincoln, J. R., and Zietz, G. Organizational properties from aggregate data: Separating individual and structural effects. *American Sociological Review*, 1980, 45, 391–408.

Macht, M. W., Seidl, F. W., and Greene, D. R. Measuring inmate morale. *Social Work*, 1977, 22, 284–289.

Marquart, J. W. Prison guards and the use of physical coercion as a mechanism of prisoner control. *Criminology*, 1986, 24, 347–366.

Marquart, J. W., and Crouch, B. M. Judicial reform and prisoner control: The impact of *Ruiz v. Estelle* on a Texas penitentiary. *Law & Society Review*, 1985, 19, 557–584.

McCain, G., Cox, V. C., and Paulus, P. B. The effect of prison crowding on inmate behavior. *Final Report, LEAA Grant 78-NI-AX-0019*, University of Texas at Arlington, 1980.

McCleery, R. H. The governmental process and informal social control. In D. R. Cressey (Ed.), *The prison: Studies in institutional organization and change*. New York: Holt, Rinehart & Winston, 1961.

Megargee, E. I. Population density and disruptive behavior in a prison setting. In A. K. Cohen, F. G. Cole, and R. G. Bailey (Eds.), *Prison violence*. Lexington: Lexington, 1976.

Megargee, E. I. The association of population density, reduced space, and uncomfortable temperatures with misconduct in a prison community. *American Journal of Community Psychology*, 1977, 5, 289–298.

Moos, R. H. The assessment of the social climates of correctional institutions. *Journal of Research in Crime and Delinquency*, 1968, 5, 173–188.

Moos, R. H. *Evaluating correctional and community settings*. New York: Wiley, 1975.

Murray, H. A. *Explorations in personality*. New York: Oxford University Press, 1938.

Nacci, P. L., Teitelbaum, H. E., and Prather, J. Population density and inmate misconduct rates in the federal prison system. *Federal Probation*, 1977, 41, 26–31.

Nelson, W. R., O'Toole, M., Krauth, B., and Whitmore, C. G. *Direct supervision models*. Boulder, CO: National Institute of Corrections Information Center, 1984.

Pace, C. R., and Stern, G. G. An approach to the measurement of psychological characteristics of college environments. *Journal of Educational Psychology*, 1958, 58, 269–277.

Paulus, P., Cox, V., McCain, G., and Chandler, J. Some effects of crowding in a prison environment. *Journal of Applied Social Psychology*, 1975, 5, 86–91.

Paulus, P. B., McCain, G., and Cox, V. C. Death rates, psychiatric commitments, blood pressure and perceived crowding as a function of institutional crowding. *Environmental Psychology and Nonverbal Behavior*, 1978, 3, 107–116.

Pennings, J. M. Measures of organizational structure: A methodological note. *American Journal of Sociology*, 1973, 79, 686–704.

Porporino, F. J., and Zamble, E. Coping with imprisonment. *Canadian Journal of Criminology*, 1984, 26, 403–421.

Press, A. When will it happen again. *Newsweek*, February 18, 1980, 95, 70.

Prestholdt, R. H., Taylor, R., and Shannon, W. The correctional environment and human behavior: A comparative study of two prisons for women. In Suedfeld et al. (Eds.), *EDRA 7 Conference Proceedings*, Book 1, 1976, 145–149.

Schnelle, J. F., and Lee, J. F. A quasi-experimental retrospective evaluation of a prison policy change. *Journal of Applied Behavior Analysis*, 1974, *7*, 483–496.

Selo, E. Review of *Evaluating correctional and community settings*, by R. H. Moos. *Journal of Criminal Justice*, 1976, *4*, 348–350.

Selznick, P. *Leadership in administration*. Evanston, IL: Row, Peterson and Company, 1957.

Seymour, J. Environmental sanctuaries for susceptible prisoners. In R. Johnson and H. Toch (Eds.), *The pains of imprisonment*. Beverly Hills: Sage, 1982.

Sims, H. P., Jr, and LaFollette, W. An assessment of the Litwin and Stringer organization climate questionnaire. *Personnel Psychology*, 1975, *28*, 19–38.

Skalar, V. Social climate in the experimental and control institutions. In K. Vodopivec (Ed.), *Maladjusted youth: An experiment in rehabilitation*. Hampshire, England: D. C. Heath, 1974.

Smith, D. E. Crowding and confinement. In R. Johnson and H. Toch (Eds.), *The pains of imprisonment*. Beverly Hills: Sage, 1982.

Sneider, B., and Hall D. Toward specifying the concept of work climate: A study of Roman Catholic diocesan pirests. *Journal of Applied Psychology*, 1972, *56*, 447–455.

Sommer, R. *Tight spaces: Hard architecture and how to humanize it*. Englewood Cliffs, NJ: Prentice-Hall, 1972.

Srivastava, R. J. *Environmental needs of juvenile group homes*. Tucson: Environmental Research and Development Foundation, 1978.

Stern, G. G. *People in context: Measuring person-environment congruence in education and industry*. New York: John Wiley, 1970.

Tausky, C. On organizational alienation. *American Sociology Review*, 1967, *32*, 118.

Thornton, D. Intra-regime variation in inmate perception of prison staff. *British Journal of Criminology*, 1985, *24*, 138–147.

Toch, H. *Men in crisis: Human breakdowns in prison*. Chicago: Aldine, 1975.

Toch, H. *Living in prison: The ecology of survival*. New York: Macmillan, 1977.

Toch, H. Inmate classification as a transaction. *Criminal Justice and Behavior*, 1981, *8*, 3–14.

Toch, H. Quo vadis? *Canadian Journal of Criminology*, 1984, *26*, 511–516.

Toch, H. Warehouses for people? *American Academy of Political and Social Scientists Annal*, 1985, *478*, 58–72.

Tupker, H., and Pointer, J. *The Iowa Differential Classification and Treatment Project*. Eldora: Iowa Training School for Boys, 1975.

Useem, B. Disorganization and the New Mexico prison riot of 1980. *American Sociological Review*, 1985, *50*, 677–688.

Walker, B., and Gordon, T. J. Environmental health needs in correctional institutions. *Federal Probation*, 1977, *41*, 34–38.

Walkey, F. H., and Gilmour, D. R. The relationship between interpersonal distance and violence in imprisoned offenders. *Criminal Justice and Behavior*, 1984, *11*, 331–340.

Waters, J. E. Psychosocial descriptions of the correctional environment: A method for evaluation and intervention. *Journal of Humanics*, 1977, *4*, 38–43.

Wener, R. E., and Kaminoff, R. D. Improving environmental information: Effects of signs on perceived crowding and behavior. *Environment and Behavior*, 1983, *15*, 3–20.

Wener, R., and Olsen, R. Innovative correctional environments: A user assessment. *Environment and Behavior*, 1980, *12*, 478–494.

Wener, R., Frazier, W., and Farbstein, J. Jails: Direct-supervision facilities have succeeded in a field better known for its failures. *Psychology Today*, 1987, 40–49.

Wenk, E., and Frank C. Some progress in the evaluation of institutional programs. *Federal Probation*, 1973, *37*, 30–37.

Whiting, C., and DeJoy, D. *Behavioral data in evaluation research: Use in correctional visiting facilities*. University Park, PA: Division of Man and Environment Relations. Pennsylvania State University, 1976.

Wormith, J. S. Personal space of incarcerated offenders. *Journal of Clinical Psychology*, 1984, *40*, 815–827.

Wright, K. N., *An organizational approach to correctional effectiveness*. Jonesboro, TN: Pilgrimage Press, 1979a.

Wright, K. N. The conceptualization and measurement of the social climate of correctional organizations. *Journal of Offender Counseling, Services & Rehabilitation*, 1979b, *4*, 137–152.

Wright, K. N. *The great American crime myth*. Westport, CT: Greenwood, 1985a.

Wright, K. N. Developing the prison environment inventory. *Journal of Research in Crime and Delinquency*, 1985b, *22*, 257–277.

Wright, K. N., An exploratory study of transactional classification. *Journal of Research in Crime and Delinquency*, 1986, *23*, 326–348.

Wright K. N., and Boudouris, J. An assessment of the Moos Correctional Institutions Environment Scale. *Journal of Research in Crime and Delinquency*, 1982, *23*, 255–276.

Wright, K. N., Harris, J. M., and Woika, N. *Improving correctional classification through a study of the placement of inmates in environmental settings*, NIJ Grant 83-IJ-CX-0011, 1985.

Yarbrough, V. E. *A study to determine the effects of institutionalization on juvenile delinquents' school motivation and learner self-concept*. Doctoral dissertation, University of Tennessee, Knoxville, 1973.

Young, M. Resident and staff perceptions of present and ideal correctional environments. *Research Report III*. Frankfort: Kentucky Department of Corrections, 1973.

Zupan, L. L., Menke, B. A., and Lovrich, N. P. Podular/direct supervision detention facilities: Challenges for human resource development. In Farbstein, J., and Wener, R. (Eds.), *Proceedings of the first annual symposium on new generation jails*. Boulder, CO: National Institute of Corrections Jail Center, 1986.

Part V

CORRECTIONS RESEARCH AND THE FUTURE

Epilogue

THE RESEARCHER'S WORK IS NEVER DONE

JOHN P. CONRAD

For most of this century, social scientists have taken an interest in the community of keepers and convicts who live in constant confrontation in American prisons. It was many years before their interest was reciprocated by those whose problems and behavior were the object of sociological and psychological study. Practical prison wardens saw no need to change their ways, and few of them found anything of interest in the early studies of sociologists, psychologists, and other outsiders prying into their affairs.

The modernization of state government changed all that. Managers of all state departments came under pressure from the fiscal authorities to plan their future operations so that responsible budgets could be presented to legislatures. For departments of corrections, that called for projections of prison population trends, which could not be studied without statistics on the movement of men and women in and out of prisons. As prison administration came under the professional scrutiny of budget analysts, more and more data were demanded of commissioners and directors. Questions proliferated: What is the optimum size of a parole caseload? Can parolees be classified according to the risks they present so that caseloads can be differentiated? What evidence is there that prison treatment programs produce positive effects on the prisoners exposed to them? What are the rates of recidivism for the principal types of offenders? Can the postrelease behavior of prisoners

JOHN P. CONRAD • 544 Reed Drive, Davis, California 95616.

be predicted? Can the disparity of sentences for offenders committing similar crimes be reduced by a system of guidelines? Is it really necessary to incarcerate so many offenders for as long as laws and policy now require? Could some offenders be safely confined in less than maximum custody conditons? If so, how many, for how long, and what will they be doing while so confined?

These and many more questions required research expertise. The contributors to this volume have brought together the results of work done and an outline of work yet to be done. My task in this final chapter is to bring together the issues that are current and some of the issues that loom all too clearly on the social horizon. Research reports almost invariably mention in their conclusions that "more research must be done" to settle the questions to which the study had been addressed. This plea, so often mocked as self-serving, is a statement of a reality of social science: A researcher's work is never done. Questions may be answered with conviction, but the answers always raise more questions. A proposition that is true and firmly established today must be reexamined soon, perhaps tomorrow, perhaps next month or next year because change will inevitably cast uncertainty on certainty.

Looking back over my 40-odd years in penology, the shifting foundations of knowledge stand out as the inconstant constant. When I began my correctional career, my seniors were sure that there were certitudes to be found in social science, just as Newton and Galileo, Darwin and Pasteur had established them in the natural sciences. It was our scientific obligation to work in an enterprise aimed at finding these certainties so that the processes of penology could become rational, predictable, and reducible to systems, just as was the case in physics, chemistry, and even in biology. We could think or ourselves as precursors of a Newton of social science. In our humble way, we were making possible a unified theory supporting a rational practice.

We know now, and should have known then, that this aspiration can never be realized. Everything we know must be seen as subject to obsolescence in a society in which change is unpredictable but inevitable. The physicist knows that the hydrogen atom of 1989 has the same characteristics as the hydrogen atom of 1889 or the same atom of 2089. More can be learned about that atom, but it is still the same atom. In social science, we are not blessed with such certainties. Our task is more exciting; we have to fashion new tools to deal with phenomena that have shaped past realities out of all recognition.

Until well within living memory, corrections occupied a place on the outer margins of national attention. The crime rate was tolerable, prisons were mostly out of sight and out of mind, and the country had more pressing issues to resolve than the deterrence of crime and the rehabilitation of criminals. The memoirs of a few picturesque wardens— Lawes of Sing Sing, Duffy of San Quentin, and Ragen of Stateville— fascinated some readers as accounts of remote and exotic places, inaccessible to ordinary men and women.

In succession, the nation's discourse had focused on Prohibition, the Great Depression, and World War II. The study of crime was the specialty of a few sociologists at the University of Chicago. Many major universities got along without any sociologists at all, let alone the departments of criminal justice and the schools of criminology that are now so common.

As for the study of corrections, the pioneering work of Sheldon and Eleanor Glueck (Glueck and Glueck, 1930) received fleeting prominence in the press because of its finding that reformatories did not seem to reform. That was a mild surprise; the public had been led to believe that a year or so in a reform school would usually straighten out a wayward youth.

Hardened criminals, of course, went to prison where they were supposed to be put to hard labor. That was what prisons were for. It was seldom brought to public notice that exceedingly few prisons could provide convicts with labor of any kind to do. A riot in a mess hall, the escape of a sensationally hardened thug, a scandal on a parole board might make headlines in a nearby newspaper but only briefly. Prisons and reformatories were autarchies where the reign of the warden was absolute. Governors, legislatures, and courts rarely ventured to intervene. Prison authorities liked it that way. Autocrats do not take kindly to interference. The walls that kept prisoners inside also kept intruders out.

As the reader of this volume has seen, all that has changed. In some states, especially outrageous scandals convinced the public that closer control of what went on was required. Prison administration became centralized in departments of corrections administered by commissioners or directors who were supposed to keep wardens and guards honest and humane. In other states, a concern for accountability called for professional administration in the capital. Legislative committees and budget analysts could not be expected to review intelligently separate budget requests from each of several prisons maintained by the state. Some departments exercised nominal control under a director with carefully limited powers. Others were elaborately staffed with bureaus and bureaucrats to supervise all aspects of prison operations. During the post-World War II years, wardens have been gradually reduced to the status of field managers, closely answerable to a commissioner in the state capital, and stripped of their previously untrammeled powers. Authority in corrections now resides in the state capitals.

The indefatigable Gluecks continued their criminological studies, many of them with important, if indirect, significance for corrections. Serious penological research began with the work of Donald Clemmer. His classic study of the prison community in 1940 opened questions that still claim the attention of sociologists (Clemmer, 1940). Clemmer was inspired by his belief that better public understanding of prisons was badly needed. A first step was to describe the prison as a community—he had no hypotheses to test. In a second edition of his famous book, published 18 years later, he noted that prisons had much improved and were different in important respects from the prison he had described. Nevertheless,

> the prison world is drab and graceless in spite of television sets and flowers on the campus. There is monotony and even stupor, in spite of group counseling and psychotherapy. Homosexuality is about as prevalent now as of old, in spite of classes of sex education and liberalized visiting. By and large there is disinterest in work, in spite of vocational training and occupational aptitute tests. And so on. The improvements [in] . . . 60 percent of [our] prisons are real but have been only in degree, for the old patterns continue. (Clemmer, 1958, p. xiii)

Nothing in that paragraph would be untrue 30 years later, but some new patterns have been added to the somber picture. Penitentiaries are still drab and graceless, but racial conflicts, prison gangs, the introduction of contraband narcotics, and desperate overcrowding have filled the cellblocks and yards with fear.

Although Clemmer's work was respected, it was not followed up until 1952–1953, a crucial time in the history of corrections and correctional research as well. That was the year when riots and lesser disturbances erupted in many prisons across the country. Their violence and contagious spread attracted a number of social scientists to the prison community as a subject for research. The work of Gresham Sykes (Sykes, 1957) and Donald Cressey (Cressey, 1961) initiated a literature of correctional research that accumulates to this day in textbooks, monographs, and journal articles. In the beginning, it aroused scant interest among practical prison officials. Cressey reported one incident that was surely representative of the prevailing response among wardens to the early findings of penological inquiry:

> We once asked a warden about the value of sociological training for prison workers, and he responded, "It is like I say around here. A man is tearing up his cell and has just attacked an officer. So I say, Well, let's go over here to the shelf and get one of these criminology books and find out what we should do. There's nothing there." There never will be anything there. Nevertheless the detailed insights by the authors of this volume show realism and

concern for the practical implications of social science theory for those decisions. The authors probably know more about prisons than do most wardens, and their research *can* be put to use by men who are skilled in day-to-
day problems of government. (Cressey, p. 11)

Despite Cressey's bravado, it was a long time before correctional
research found a welcome from penal managers. An example from personal experience: I had my first research assignment in the mid-1950s,
when I directed a project to study the effectiveness of small caseloads
in parole operations—the California Special Intensive Parole Unit (SIPU)
experiment. In a progress report I referred to SIPU as a research project.
My superior, the chief parole officer, read the report, summoned me to
his office and, more in sorrow than in anger, warned me never to use
that word again. It would demoralize the staff and the parolees themselves if the impression got abroad that the Division of Adult Paroles
was engaged in research, and the officers and parolees were just so
many guinea pigs.

A year or two later the California Department of Corrections had
added a research division and became host to a long succession of research projects that continues to the present time. Few, if any, correctional agencies now eschew research. Technology has enabled them to
maintain statistical accounting of the flow of prisoners in and out of the
institutions and to keep track of the programs administered. Many are
now equipped to conduct sound and credible assessments of the usefulness of these programs.

From a series of clumsy, ill-designed program evaluations, typo-
logical investigations, and studies of predictive methods, the stream of
correctional research has become increasingly useful. Maybe it was true
at one time that a troubled warden could look in one of those criminology
books and find that there was "nothing there." It is no longer true, even
for a warden who has a cell-wrecking, assaultive prisoner on his hands.
In this volume, the editors have assembled a group of able researchers
to review the progress that has been made and to define the issues in
correctional research as they now stand.

Unlike some who are allowed the closing pages of a volume like
this, I shall not trespass on the contributors' turf. Their thorough studies
of their topics stand alone without amplifying comment from me. It is
enough to say that these essays describe the way things are and how
they got that way. They also point cautiously to change in the offing
and to alternatives to the present state of affairs. We are concerned here
with the issues of research and policy. What do we need to know to
create a penological policy in which the courts, the managers, and con-
scientious professionals can have confidence in what they are doing?

How can the outlandish costs of corrections, now mounting annually, be brought within reasonable bounds? Some of the answers are explicit in the essays that have been presented in this volume. They also suggest the issues of the future, the issues that managers must confront and will need research assistance to resolve. Some of the questions that must be settled to achieve a sound and hopeful penal policy are:

- Can the rehabilitative ideal be revived? Should it? What kinds of programs and services are essential if rehabilitation is to be a realistic objective?
- Could the private sector contribute a more economical and more effective model for prison operations? If so, what obstacles and policy problems must be resolved? What kinds of facilities could be best managed by private entrepreneurs? Experience with the privatization movement is accumulating, but we still lack rigorous data on the performance of correctional entrepreneurs. Until we have statistical corroboration of plausible expectations, policymakers cannot be sure how far the state should go with private correctional services.
- What female offenders should be incarcerated? What kinds of controls would be appropriate and effective for the classes of women who need not be sentenced to prison but on whom some sanctions or controls should be imposed? Are the conventional programs for women felons still appropriate—or should new and more varied vocational and industrial training be devised and offered?
- How can sentencing practice be reformed? Can the formulation of guidelines for sentencing authorities solve the problems of disparity and assure a balance between prison capacity and actual population? The new federal guidelines for the courts have been widely criticized for the effect they will have in increasing strains on the already overpopulated federal prisons. Can a better model be devised?
- Can principles be defined by which prison industry can be a constructive force to eliminate the curse of prisoner idleness? If so, what are these principles? What are the hazards in applying them? Is there a role for private enterprise in the management of prison industries?
- What are the proper and achievable objectives of prisoner classification and how may a system be constructed to realize those objectives? What kinds of information are required for a fair and effective system? How is this information to be collected?
- Can administrators and social scientists in partnership transform

the prison from a dangerous and often destructive environment to a condition in which the norms of the larger community outside the walls are supported? If so, how? What would such a prison be like?

- To what extent can the role of the prison guard be modified to allow for the delivery of human services? Will their assignment to service functions result in untenable ambiguity?
- Although the interventions of the courts in the 1970s have resulted in major changes in penal policies and practices, signs are accumulating that prisoner access to the courts for remedies for abuse will be sharply reduced. Can grievance procedures be created that will provide for correction of unfair or abusive treatment?

None of these issues is new. Both scholars and administrators have been pondering them for many years. Pessimists make the case that in spite of all the efforts to improve, prisons are probably worse than ever, although worse in different ways. I am an undaunted meliorist, confident that even the prison, that most dismal of public institutions, has been substantially improved and can be further improved. As a realist, I know that there are processes that will erode the quality of any human institution, even the most benign. Only external vigilance and effective intervention can assure that improvements do not crumble away in the hands of fallible managers.

The prison holds society's rejects, men and women who have little going for them. Increasingly, they come from those sections of our cities where an underclass subsists on crime, hustling, and welfare. Karl Marx referred to the underclass as the *Lumpenproletariat*, the casualties of capitalism, and held out no hope for them. I refuse to concede that he was right. In a dynamic polity, there can be no place for hopelessness for any element of the people. Americans must believe that their country can be safe, lawful, industrious, and hopeful for all Americans. We cannot give up on our national social and economic problems and declare them insoluble.

Likewise with our prisons, which must also be safe, lawful, industrious, and hopeful. These objectives may often seem unattainable. Unless our entire government, particularly the officials who occupy policymaking posts in criminal justice, works toward the achievement of these goals, the American prison will inevitably get worse through the remorseless processes leading to stagnation.

Although this volume illuminates those issues on which research has shed some light, we cannot claim to have swept up all the corners and defined all the issues. Don Cressey's warden still haunts us. He looks in the criminology book for the answers he needs and cannot find them. New issues on which scholars have barely touched bedevil this frustrated warden and, even more so, the commissioner of corrections responsible for the policies that govern prison management. Hoping that a future volume of this kind will offer usable answers to questions that now have no good answers, I will enumerate these questions and discuss their salience.

1. OVERCROWDING

The complexity of this problem is little short of maddening. As sentencing legislation becomes more severe, the prison intake swells, and more prisoners must be accommodated than had been planned when the prison was built. *First question:* Can sentencing policy be properly adjusted to prison capacity? If so, by what means? *Second question:* What rational principles can be devised to establish appropriate sentences that will maintain protection of the public, assure that serious crimes have serious consequences, and at the same time prevent the waste of costly prison space for the confinement of criminals who can be dealt with by cheaper means?

These questions do not exhaust this ominous problem. We have not yet considered what density of humanity constitutes overcrowding. I recognize overcrowding for sure when I see gross examples, but I also know that moderate crowding leads to intolerable levels of overcrowding. Double celling in the cellblocks and triple bunking in the dormitories are expedients that will be followed by convicts sleeping on the corridor floors. Control is lost, and management is preoccupied with regaining it. Policies and practices are distorted by the need to manage this abnormal and dangerous condition. *Third question:* What is the minimum space required for a maximum custody prisoner, and how do we arrive at that minimum? *Fourth question:* How much personal space should be allowed for minimum custody prisoners who may enjoy much more freedom of movement? *Fifth question:* What is the maximum number of prisoners who should be assigned to a dormitory? How can assignment to a dormitory be made attractive to a prisoner accustomed to the privacy of a cell to himself?

2. PRISON GOVERNANCE

The creation of state departments of corrections in the 1940s and 1950s met the requirements of modern public administration with a model that on paper is fairly uniform across the country. The familiar solid lines of authority and the dotted lines of staff advice are clearly delineated. How the model is used depends on such variables as culture, the personalities of senior officials, financial support, the requirements of court decrees, and the size of the prisoner population—as well as many others. Anyone with opportunities to observe more than one prison system will be well aware that the differences from state to state are large and significant.

The study of these differences has begun to draw the attention of political scientists. An exploratory study by John DiIulio described three models of governance from detailed investigation of administrative styles in the prison systems of Texas, California, and Michigan (DiIulio, 1987). Much attention was given to the bureaucratization of corrections and recognition of the primacy of control if the quality of prison life is to be maintained at an acceptable level. DiIulio holds that *quality of prison life* consists of three "strategic features": *order, amenity,* and *service.* By *order,* he means the prevention of misconduct endangering the safety of individual prisoners and guards. By *amenity,* he means "anything that enhances the comfort of the inmates: good food, clean cells, ample recreation, color television." By *service* he means "anything that is intended to improve the life prospects of the inmates: . . . remedial reading, vocational training, work opportunities."

Whether these three "strategic features" exhaust the essentials is not important at this stage of the development of this new paradigm. (I have already proposed that prison standards must meet the requirements of lawfulness, safety, industriousness, and hopefulness—almost but not quite the same as DiIulio's "strategic features.") What is important is the necessity for further empirical study of governance. Prison management has become more complex with technology, standards of care, and the requirements of modern principles of public administration to which commissioners and wardens must adapt. At the same time, the vastly increased prisoner population has imposed an unwieldy load on administration and facilities, calling into question the traditional roles of the entire staff. DiIulio describes three "models" in each of which the widely differing roles of commissioners and wardens are seen as crucial determinants of the effectiveness—or ineffectiveness—of control.

Studies such as DiIulio's are overdue and may be said to have begun in the nick of time. We need to reconsider the job descriptions of commissioners, wardens, and their immediate staffs if the currently overloaded systems are not to deteriorate. Questions like these need to be explored:

• What duties must the commissioner perform personally? What responsibilities should he delegate to which subordinates? How close must be his contact with operations in the prisons?

- How large and diverse a departmental staff should support the commissioner?
- In view of the crucial part the parole board plays in determining the size of prison populations, should it be an independent entity? If so, what kind of supporting staff should be provided to it? To what extent should the parole board be expected to rely on the commissioner's staff?
- Where prison terms can be reduced by allowing for "good time," what rules and procedures should govern allowances and cancellations?

Questions like these have long floated unresolved and inadequately stated. Their resolution is urgent in the present climate of penological uncertainties.

3. THE PRISON GANG

In his magisterial study of Stateville, James Jacobs described the structure and functions of gangs at that Illinois prison (Jacobs, 1977). Faced with the presence of gangs in his institution, a wise warden will turn to Jacobs's still instructive study. He will not find a prescription for their control, but he will find a basis for understanding why prisoners join gangs and how they are organized for control of and services to members. We still use desperate measures. Consider these two examples from my own observation.

Recently I visited the Michael Unit of the Texas Department of Corrections. This is a new, state-of-the-art facility that will impress any experienced penologist with the massive but sophisticated security that has been provided in its architecture. One 500-man cellblock has been dedicated to the housing of members of prison gangs. The rule is that any prisoner identified as a gang member, whether a "commander" or a mere "soldier," must be housed there for the duration of his term, which may be for many years. One staff member is assigned full time to the identification of gang members, surveillance of gang operations, and organization of information concerning gang communications and activities. It is hoped that this severe policy will in time deter prisoners from enlisting in a gang. With gang members safely removed from the general population, it is supposed that the narcotics traffic supporting these combinations will abate, and the homicides that enforce gang discipline will be less motivated and more difficult to carry out. The policy is new, and the effects have not yet been established.

At California's supermaximum custody prison at Folsom, the problem of the gang dropout is peculiarly intractable. Quite naturally, a man who has decided that he has had enough of the Aryan Brotherhood or the Black Guerrillas or the Mexican Mafia—whichever has claimed his allegiance—becomes automatically an object of concern to gang leaders. Their reasoning is logical: If he is no longer one of us, he will probably be a snitch and therefore must be subjected to extreme measures. That calls for the administration to place the defector in protective custody, adding thereby still another soul to be accommodated indefinitely in costly maximum custody conditions and in almost complete idleness. Not long ago I read the extraordinarily bulky case file of one such man, a dropout from the Aryan Brotherhood. His jeopardy was plainly confirmed by a violent and nearly successful attempt on his life by one of his former associates while he was escorted from a shower by not one but two officers. Not unnaturally, his status is now described as "extremely heavy PC." Because he is a life prisoner with many years of life expectancy, he will be a costly burden on California taxpayers for many years to come. What else can be done with this wretched man?

The dilemmas presented by prison gangs have been with us for nearly two decades. Some states have been blessedly free of them; others have been grievously afflicted. Their power is formidable. By various means, they manage the importation and distribution of narcotics and make a good enough thing out of the traffic to offer subsidies to cooperative correctional officers. In some prisons, their power has extended to the assignment of prisoners to desirable jobs or to their placement in protective custody. For at least 20 years, prison officials have been aware of prison gangs and the dangers and disruptions they present. A satisfactory method of control still eludes us. Bloody experience has left no question of their lethal codes of conduct.

To describe the gang and its attractions for the underclass prisoner is an interesting exercise in social psychology from which much can be learned about the need that such a prisoner feels to belong to a disciplined organization. So far, scholars have failed to provide credible guidance for the control of the gangs' activities. Administrators have learned that they cannot safely co-opt gang leaders and their supporters. To allow them the freedom of the prison yard is to endanger other inmates and to risk the corruption of correctional officers. To lock all gang members up for the duration of their sentences is to assure their release from the unnatural conditions of maximum security directly to the freedoms of the community—the worst possible transition.

What is the best answer? No one knows. What is needed is a cautious series of experiments with graduated freedoms within a small institution, beginning, perhaps, with junior "soldiers" who can be more easily detached from their commitments than those who have achieved some status. So far as I know, experiments are not even being conceived, and such desperate measures as those I have mentioned are considered common sense, the only realistic control.

4. CONVICTS IN SEGREGATION

Every prison system I know of, including some relatively benign prisons in northern Europe, contains men and occasionally some women in a sequestered block or wing known to correctional bureaucrats as "Administrative Segregation" or a "Security Housing Unit" (SHU), or an "Adjustment Center"—or, to the convicts themselves, as *The Hole*. Regulations in some systems limit the stay of any prisoner in The Hole to no more than some arbitrary period—6 months, a year, 2 or 3 years. Release from The Hole in such systems may be extremely brief, allowing enough time for a case review to determine that order and safety require his or her immediate return to The Hole.

Other prisons require a periodic review of the prisoner's progress toward maturity. Sometimes these reviews are to be conducted weekly, sometimes monthly. As the régime in segregation units calls for inactivity as the norm, "progress" can be gauged only by the decreasing frequency of undesirable incidents. Indeed regress is the only change usually found; a man hurling feces at a guard may be locked in a cell with a solid steel door, as may another who howls obscenities all night. Lesser offenders may be placed on the "diet loaf."

Not much work has been done to improve this state of affiars. Like most prisoners, those in segregation units will eventually be released, after the worst possible preparation for a return to the streets.

Other programs are conceivable for these exceptionally difficult men and women, but initiative and imagination have not been sufficiently devoted to their problems. In Texas, for example, condemned row prisoners are allowed to choose work in a clothing factory. Most of them seem glad to get out of their cells and to be doing something to distract them from the awful predicament in which they have found themselves—even though their labors are unpaid. It should be possible to arrange voluntary workshop programs along these lines for segregated prisoners. In some states, daily contacts with skillful counselors often help such men and women to extricate themselves from a situation in which hope is literally impossible to imagine.

Neither of these suggestions nor others that may occur to the reader will necessarily transform most of these convicts into upstanding pillars of the prison community. They are unreliable human beings at best and often dangerous to prison employees and fellow convicts. Nevertheless, they should be offered ways to change. My point here is that no one is thinking about the problem presented to society by these men and women and the units to which they are consigned. There is an urgent necessity to innovate, and ideas do not loom on the landscape. I am reminded of a warden who once remarked to me, "these donkeys in The Hole are 10% of our population and take 90% of our time. It ought to be the other way around. We ought to let them stew in their own juice and help those who want to be helped." That 10% will continue to take an inordinate amount of time until some ingenuity and concern create a basis for hope and choice for them.

That is a short list of outstanding issues that call for resolution. I have not included the prisoners who require protective custody because of the inability of the staff to assure their safety by means other than placing them in full-time segregation. The values of "boot-camp" exposure to prison, shock probation, and shock parole deserve much more attention from research than they have been given. We are accumulating enough experience with the administration of "good time" to make a study of its benefits, if any. If we can find Cressey's warden, I am sure that he will think of more guidance that he would like to have from the contributors to this volume.

Years ago a distinguished sociologist remarked to me that sociological studies had arrived at a point at which he could foresee that one major push might settle for good and all the theoretical and operational problems of the prison. He went on to say that that would be an exhilarating development, stimulating his profession to greater efforts toward the understanding and final resolution of other social problems. I was not in a position to suggest that he prepare a proposal for foundation support, but I admit that I was impressed. It did not occur to me to ask him how such a project would provide for the inevitable but unpredictable changes that the years would bring about in the prison, as well as in the larger society.

Fortunately or unfortunately, change is the inconstant constant. As the pre-Socratic philosopher, Heraclitus, observed, five centuries before Christ, one cannot step into the same river twice. The rivers that converge in the prisons of America have swollen to flood proportions. Issues that were unimaginable when I first engaged in penology now occupy most of our attention. The contributors to this volume have shown how much as been done in the social sciences to rationalize correctional practice. That there will always be more to do to keep afloat in the river does not diminish the importance of what we have reported in these pages. The researcher's work is never done.

5. REFERENCES

Clemmer, Donald. *The Prison Community*. New York: Rinehart, 1940. Second edition, 1958.

Cressey, Donald R. (Ed.). *The Prison*. New York: Holt, Rinehart and Winston, 1961.

DiIulio, John. *Governing Prisons: A Comparative Study of Correctional Management*. New York: The Free Press, 1987.

Glueck, Sheldon, and Glueck, Eleanor. *500 Criminal Careers*. New York: Knopf, 1930.

Jacobs, James B. *Stateville: The Penitentiary in Mass Society*. Chicago: The University of Chicago Press, 1977.

Sykes, Gresham. *The Society of Captives*. Princeton, NJ: Princeton University Press, 1957.

INDEX